The Odyssey of the Ship with Three Names

The Center for Basque Studies
University of Nevada, Reno
Occasional Papers Series, No. 23

The Odyssey of the Ship with Three Names

Smuggling Arms into Israel and the Rescue of Jewish Refugees in the Balkans in 1948

Renato Barahona

Center for Basque Studies
University of Nevada, Reno

This book was published with generous financial support from the Basque government.

Occasional Papers Series, No. 23

Series Editors: Joseba Zulaika and Cameron J. Watson

Center for Basque Studies
University of Nevada, Reno
Reno, Nevada 89557
http://basque.unr.edu

Book design: Kimberly Daggett
Cover design: Daniel Montero
Front cover photo: Photograph 5, see p. x for caption
Back cover photos, top to bottom: Photographs 32, 34, 10, and 30, see pp. x–xi for captions

Library of Congress Cataloging-in-Publication Data

Barahona, Renato, 1944- author.
  The Odyssey of the ship with three names : smuggling arms into Israel and the rescue of Jewish refugees in the Balkans in 1948 / Renato Barahona.
    pages cm. -- (Center for Basque studies, occasional papers series ; No. 23)
  Includes bibliographical references and index.
  Summary: "Singular history of the S.S. Kefalos, a tramp steamer crewed mainly by exiled Spanish Republicans that, among its many lives, transported arms and refugees from Mexico and the Balkans to the fledging state of Israel after World War II"-- Provided by publisher.
  ISBN 978-1-935709-52-7 (pbk. : alk. paper) 1. Kefalos 1917-1948 (Ship) 2. Jews--Palestine--History--1917-1948. 3. Palestine--Emigration and immigration--History--20th century. 4. Jewish refugees--Palestine--History--20th century. 5. Illegal arms transfers--Palestine--History--20th century. 6. Holocaust survivors--Palestine. 7. Historic ships. I. Title.

DS126.4.B355 2014
304.8'5694049609044--dc23

                              2014014314

To the memory of the crew

Contents

List of Photographs

(Photographs begin following page 157)

Acknowledgments

From the outset of this investigation I had the uncommon good fortune to be guided and assisted in every possible manner by two incomparable mentors, Carlos Blanco Aguinaga, my late father, and Commander (ret.) Yehuda Ben-Tzur, Palmach/Palyam — www. palyam.org. These partners and collaborators, as I refer to them in e-mails, have been at the heart of the book project from the start — strong and steadfast through the last four years. Neither one has been shy about pointing out my errors, and on more than one occasion, either one or both, have suggested alternative — and often better — interpretations for wrongheaded analyses on my part. Each of the two has brought considerable experience and expertise to the project. For instance, my father led me through the end of the Spanish Civil War and its aftermath, his exile in Mexico, the social and political conditions in that country during the late 1940's, and his subsequent voyage to Israel. Yehuda, on the other hand, has been my guide on a wide range of Israeli matters from pre to post-Independence times. With extraordinary patience and unselfishness, he has explained to me crucial aspects of Israeli society, politics and culture, especially in the decade of the 1940s. In short, he cast light on what was often an impenetrable labyrinth; moreover, he has translated numerous documents from Hebrew, made countless contacts in the search for information, and, in the process, secured a vast number of original materials, which otherwise would have remained unknown. Without these two men's vast collective knowledge and wisdom, this book could not have been written.

I am particularly grateful for the extensive cooperation from numerous archivists and archives. In particular I wish to single out the magnificent assistance of Camille Servizzi at the American Jewish Archives (AJA), and of Peter E. Hanff, Deputy Director at the Bancroft Library. At the latter institution, I was also aided by Susan Snyder, Head of Public Services. At the National Archives and Records Administration (NARA), I was rendered invaluable help by numerous individuals whose names appear below. The Federal Bureau of Investigation and U.S. Department of Justice have been cooperative to the extreme, acceding regularly to requests for files and materials. The same is true of Irargi, the central archives of the Basque Government (known in Castilian and Basque as the *Centro de Patrimonio Documental de Euskadi, Eusko Jaurlaritza. Gobierno Vasco*).

I am greatly indebted to the individuals and families who have provided me with important documents and first-hand information for this study. Among the most generous have been Robert Allen, Bonnie Arthur, Cecil Asman, Isabel Carroquino, Angela Mallory Dega, Eric A. Forbes, David Gritzewsky and Family, Roberto Hernández Gallejones (Archivero Municipal, Portugalete); Nancy Ratner and Family, Wm. A. Schell, Betty M. Slater, and Edward Von der Porten. Not only have they graciously shared significant materials with me, they have patiently answered every query of mine no matter how seemingly trivial or obscure. Bree Kessler carried out crucial research on my behalf at the United Nations Archives in New York, and through hard work, found extremely valuable documents that helped to explain much.

I am also thankful to the numerous persons and institutions that have assisted me with key information, leads, advice and direction: Susan Abbott (NARA); Cristiano D'Adamo; Michlean Amir (United States Holocaust Memorial Museum); Paul Arpaia; Tommaso Astarita; Haim Avni (Avraham Harman Institute of Contemporary Jewry, The Hebrew University of Jerusalem); Roberto Ballabeni; Douglas Ballman (USC Shoah Foundation, Institute for Visual History and Education); Peter Barker; Yehoshua Barlev; Ruth Barriskill (Guildhall Library, Printed Books Section, Aldermanbury, London); David Bercuson (University of Calgary); Charlotte Bonelli (American Jewish Committee Archives); Peter Brueggeman (Scripps Institution of Oceanography Library); Matthew Butram (U.S. Department of Transportation, Maritime Administration); Ricky-Dale Calhoun (Kansas State University); Ron Carlson (Project Liberty and Armed Guard Website, www.armed-guard.com); Antonio Cazorla-Sánchez (Trent University); Leonardo Cohen Shabot (Ben Gurion University of the Neguev); Anne Cowne (Corporate Communications, Lloyd's Register); Nadav Davidovitch (Division of Public Health, Ben Gurion University); John Deeben (NARA); Lisa Donitz (Alumni Records, United States Merchant Marine Academy); Remi Dubuisson (United Nations Archives and Records Management Section); Ilene Roberta Ellis, Gail E. Farr (NARA); Terry Feinberg (*The Salinas Californian*); Filippo Fenelli (ONI, *Officine Navali Italiane*); Alicia Gojman de Backal (*Centro de Documentacion de la Comunidad Ashkenazi de Mexico*); Ralph Goldman; Sara Grizanti (Photo Archives, USHMM); Torsten Hagneus; Heather Halliday (American Jewish Historical Society); Elise Hamner (*The World,* Coos Bay, Oregon); Eldad Harouvi (Palmach Museum); Carmelita Harris (Assessor/Recorder Office, San Francisco); Scott Henry (*Marin Independent Journal);* Shannon Hodge (Jewish Public Library Archives, Montreal); Laura Jo Hofsess (Jewish Public Library Archives, Montreal); Mike Holdoway (www.convoyweb.org.uk); Isabel Ibañez (*El Correo Digital*, Bilbao); Sandrine Ingram (Family Research Department, Central Zionist Archives); Linda Johnson (California State Archives); Elliott Kantner (UCSD Library); Paul Kaye; Jan Tore Klovland (Norwegian School of Economics and Business, Administration, Bergen, Norway); Wendy Kramer (San Francisco History Center, San Francisco Public Library); Kim Y. McKeithan (NARA); Roberto Kerexeta (Irargi); Wendy Kramer (San Francisco Public Library); David A. Langbart (NARA); Carol Leadenham (Hoover Institution Archives); Orly Levi (Haganah Archives); Richard S. Levy (University of Illinois at Chicago); Leland R. Lewis; Nissan Liviathan; Cynthia Livingston; Dewey Livingston; Javier Lorea (*Ayuntamiento de Peralta*); Ralph Lowenstein (University of Florida); Arieh Malkin (Machal. Aliya Bet); Ramón Martín Suquía (*Gipuzkoako Protokoloen Agiritegi Historikoa / Archivo Histórico de Protocolos de Gipuzkoa*); John

Matthews (Interlibrary Loan, University of Illinois at Chicago); Richard Maxwell (Queens University, New York); Margot McCain (Portland Public Library); Niksa Mendes (Maritime and History Museum of the Croatian Littoral Rijeka); Michael Meszaros; Lara Michels (Judah L. Magnes Museum); Mark C. Mollan (NARA); Janie Morris (Rare Book, Manuscript, and Special Collections Library, Duke University); Kristin Morris (San Francisco Museum and Historical Society); Jocelyn Moss (Marin History Museum); Benjamin Oko, Ana M. Ortiz (Interlibrary Loan, University of Illinois at Chicago); Kelly Page (Maine Maritime Museum); Stanley Payne (University of Wisconsin); Timorah Perel (Reference and Information Services, Yad Vashem Holocaust Resources); Alfredo Pérez Trimiño (*Monografías Históricas de Portugalete, http://monografiashistoricasdeportugalete.blogspot.com/*); Wayne Peterson (Deputy Court Clerk, San Francisco Superior Court); Rick Peuser (NARA); David Pfeiffer (NARA); Achille Rastelli (AIDMEN/*Associazione Italiana di Documentazione Marittima e Navale*); Marianne Reynolds (Public Library of Cincinnati and Hamilton County); Joseph Rom, (Palyam); Arieh Rona; David P. Rosenberg (Center for Jewish History); Willi Rostoker; Jelena Rubić-Lasić (Ministry of Culture of the Republic of Croatia); Rochelle Rubinstein (Deputy Director, Archival Matters, CZA); Vicente L. Sanahuja (Vidamarítima); Laurence Schecker (Federal Communications Commission, United States); Itzhak Shander; David P. Sobonya (FBI-Records Management Division); Samuel D. Spivack (Drake Navigators Guild); Neil Summers (Jack Chapman Collection); Frances Thompson (UCLA Public Records Coordinator); Laurie Thompson (Anne T. Kent California Room, Marin Civic Center Library); Mark R. Thompson (Portland Harbor Museum); Randy Thompson (Senior Archivist, NARA, Riverside); Gloria Pilar Totoricagüena; *Untzi Museoa-Museo Naval*, San Sebastián; Becky Vance (Society of Former Special Agents of the FBI, Inc.); Peter C. Wagner (U.S. Department of Transportation, Maritime Administration); Kevin Wilks (Center for Research Libraries, Chicago); Captain Hillel Yarkoni; Etti Yotvat (The Jerusalem Report); Jorge Zapata López; Alexandra Zapruder; and Nagore Zelaia (*Artxiboa — Bermeoko Udala*).

Finally, it would be unconscionable not to express my enormous gratitude to the members of my immediate family for their unshakable support, encouragement, and patience: my mother, Iris, my sisters Alda and Maria, my wife Kathy, and my son Ernesto. After so many years on this project, they will be greatly relieved not to hear me discuss anymore what my son Ernesto for quite some time has simply, if humorously, referred to as "the boat."

Introduction

Israeli agents of Haganah — the main Jewish underground in Palestine — purchased in the United States in spring of 1948 the cargo ship *S.S. Kefalos* to smuggle arms into Israel. The vessel was registered in Panama under the ownership of the fictitious Manuel Enterprises, Inc., an Israeli shell company. The daring plan was to sail the vessel from New York to Tampico, Mexico, to load the arms and transport them from that port to Israel. The crew of the *Kefalos* was heavily composed of Spanish Republican refugees and Spanish was one of the predominant languages aboard. The *Kefalos* sailed from New York on 13 June and arrived in Tampico under false pretenses eleven days later (24 June). Loaded with arms, the vessel then left Tampico on 3 August, though it quickly changed its name and appearance in an attempt to elude British vigilance when it crossed Gibraltar and U.N. Observers in Tel Aviv. The ship's new name was revealing: it was re-baptized the *S.S. M*[artin] *A*[lonso] *Pinzon*, named after Columbus's navigator. Throughout the secret operation there was extensive cooperation between seemingly disparate diasporas. Jews (Israeli, European, North American, and Mexican) worked closely with Spanish crew members, many of them Basque, to assure the success of the enterprise. The Israeli code name for the vessel was *Dromit* ("southerner"; Dromi was an alias for Mexico). The ship arrived in Israel thirty-five days later on 8 September 1948 and quickly unloaded vitally needed arms. Israeli authorities then decided to reconvert the *Kefalos* to a semblance of a passenger ship to rescue Jews stranded in the Balkans. Restructured in Naples in September-October, 1948, the vessel then made two voyages from Bakar (modern-day Croatia) to Haifa in late 1948 with over 7,700 refugees. All this seems straightforward and simple enough now, but six years ago I ignored nearly all but the most basic facts of the improbable saga of the rust bucket, as it was endearingly known to many of those who sailed aboard it.

At the heart of this book are two fundamental questions: a logistical and military one (the transport and smuggling of arms for Israel's War of Independence); and a humanitarian one (the rescue of Jewish refugees in the Balkans). The monograph examines how each of the objectives was successfully accomplished. To do this it was essential to have excellent coordination, from Haganah's organizational leadership at the top, to a veteran and skilled captain, down to a loyal and adept, and politically committed crew whose sympathies for the Israeli cause never wavered. The monograph also makes the case that the *Kefalos* enjoyed a good measure of luck at crucial times in its voyages. In sum, this work aims to cast light on the procurement of arms by Israel during the War of Independence, on post-Holocaust refugee issues, and on the cooperation between disparate Jewish and Spanish Republican diasporas. But there is another significant — if not always apparent — facet to the odyssey of the *Kefalos* that transcends the juncture of events in 1948: the intersection of Spanish and Jewish cultures across time and space. Perhaps the best example of the persistence on this *longue durée* is revealed by the fact that during one of the trips from the Balkans to Israel, some of the Jewish refugees conversed with the Spanish crew in Ladino (medieval and early modern Judeo-Spanish). This continuity was also powerfully displayed in an anecdote vividly recalled by my father: after unloading its arms, and as the ship was getting to leave Tel Aviv on 12 September, and the plank was being raised to leave, someone on shore yelled out to him *"adiós paisano!"* in perfect Castilian.

I have known about the *Kefalos* since I was a child. My father, Carlos Blanco Aguinaga, a crew member, would sometimes talk about it but never extensively or in detail. Still, it was clear to the family that his journey aboard this vessel had been an important chapter of his youth. And yet, strangely, he had no photographs of the *entire* ship even though he had two very hazy ones from a small newspaper clipping of the freighter in Tampico and another photograph of the crew on deck during a safety drill (photograph 34). In spring 2008 I was teaching a course on nineteenth-twentieth century Spain, and sometime in late March or early April, I was discussing the end of the Spanish Civil War, always for me a sad undertaking. During one of the classes I explained to my students the Republican exile to Latin America and to Mexico in particular. To illustrate the matter more fully, I showed some photographs of the ships like the *Sinaia* that had taken the refugees to their destination in the New World. In my search I somehow had the idea of finding a photograph of the *Kefalos*.

In the era of the Internet this surely would prove an easy endeavor, and yet it was not. And what started, innocently enough, as a straightforward quest, turned into a major historical investigation that has lasted six years and consumed a great deal of my life. If Jonah was swallowed by a whale, I was swallowed by the *Kefalos*. But I confess not to regret a single moment of the time I have spent researching the boat, even when it put on hold other ongoing and nearly completed projects. In many respects, as I delved more and more deeply into the odyssey of the ship with three names, I was able to reconstruct and relive the many facets of the vessel's implausible journey. Along the way I not only learned about matters profoundly alien to this early modern historian, but during the investigation, I met a number of fascinating individuals who have guided my work and provided me with important first-hand information on some of the principals of the *Kefalos*'s story.

One of the first things I had to do was to accurately identify the ship's captain, Adolph S. Oko, Jr. When my search for Captain Oko began, I completely overlooked the 'Jr.' part, even when my father's discharge papers read A. S. Oko, Jr, though, in my defense, a feeble one at that, the 'Jr.' is completely inside of, and overlapped by, the ship's official seal, making the reading unclear. So I Googled away endlessly, looking for Adolph S. Oko, and of course repeatedly encountered the captain's father, Adolph Sigmund Oko, the celebrated bibliographer and Spinoza scholar associated for so many years with Hebrew Union College. Of course there was another Adolph

Sigmund Oko, but his papers at the Bancroft Library failed to show that he was the son of the famous librarian at Cincinnati. Eventually, I figured out that there were indeed two Okos. But confirmation of this arrived through an improbable source: the Inverness Yacht Club (Marin County, California). According to the Club's web page, "Oko had proved himself an audacious sailor on waters deeper and wider than Tomales Bay. After World War II, he ran the British blockage of the Mediterranean in his rust bucket, the *Kefalos*." Armed with this information, not entirely correct by the way, I contacted the Club and received a gracious, helpful reply from one of Captain Oko's friends and associates, Edward Von Der Porten, who not only provided important information on 'Oke,' as his wife and many of his friends fondly called him, but also furnished me with a transcript of an important lengthy taped interview that Edward and his wife Saryl had conducted with Oko in December, 1960. Several extremely significant leads and finds followed in short order.

Now that I had identified the correct Oko, I set out to gather additional facts about him. A natural start was through his father's records; I contacted the American Jewish Archives and inquired. In May, 2008, the AJA replied that they had nothing in the collections of Oko Sr. regarding his son, but added that the Archives held "a microfilm [...] which contains correspondence and papers relating to the rescue of European Jews by Captain and Mrs. Adolph Oko — 1948–1949." Moreover, the microfilm was accompanied by obituaries, editorial comments, and twenty-seven photos of the *Kefalos* that had belonged to the Okos. Once I obtained the materials on loan, it became immediately clear that this was a discovery of the highest order. Not only did I now have excellent photographs of the ship, I also possessed one of the main foundations of the investigation.

Also in April-May, 2008, while looking for the *Kefalos*, I established my first contact with Commander Yehuda Ben-Tzur, a veteran of the War of Independence, a retired Israeli naval officer, and a former director of the Israeli Defense Forces Naval Academy. Commander Ben-Tzur, is one of the co-directors of Palyam.org, a "site dedicated to preserving the heritage of the Palyam & Aliya Bet." I was initially attracted to the page by a brief piece on the *Kefalos* written by Ben-Tzur himself. My association with Yehuda Ben-Tzur has proven invaluable; a bottomless pit of information and knowledge, and an individual of seemingly endless contacts, he has served as my guide and mentor of all matters related to the war as well as to numerous aspects of Israeli society and government during the 1940s and 50s. Not only has Yehuda been extremely generous with his time despite his many other commitments, he has provided me with important facts that have vastly enhanced this project and enriched my understanding of complex matters that were well beyond my initial state of comprehension. And he has not been shy about correcting my mistakes or wrong-headed assumptions when it was required. Despite the physical distance that separates us, we have been in constant contact through e-mail. In fact, along with my father, the three of us have exchanged hundreds, perhaps even thousands, of communications since beginning our joint collaboration in the spring of 2008.

After an in-depth consultation of the materials from the AJA was completed, leads multiplied, and what began as a trickle became a torrent of information. Through Ancestry.com I was able to develop hundreds of leads on numerous facets of the crew: prior sailing histories, ages, personal information, nationalities, places of birth, and so on. Also through this site and its web of interlocking references, I began to piece together important parts of the lives of Captain Oko and his wife Gladys. Many of the missing biographical facts of their lives I slowly filled in with countless queries to state vital records offices, articles and publications, newspapers and obituaries, local libraries, and friends and acquaintances. Of course, as is so often the case in historical research, there were many dead ends, but fortunately also innumerable leads that led seamlessly directly to other vital information. Such was the case, for example, of the ship itself.

Once I was able to ascertain some basic facts about the vessel's origins, owners, travels, transfers and sales, and overall history, I could verify many key elements of the *Kefalos* through patient inquiries at the National Records Administration (NARA). The NARA's very helpful, if overworked, staff provided invaluable details of the ship, particularly during WWII and its transfer to new owners after the War. It took some doing, but with the help of NARA and sites devoted to maritime matters, I was able to trace with a fair degree of exactitude the entire history of the *Kefalos* from its construction to its scrapping in 1963. Other federal and state government agencies answered my petitions for documentary assistance. For example, I requested, and obtained, from the U.S. Coast Guard the service records of Oko during 1942-1946. And since I knew from the secondary literature that several individuals connected to the *Kefalos* enterprise had been indicted and tried for violations of the Neutrality Act and other federal provisions, I filed numerous Freedom of Information Act (FOIA) petitions with the FBI for documents related to many of the individuals in question. Though often heavily redacted, and often slow in arriving, the FBI files proved an extraordinary source of information on the ship, its crew, and how the arms it smuggled to Israel had been secured in Hawaii and in Mexico by Haganah operatives through a variety of legal and illegal means.

However, not all the documents have been gathered through the Internet or received in regular mail. In early 2009 and 2010, I consulted twice in person several important trials at NARA (Laguna Niguel, California). And in the summer of 2009, I found and researched the captain's extensive personal papers at the Bancroft Library in Berkeley. These holdings include drafts of an unfinished book manuscript about the *Kefalos* that Captain Oko started to write in 1957-8 but never completed. Titled "And It Was So," this work contains a wealth of information not found elsewhere. But these two important collections were not the only ones to hold crucial sources on the vessel. In the course of the investigation, other essential documents came to light, notably at NARA, the Haganah Archives, the Central Zionist Archives, the Palmach Archives, and in public and private Spanish collections. For example, through contacts with local and municipal archives in the Basque region, I have obtained significant information on a handful of crew members. To give the reader an idea of the sheer quantity of documents gathered so far, as of this writing, there are now three large boxes of hard copies and files, close to 6,000 e-mails exchanged between myself, my father, Yehuda Ben-Tzur and numerous other entities, and close to one hundred folders of *Kefalos*-related materials in my computers' hard drives.

One of the most satisfying results of the research has been the collection of important photographic evidence. A substantial number of original photographs have been gathered for this book. Drawn mostly from private collections, the vast majority of them have never been seen or studied. Many of the photographs are stunningly beautiful, especially those taken by the Okos primarily on the voyage from Tampico to Tel Aviv, as well as other expressive ones of the refugees by the Okos and other photographers on the journeys from the Balkans to Israel. There are also a number of unrelated, unidentified photographs of unknown provenance. In all, there are approximately some sixty to seventy photographs, including newspaper ones. I've had to make hard choices on which ones to select for this book, and therefore have limited myself to a small number of photographs that illustrate and enrich key points of the narrative.

For the most part this book follows a straightforward chronological order. Chapter 1 traces the history of the *Kefalos* from its construction to its transfer to Israeli ownership (1917-1949). The prominent role of the vessel as the *S.S. Larranga* during WWII is underscored. Chapter 2 examines the intertwined lives of Oko and Gladys. The couple was inseparable from the time they met in the early 1930s until Oko's death in 1963. At chapter's end I discuss the important document titled "Instructions to Master." This was a set of orders likely given to Oko in New York by Teddy Kollek, at the time the chief Haganah operative in the U.S., amidst much cloak-and-dagger secretiveness. The instructions were effectively the captain's operational orders for the mission. Years later, Oko reviewed the yellowing, two-page list, and remarked critically, if with a touch of nostalgia, that it read like a "dime novel [...] so obvious and awkward." After the crew enlisted formally before the Panamanian consul, the ship — code-named *Dromit* by Haganah — left New York on 13 June ostensibly for South America (Buenos Aires or Montevideo), one of the numerous subterfuges employed by Israeli operatives during the enterprise.

Chapter 3 details the ship's lengthy, and largely involuntary, stay in Tampico and the manner in which Haganah's network procured arms by all necessary means. This chapter begins with the ship's eventful forty-day stopover in Tampico (24 June-3 August). The *Kefalos* had arrived at port under patently questionable circumstances, alleging the need for repairs and special parts. Newspaper publicity in mid-July torpedoed all secrecy, resulting in widespread public scandal and controversy. The U.S. government had substantial intelligence on the doings of the *Kefalos*. Adding to the captain's troubles, many of the arms were late in arriving at Tampico, and he suffered from dysentery during most of his stay there. After all the preparations had at last been finalized, according to the list prepared by the captain, the ship carried thirty-six crew members and two passengers upon departure, and the vessel left Tampico with a substantial cargo of arms and sugar. Significantly, with patently false port documents, the vessel departed for Shanghai, via Genoa, still officially as the *Kefalos*, even though there's substantial evidence that many, including the captain, had begun to refer to the ship as the M.A. *Pinzon*. While Oko and the crew waited impatiently at Tampico, from Hawaiian salvage yards to Mexican armories, Haganah operatives had obtained a sizeable arms cargo through a variety of ways, ranging from outright theft to purchases secured and/or accompanied by bribes to Mexican officials. Among the best known of these actions was the celebrated *Idalia* episode. In a caper worthy of a Hollywood B-movie thriller, Herman "Hank" Greenspun commandeered a schooner owned by Leland R. Lewis in Wilmington/San Pedro, California, loaded it with arms stolen in Hawaii, and with a total crew of five, forced it to travel to Acapulco, Mexico, where the cargo was unloaded with the assistance of the Mexican Navy. The arms were then trans-shipped by train to Tampico, along with other armament procured in Mexico City.

Chapter 4 explores the ship's crew, one which by all accounts had a markedly Spanish Republican flavor. (Through painstaking research, as of this writing, I have been able to gather biographical data on thirty-four of the thirty-eight crew members and passengers on the way to Israel.) Over half of the crew was composed of Spanish refugees (many of them Basques), and Spaniards traveling with Latin American passports. In a possible overstatement, but a highly significant one, according to Captain Oko, Spanish was the freighter's predominant language. My father often acted on board the ship as a translator between Spanish and English speakers. Nearly all testimonies are unanimous in underscoring the loyalty and discipline of the Spanish crew during the mission. To the captain's enormous regret, one of the Spaniards he admired most, Mariano Manresa, was ill with cancer, and even though he traveled from New York to Tampico aboard the ship, his condition forced him to abandon plans to make the journey to Israel as he wanted and planned to do. This chapter also discusses another important element of the crew: the five Jewish individuals recruited and placed on the ship by Haganah. They were Al Ellis, Robert Keller, Arieh Kesselman, Nathaniel Ratner, and Jack Rothman. Of the five only Rothman, the radio operator, had been on board since New York. The others joined the ship at Tampico. It is important to note that Ellis and Ratner had been part of the *Idalia* crew. Though their role and significance on board are subject to a good deal of conjecture, it seems evident that Haganah wanted to maintain a strong presence on the *Kefalos*, probably to keep an eye on Captain Oko, an independent-minded and strong-willed individual who was not entirely trusted by the Israelis.

Chapter 4 also provides an account of the long thirty-five day voyage to Tel Aviv, how the ship's appearance was transformed by the carpenter in an attempt to fool the British; its slow, steady speed (8.5 knots an hour), and the daily tedium of life on board. There were important questions in everyone's mind of what might happen when the *Kefalos* crossed Gibraltar, and yet, to universal relief among the crew, the British let it pass without incident. But even after Gibraltar, the voyage was not without danger. Near Pantelleria — a small island roughly midway between Tunisia and Sicily — the vessel nearly crashed into some shoals when it accidentally strayed off course. The captain's log shows that he charted a careful course for Israel to avoid the most obvious perils. However, other difficulties quickly arose: there were radio problems and Israeli listening stations lost all contact with the ship, causing a mad scramble among Israeli officials to locate it. Additionally, the ship experienced severe water and fuel shortages; with some of the gauges nearly on zero, the vessel arrived in Tel Aviv on 8 September. The freighter's valuable cargo was quickly unloaded: arms were taken to shore rapidly and at night; sugar was carried to land slowly and at daytime. The much-needed arms were rushed to the Negev where they played a decisive role in Israeli operations. The ship hurriedly left Israeli on 12 September amid suggestions of impending additional U.N. inspections that might well have turned up violations of the Second Truce. As a footnote, Israeli officials gave stern orders that the name *Pinzon* was not to be mentioned again. That did not prevent Israeli officials to continue calling the vessel the *Pinzon* for some time, and Captain Oko later to refer to *himself* as the master, not of the *Kefalos*, but of the "S.S. *Martin Alonzo* [sic] *Pinzon*."

Chapter 5 explores an important change in the ship's mission. There were significant disputes among Israeli officials about the vessel's future. After heated discussions, they decided to change the use and purpose of the *Kefalos*. Instead of carrying arms, the rust bucket would be used to transports passengers. Dispatched to Naples quickly, the *Kefalos* spent fifty days in that port (22 September–8 November); there it was retrofitted to carry people. As in Tampico, the lengthy stay in Naples was not without complications; numerous expenses were approved by the captain and Israeli aides, and bills rapidly piled up. Predictably, Oko's frustrations due to delays and conflicts with Israel's representatives in Italy resulted in continual tensions — frictions with loose ends that lasted for years. In a surprising development, while the *Kefalos* was undergoing substantial transformations and repairs, the real M/V *Pinzon* arrived in Naples, where the two ships coexisted for a couple days. At least one other important event occurred for the *Kefalos* at that port: while taking the ship to open waters for a test practice to ascertain its seaworthiness, the *Kefalos* encountered an Israeli chartered arms ship, the M/V *Scio*, in severe difficulties. The *Kefalos* towed it to Naples, earning in process some money as well as the gratitude of Haganah officials. Naples also saw some changes in the personnel. As several crew members left for other destinations, some of them were replaced by other Spaniards recruited from Campo Bagnoli in Naples, a camp for displaced persons administered by the International Organization of Refugees.

Chapter 6 delves into the two rescues of refugees or immigrants (*olim*) in Bakar. During the first one (8–23 November), the vessel traveled around the 'boot' of Italy and up the Adriatic, arriving in Split-Bakar (present-day Croatia). At the latter port over 4,000 came on board. It was during this difficult journey with extremely poor conditions on board that, according to the captain, Spanish crew members conversed in Ladino with some refugees. Despite the travails, there were numerous positive aspects of the refugees' conduct during voyage: social harmony, music, marriages and births. But shortly after leaving Bakar, a strong storm kicked up, and Captain Oko, fearing that the vessel was not sea worthy, and worried about the passengers' safety, took shelter off the Italian coast. The refugees insisted on proceeding directly to Israel, but the captain resisted their demands. The captain, with Nathaniel Ratner's assistance, overcame the attempted takeover and near mutiny by olim, and ship arrived safely in Haifa.

This chapter also surveys the second rescue of refugees (28 November–25 December). This trip to the Balkans was quite possibly more eventful than the first. The ship arrived in Bakar on 8 December. There the vessel waited several days for the first group of refugees to arrive. A host of complications and dangers at port ensued. The *Kefalos* was ordered by local authorities to leave the dock where it was moored to make room for another ship, an arms vessel. Ratner and Oko employed a host of delaying tactics to ensure that no refugee was left behind. All refugees came on board and the ship sailed before a port ultimatum expired. The *Kefalos* left overloaded, with horrendous conditions on board, and amidst a raging storm. The sea eventually calmed, but a voyage of eight days under normal conditions took nearly eleven. There were complaints about food, and even a threatened hunger strike by the refugees. Again Ratner played a key role in quieting things down. The refugees arrived weakened and battered when the *Kefalos* put into Haifa on Christmas Night, 25 December. According to Oko, nearly 3,800 olim arrived on the second voyage. During the two trips from the Balkans the ship had rescued 7,737 refugees. This chapter also briefly details the ship's final days under Oko's orders. In early January, 1949, with the vessel still at Haifa, Oko was "requested" by Israeli shipping officials to hand command of the *Kefalos* — also pointedly called *Pinzon* in parenthesis — to Captain Joseph Golandski. After transfer from Panamanian to Israeli registry, the vessel quickly officially became the *Dromit*. The crew's outstanding pay was settled at the same time at Haifa.

The conclusion examines the reasons for the mission's favorable outcome. Chiefly, it was the close cooperation between Jewish and Spanish Republican diasporas that ensured the success of the *Kefalos*'s military and humanitarian goals. Overall, it was an impressive operation, one assisted by a combination of significant factors and circumstances: imaginative and bold planning, excellent coordination and financing, the crew's unbending dedication and enormous sailing skill, and more than a fair amount of good fortune. Finally, the book closes with a brief epilogue of the aftermath of the *Kefalos* saga and the fate of some of its main protagonists: Oko and Gladys,

the crew, the American Jewish volunteers and the Haganah operatives and their associates in the United States.

Even though I hope that this modest book advances our understanding of the vessel's extraordinary adventure, while casting light
on larger historical issues, it is evident that there's much we ignore
about a host of key ancillary matters. For example, how was it that
so many Spanish Republican sailors (Basques in particular) came to
sympathize with the Israeli cause? What did most of the crew do after the ship's journeys came to an end? Why did the Mexican government decide to assist Israel — even if admittedly under the table, and
with more than a fair amount of questionable motives? What was the
precise role of Mexican officials in this arms procurement process?
Why is the bibliography virtually non-existent on U.S. government
trials of those tried for a host of violations of the Neutrality Act and
other provisions? Why the deafening silence on these matters when
some of the most flagrant arms smuggling transgressions were related to the vessel at the heart of this book? These and other pertinent
interrogatives await investigators; their findings will undoubtedly
augment considerably our knowledge of the odyssey of the ship with
three names.

1

The Rust Bucket

We went to Portland, Maine to accept delivery of the vessel, and to bring her to Todd's dry dock in New York. I will never forget my chief mate's remark (Mr. Eric Forbes) when he saw the vessel for the first time: "This isn't a ship, Captain, and she'll never be a ship. Have you been smoking opium?" I advised Mr. Forbes that what she lacked we would supply. That men make a ship.

— "A. S. Oko Jr., "THE KEFALOS"

I took delivery of a vessel, and she was a sad rust bucket in Portland, Maine.

— A. S. Oko Jr., "1960 account"[1]

The *Kefalos* started its life as the T/S *Dicto*. It was built at Bethlehem Steel Company, San Francisco, California (formerly Union Brass & Iron Works [1849–1906], Union Iron Works [1906–1917], incorporating Risdon Iron Works [in San Francisco] and United Engineering Works [in Alameda]).[2] The vessel was delivered in July 1917 to B. Stolt-Nielsen (Haugesund, Norway); the company paid 3,500,000 Norwegian kroner for the ship (U.S. $1,035,502 in 1917 dollars).[3] Fitted with a General Electric Company steam engine, the *Dicto*, a cargo ship, had a gross weight of 3,892 tons and a dead weight of 5,950 tons (estimates of these weights vary little over the years). A small vessel, its dimensions were hardly imposing: it measured 341 feet in length, 48.2 feet in width, and 24.5 feet in height. Little is known to this writer about activities of the *Dicto* following 1917, although, as a possible harbinger of things to come, the ship was quickly pressed into humanitarian actions, participating in Belgian relief in 1918 and 1919.[4] After a little over eleven years in the possession of the *Dicto*, B. Stolt-Nielsen sold the ship in November 1928 to E. B. Aaby in Olso for 230,000 kroner (U.S. $61,300).[5] Though the reasons for the vessel's serious devaluation remain unknown, it seems likely that there were substantial problems with key elements of its turbine engine. Its new owner in 1929 took out the turbine machinery and replaced it with a triple expansion steam engine (3 cylinders, diameter 24", 38", and 64"; stroke 42"), built by McKie & Baxter, Ltd. (Glasgow, Scotland).[6] The ship's two original boilers, however, were kept. The overhaul in the machine room gave the ship new life and allowed it to sail reasonably well for the next twenty years.

In 1933, E. B. Aaby sold the vessel to the American Foreign Steamship Corporation (New York, New York), and the ship formally became part of the American Cardinal Steamship Corporation.[7] Eventually, the freighter was simply named the *American Cardinal* and sailed as such during the next three years.[8] The ship was then purchased in 1936 by Maltran (C.D. Mallory Corporation), and renamed *Mallard* in September of that year.[9] Under Mallory, the *Mallard* apparently was primarily involved in two-way coastal trade along the eastern seaboard and southern United States.[10] And in this manner and ownership the *Mallard* sailed until late 1941, when it was requisitioned by the U.S. government, as direct entry into World War II seemed inevitable. A new certificate of registry was issued in New York on 5 December 1941, and the ship's name was changed to *Larrañaga*. However, as the certificate specifically asserts, the name occurred by authority of a telephone communication from the U.S. Bureau of Marine Inspection and Navigation.[11] This communication resulted in considerable bureaucratic confusion in subsequent years; in effect, the ship sometimes appears as *Larrañaga*, its intended new name, but more commonly as *Larranga*.[12] The vessel was about to enter several years of arduous service on behalf of the United States and its allies during World War II as a cargo vessel.

The *Larranga*'s integration into the war effort during the early periods of conflict was not devoid of complications, and turf struggles between various branches of the U.S. government ensued.[13]

But once the disputes were settled, the ship's functions and objectives were more precisely defined, and the vessel [photograph 1] was armed for self-defense. The *Larranga* appears to have acquitted itself quite honorably during the war.[14] Probably the best way to judge the ship's wide-ranging service on behalf of the Allied cause in the North Atlantic — between such ports and adjacent areas as Boston, Halifax, Newfoundland, Reykjavik, and Murmansk — is through an examination of its participation in fifty-six convoys, one voyage as an escorted vessel, and twenty-one trips as an independent cargo ship.[15] There is even an often-repeated, though unverified, account that the armed guard "got its first taste of battle when it fired three rounds as [sic] a surfaced submarine on Christmas eve, *perhaps* scoring a hit on the second round."[16] From March 1944 until September 1945 the *Larranga* was "under charter to the government of Iceland."[17] The ship's last recorded voyage as part of its duties in the War Shipping Administration appears to have occurred in late December 1945, when it departed from Brest, France.[18] As the war ended, nearly thirty years of continual sailing had exacted a heavy toll on the vessel, and the *Larranga* was in horrendous condition.

On 3 March 1946, the cargo ship entered the naval reserve fleet and was laid up in Virginia at the James River facilities for inactive U.S. Navy auxiliary ships. The reason for the lay-up was telling: the vessel was labeled as "obsolete for any use." The cost of repairs to enter the reserve fleet was estimated at $125,000.[19] The War Shipping Administration, which owned the *Larranga*, in a memorandum to the U.S. Maritime Commission dated 14 May 1946 gave the commission the authority to advertise the sale of the vessel.[20] In late December of that year, the U.S. Maritime Commission invited bids for the sale of several ships at the James River reserve fleet, including the *Larranga*.[21] The sale should have proceeded fairly rapidly. However, all of initial bids were rejected as too low by the commission, and a new invitation for bids was announced.[22] The bidding for the first round had been restricted to U.S. citizens, and the highest bid was only $80,000. In the re-advertisement, the restriction was dropped, and the sale was, in effect, open to buyers of any nationality. The new round of bids proved more successful, and the commission approved the sale of the *Larranga* to Michael P. Bonicos on 4 April 1947 for $102,560.98.[23] The ship was withdrawn from the reserve fleet on 24

June 1947,[24] and it was "surrendered" to its new owner at Newport News, Virginia, on 30 September 1947.[25] Shortly after acquiring the vessel, Bonicos renamed it *Kefalos* and placed it under Panamanian registry.[26]

Even though details about the new owner are relatively scarce, Bonicos's life is not entirely a blank slate. Born in Cephalonia, Greece in March 1888, Bonicos had more than a passing familiarity with the sea. His name appears in a smattering of ship crew manifests, beginning in 1917. For example, in a 1917 ship arrival in New York, the twenty-nine-year-old Bonicos had the position of machinist on board the *Alicante*, a vessel whose port of departure was Barcelona. And in 1919, arriving in the same port from Rotterdam on board the *West Gambo*, Bonicos had risen to the position of first assistant engineer.[27] In 1917 and 1918, however, Bonicos was living and working in Philadelphia, and his 1917 registration card lists him as a repairman at a steel company.[28] On 27 September 1918, Bonicos wrote the U.S. Department of Labor (Immigration Service), stating his desire to return to Greece "to enter the Greek Navy," and identifying himself as a marine engineer.[29] Bonicos appears to have traveled to Europe, returning to the United States in 1920, and shortly thereafter, in 1921, he began naturalization proceedings.[30] In the 1930 U.S. Census, Bonicos, now forty-two and married to a young Belgian woman, was living in Manhattan and was listed as a "marine engineer."[31] By 1942, Bonicos was residing in Brooklyn at the same address as when he made the highest bid to purchase the *Larranga*.[32] After the purchase date, the information concerning Bonicos becomes spotty at best, and little is known about him from 1942 until 1947 and 1948.

Under Bonicos's ownership (September 1947–May/June 1948), the *Kefalos* left few traces in maritime documents, as well as many unanswered questions. For example, was it owned solely by Michael P. Bonicos, or in partnership with one of his brothers? The official papers of the sale only allude to Michael, but Oko, a fierce critic of Michael and his slightly younger brother, Gerassimos, a ship captain, wrote that the *Kefalos* "had been in disuse, was under threat of a [law]suit, and had been purchased by a couple of international characters, the Bonicos brothers."[33] The captain was furious at the Bonicos for the state in which he found the vessel when he first encountered it. In a memorable – if highly exaggerated – passage,

Oko lyrically described the pain of an abused and neglected vessel, and even posed an improbable question: "Can a ship commit suicide?"[34] "According to Oko, the *Kefalos* had "deteriorated under the corrosive treatment given her by the owners [the Bonicos], [...] and manned her with crews so mistreated that resentment turned to such virulent brew of hate that the last departing seamen soiled the decks and defecated on the floor of their quarters as a parting insult to the ship and its owners."[35] Oko castigated Bonicos for having the *Kefalos* make eight voyages during the previous period "with holds filled to capacity and never so much as a thank you repair. She had been run as a starvation ship and manned by crews driven to desperate extremes."[36] But how had the new owners been able to get away with such flagrant mistreatment of the ship and its crews? The answers were straightforward, according to Oko, a seaman with substantial maritime experience. The Bonicos, asserted Oko, had shown an utter "disregard of accepted seafaring practices," and since the vessel had been "placed under Panamanian registry but operated chiefly from "American ports," the owners had been able to side-step "governmental regulations of both countries."[37] A case in point was the cargo ship's last nightmarish voyage under Bonicos: "China clay had been loaded in England, without benefit of papering or any protection from the insidious dust so fine-textured that it silted into every crack or crevice and coated every surface with the choking clay," permeating the entire ship.[38] Not papering the cargo, according to Oko's scathing indictment, was all in an effort to save money. In sum, a ship that "had borne many names, served various European and American flags, passed from one owner to another, and carried innumerable types of cargo under varied conditions of war and peace [...], a 'common carrier,' serviceable, honest, and dependable, but with no pretensions to style, beauty, or spectacular achievement" had been exploited and rendered nearly useless by the Bonicos.[39]

Oko's intense dislike — bordering on hatred — for Captain Gerassimos Bonicos, in particular, came close to boiling over during a face-to-face confrontation aboard the *Kefalos* when the ship was inspected at Todd's Dry Dock in Brooklyn in early June 1948 (more on the circumstances of this unlikely meeting below). Captain Bonicos had asked to be taken on as a passenger aboard the *Kefalos* on its delivery run from Portland, Maine, to New York (3–6 June). Oko was not pleased by this but felt bound to extend a "captain's courtesy" to Bonicos, a favor he came to regret.[40] A large party — which included Israelis, men from Todd's, Oko, Bonicos, and possibly others — was going over the vessel at the dry dock on 7 June to ascertain what repairs were needed to make the *Kefalos* completely seaworthy again. Having Captain Bonicos there was a mixed blessing for Oko. The new skipper of the ship freely admitted Bonicos was getting under his skin and would rather not have him along, "except that as the man most familiar with the *Kefalos*, and the only one who could give any first-hand facts of [...] the two previous years, it was logical to have him on the survey."[41] However, when Oko asked Bonicos about specific problems with the vessel, he was "intent on being non-committal" and provided little information. The "repeated evasions of responsibility irked" Oko, and his resentment gradually built up. When the group reached the bottom of the dry dock and inspected the bottom, Oko noticed "a twenty-foot break in one of the fins [...] at the turn of the bilge." He immediately knew that the ship had run aground somewhere, and asked Bonicos how it had happened. According to Oko, Bonicos laconically replied, "Oh, long time ago. In the Platte."[42] [Photograph 2] From there, the conversation became more heated. Oko inquired if Bonicos had placed the *Kefalos* in a dry dock to inspect the damage. His answer, "Dry dock? Why bother?" set Oko off. Accusingly, Oko then said, "you ran her aground and didn't *bother* to inspect her bottom?"[43] In Oko's vivid description, Bonicos asserted matter-of-factly, "All ships go aground in the River Platte," and rolled his eyes upward. Oko exploded: "Look, you lousy son-of-a-bitch." Starting toward Oko, Bonicos angrily replied, "Nobody calls me a son-of-a-bitch." But Oko grabbed a metal spike, "for use in driving blocks home," and shot back at Bonicos, "One step, and you're a dead pig!"[44] Both men were shaken by the looming threat of violence; Bonicos apparently backed off, and Oko, realizing that he had come close to driving the spike into Bonicos's head, thought it best to get off the dry dock. Turning to one of the chief Israelis and the rest of the group, Oko's parting words were telling: "It's your baby," he said, and he walked off.[45] Oko confessed that he was haunted for years for having come so close to mayhem and committing murder.[46] But how and why had matters become so tense and nearly fatal aboard the *Kefalos* in early June 1948? The short answer is that in the spring of 1948 in the United States, the Israeli agents of Haganah — the main Jewish underground in Palestine — bought the cargo ship *Kefalos* from the Bonicos to smuggle arms into Israel from Mexico. Oko had taken command of the vessel on behalf of the Israelis at Portland, Maine (most probably), on 1 June 1948, and had then sailed it to New York on 3–6 June, where it underwent extensive repairs at Todd's for the next days. The long answer, however, is far more complex and significant.

The purchase of the *Kefalos* by Elie Shalit and Rafael Recanati is shrouded in considerable mystery, as might well be expected of an off-the-books transaction. No bill of sale has turned up, and even the exact date of when the vessel was bought remains uncertain. Some of the main aspects of the sale, however, are known. First, it was engineered by a shell corporation by the name of Manuel Enterprises, Inc., whose main operating office was in New York City (2 Broadway); the vessel, however, was registered under Panamanian flag. The ship's letterhead in Spanish read "Manuel Enterprises, S.A., 7 Front Street, Panama City, Panama, C.Z.," and underneath the words "S.S. Kefalos."[47] Second, Shalit and Recanati asked Oko in late May 1948 to inspect a vessel that they were interested in buying. (As will be explained in Chapter 2, this was not the first time that the Israelis had approached Oko for a possible mission.) Oko immediately flew to Portland, Maine, took a quick look at the vessel, and reported to Manuel Enterprises that the ship was "of a suitable type, but in disreputable condition." He then asked the prospective buyers how much they were "thinking of paying for her and what they knew of her history."[48] Their answer must have been jarring to Oko: the principals at Manuel Enterprises informed him that they had already bought it, and asked if he would take command of it. While Oko was probably unenthusiastic about taking command of it, he posed only one condition: that his wife, Gladys, come along as a purser. If this was possible, "I'm your boy," Oko told Shalit and Recanati.[49] They were agreeable to Oko's request: "Who you sign on as crew is up to you, Captain," they replied. Oko then offered to move things along quickly: "Then I'll be back with her and a skeleton crew from the *Adelanto* — a West Coast ship that the captain had owned for a short time — to take over the *Kefalos* within a week."[50]

Had matters been settled, and was everyone pleased? Certainly not. The ever-thrifty and practical Oko soon learned that Manuel Enterprises had paid excessively for the ship ($190,000), and he was terribly unhappy that Shalit and Recanati purchased the *Kefalos* without knowledge of its actual condition and without any evidence of repairs to the ship by the previous owners. Oko informed the new owners that the Bonicos had purchased the cargo ship from the U.S. Maritime Commission at the end of World War II for only $102,000.[51] In effect, the Bonicos brothers had made a handsome profit on the sale of the *Kefalos* after ruining her during their brief ownership. Clearly, Manuel Enterprises had been taken advantage of by the Bonicos, something that undoubtedly hurt Oko even more. But there was no turning back now; as he had told Shalit after the near violent incident with Captain Bonicos, it was their "baby" now, and because of its rundown condition, the rust bucket would require extensive and costly repairs for a host of reasons that had already become painfully clear to Oko in early June. Oko's association with the men of Manuel Enterprises and their superiors was off to a shaky start, and the relationship did not improve much over time.

Despite documentary shortcomings, it is possible to sketch the main outlines of how the purchase of the *Kefalos* was carried out. According to U.S. government files — primarily those of the Federal Bureau of Investigation (FBI) — on 5 June 1948 a payment of $300,000 from a company in Geneva (Pictet & Cie) "was made to Shipowners Agency, New York City, in connection with the purchase and repair of the SS Kefalos."[52] Shipowners Agency, a company with close ties to the Israelis, and working in conjunction with Haganah, "was requested to and did handle the sale of the SS Kefalos to the Manuel Enterprises, Inc." Two attorneys and an official of the Chase National Bank, all three from New York City, informed the FBI that the purchase "was made with funds from the account of Pictet & Cie [...] upon the authorization of one Dr. Erwin Haymann (or Hayman), of Geneva. Others connected with this sale representing Manuel Enterprises, Inc., were Mr. Recanati, Elie Shalit and Miss Diane Schweitzer."[53] Dr. Haymann, according to the U.S. Federal Communications Commission, "was reportedly an officer of a firm which procured war materials for Israel."[54] Dr. Hayman's name would also turn up as the person upon whose orders the Chase National Bank of New York City and the Banco del Ahorro Nacional of Mexico City "paid large sums" to defendants who participated in operations to export arms illegally to Israel in violation of the Neutrality Act and other U.S. government laws.[55] In sum, Haganah officials in Geneva transferred large sums to friendly associates in the United States, such as Shipowners Agency, and with the assistance of U.S. banks bought the *Kefalos* for Manuel Enterprises and paid for the ship's repairs at Todd Shipyards Corporation during early June 1948. Did Manuel Enterprises, therefore, own the ship in its entirety? Apparently not. In a complicated arrangement, Oko held 50 percent of the fictitious company's shares, and a certain unidentified "D.S." (most likely Diane Schweitzer) held the other 50 percent.[56] Not surprisingly, Diane Schweitzer worked at both Shipowners Agency and Manuel Enterprises.[57] Joined at the hip, the two organizations closely coordinated their actions. Shipowners Agency gave every appearance of a legitimate, above-board business, while Manuel Enterprises demonstrated no such pretense. Tightly controlled by Elie Shalit and associates, Manuel Enterprises operated completely in the shadows, leaving no traces beyond its letterhead.

Oko's encounter in the spring of 1948 with Shalit and Manuel Enterprises was not his first with Israeli representatives. Two years earlier, Marvin Lowenthal, a friend of Oko's father, had put the captain in touch with some "Israeli shipping boys in New York."[58] Oko first met Ze'ev "Danny" Shind of Haganah. Their meeting did not go well; Shind did not make a good first impression on Oko. Shind asked Oko what his interest in Israel was. The captain replied, somewhat defensively, noting his last name and telling Shind that by now he'd be a refugee in Israel had he survived the Holocaust. Unconvinced, Shind told Oko dismissively that this was "a purely emotional reason." Oko confesses to have been annoyed by Shind's treatment. Despite the fact, however, that they initially had "not hit it off," there were additional meetings between Oko, Shind, and Shalit. According to Oko, Shind and Shalit then asked him to take command of a vessel they had acquired that was in Baltimore (possibly the President Warfield) and was ready to be used to transport refugees from Marseille, France, to Israel.[59] Oko was amenable to the offer and told them, "Give me six weeks to put my affairs in order on the West Coast and I'm with you." The answer did not sit well with Shind, who replied, "You want six weeks? We are not interested in you." Shalit tried to smooth things over, but Shind's rude dismissal doomed whatever possibilities may have existed to work with Oko in 1946. Oko returned to California, and for two years, in his words, "sharpened my urge to serve fellow members of my minority in Israel."[60] (Oko's Jewishness is discussed in Chapter 2.) When contacted by Shalit and Recanati in May 1948 and informed that "a state of emergency existed in Israel with loopholes under the United Nations truce [and that] they had a vessel in prospect,"[61] Oko did not hesitate; he was clearly eager to get involved and ready to go.

So many things to do and in such a short period of time. In approximately three weeks (from 21 May to 13 June), Oko had to inspect the ship and report to Manuel Enterprises on its condition (dealing with its previous owners and the new ones). He had to gather a skeleton crew from his ship *Adelanto,* which was on the West Coast, and transport the nucleus of trusted seamen to Portland, Maine, take command of the *Kefalos* there, and deliver it to New York, where all of the necessary repairs to the vessel would be made. Oko would need to conscript the new crew and register them with the Panamanian Consulate. [Photograph 8] He would also need to make certain that the *Kefalos* was adequately supplied in every respect for the long voyage, and ultimately, the clandestine operation that would ensue. And as if this all were not enough, Oko would be faced in the process with innumerable challenges ranging from confrontation to compromise; promises of cooperation that did not materialize; and an infernal race against time to get out of New York as fast as possible. These daunting tasks might well have overwhelmed a weak and disorganized individual, but Oko, if high-strung and somewhat neurotic, always proved resilient, practical and resourceful. Time and again, then and later, the captain demonstrated a disciplined determination and an endless capacity for hard work; he continually made to-do lists and followed through with each item. Perhaps more importantly, Oko never acted alone; he always enjoyed the unstinting support and loyalty of his men, whose respect and trust for him often seemed boundless. As an experienced sailor, he understood them well, and treated them not as underlings to be ordered about and abused, but as proud hard-working seamen. Above all, there was Gladys, always by his side, steadfast, loving, and supportive.

After a meeting between Shalit and Oko on the West Coast on

or about 10 May 1948, preparations moved swiftly. By 21 or 23 May, Oko had left for the East Coast to carry out the ship's inspection and arrived back in San Francisco on the 28th of the month.[62] Upon returning, Oko called "together members of the maintenance crew of the SS Adalento [sic]," and, according to Oko's secretary, Mrs. Koo Okamoto, they "were told that they would be engaged in running arms to the Jews in Palestine."[63] In "And It Was So," Oko provides vivid and moving descriptions of the trusted men he gathered for the mission:

> To the eight men of the skeleton crew [...] from the Adelanto, I said nothing more than I had found a ship on the East Coast and wanted them aboard with me [...] [T] hey were smart sailors, all of them — from my hard-slugging, hard-drinking, marlin-spike seaman of a first mate [Forbes] and my Spanish guerilla Second [Manresa], who had been captain of the yacht Vita that carried Loyalist gold to Mexico when the Republic fell, on down to the illiterate but completely trustworthy ship's carpenter, Corino. They were men who knew ships and the sea. Men geared to take things in stride.[64]

According to Oko, "the men I wanted needed no persuasion. They asked no questions."[65] Without wasting much time, "We slipped out of San Francisco before dawn on Memorial Day, Gladys and these eight men I knew I could trust and I, with no good-byes and nothing but a business address in New York for urgent forwarding of mail."[66] But who were the eight sailors so admired by Oko? Although the captain did not make a full list of this nucleus, the names of all the seamen are known based on FBI documents dated 9 September 1948: Félix Apaolaza, José Blanco, Francisco Corino, Eric Forbes, Peeter Ilves, Julio Larrauri, Mariano Manresa, and Carlos Sánchez.[67] It is significant that of the eight men who flew east with Oko and Gladys, six were Spanish Republicans. If the FBI documents are to be believed, according to Mrs. Okamoto, Oko also instructed Manresa "to fill out the crew in New York with [Oko's] old sailing friends who had the same political leanings as his own."[68]

Traveling to Portland, Maine, had been the easy part; leaving port with a ship "in wretched condition" and delivering it safely to New York proved to be quite a different matter.[69] As Oko relates, fortuitously it was dusk when his party first set foot on the vessel, "which was good because no one quite expects [what] to believe what he sees in half-light. Believe me, the Kefalos looked the slut."[70] The "dank swamp smell that rose from her bilges" was nauseating. The next morning in full light, Oko's men were able to take a good look at what confronted them: tangled lines, winches that did not work well, an engine room that made the chief engineer look "paler than usual" when he emerged from his first look at it, dirt and grime everywhere, and uninhabitable quarters. It was enough "to make a seaman shudder." According to Oko, "as the Kefalos lay in Portland, she was an indictment of willful disregard of accepted seafaring practices — far below the level of ignorant neglect." (Oko graphically documented the ship's disastrous condition with a stunning photograph [Photograph 3].) Significantly, the vessel had not even been fumigated since December 1947.[71] Special machinery was brought alongside to clear the water lines and get steam to the boilers, and gradually, some of the stench was cleared. Meanwhile, the ship was stocked and its galley scraped of grease, and since the crew's headquarters were unfit, cots were set up at mid-ship. Gladys went to work with disinfectant and cleansers to make the captain's cabin habitable, while also supervising the cleaning elsewhere. In Oko's words, "all hands worked overtime to get the ship even superficially in shape."[72] There remained, however, a crucial problem: the *Kefalos* lacked a complete crew to sail it to New York. Shortly after its arrival in Portland on 1 April, disgruntled sailors, some of whom had not been paid for as long as seven months, walked off the vessel, declared a strike, and brought legal action against the ship owners — matters that would drag on for weeks.[73]

Word was sent around that a delivery crew was needed and that bonuses would be paid, along with their return to Portland. Even so, despite "a generous supply of seamen in Portland [...], there was no rush to sign on the Kefalos," so poor was its reputation. In fact, only one member of its former crew, the Polish radio operator, John Pluskewitcz, agreed to come on board.[74] Fortunately for Oko, the ship's former captain, Gerassimos Bonicos, whom Oko had agreed to take along to New York, disappeared as soon as the arrangement had been made, and only reappeared as the ship was about to leave Portland. "Otherwise," surmised Oko, "we might not have been able to get a full complement of crew for the delivery run." The press of time had prevented Oko and his men from tackling some important problems that remained, and on 3 June, after two full months at port, the *Kefalos* "wallowed out of Portland harbor on schedule."[75] On board was an experienced pilot, Captain Perry, who was assigned to take the vessel down the coast. Nevertheless, Oko was profoundly aware that as she headed south the vessel "was far below the norm of performance that any responsible skipper would reasonably demand." He was worried about the electrical circuits, winches, and dozens of other details. To his experienced ears, the "engine sounds [...] seemed to be slightly off beat." But there was no turning back; Oko wondered how long the U.N. truce would remain in effect, and if he could get to Israel on time.

Not long after leaving Portland, the first crisis arose: upon entering Cape Cod Canal, and as fog closed in on the ship, the "navigation and engine room lights blew out."[76] Oil-burning lights were brought out and set up, but the ship was forced to travel at reduced speed in the fog in a "tight traffic lane." After not sleeping well, Oko awoke the next morning to find that the engine had stopped. Then came Captain Perry's ominous words: "Oil fire in engine room. Can you get to the radio shack?"[77] After quickly ascertaining the ship's position, Oko saw the radio operator "frozen at the sending key." The captain grabbed a piece of paper and wrote on it: "OIL FIRE IN ENGINE ROOM OFF HUMOR ROCK GAS BUOY. IMMEDIATE ASSISTANCE REQUIRED. MASTER KEFALOS." Pluskewitcz sent out an immediate S.O.S. to the Coast Guard. Everyone sprang into action; Ilves, Apaolaza, Forbes, Perry, and of course Oko, who was still in his pale blue pajamas. (The pajamas would be used later to make an Israeli flag.)[78] Through their combined and courageous efforts, especially those of chief engineer Ilves, the fire was quickly extinguished. From start to finish, the harrowing incident had lasted less than half an hour. According to the ship's radio records, only 27 minutes elapsed between the first S.O.S. to the sending of the following message: "NEED NO MORE ASSISTANCE. HAVE FIRE ABOARD APPARENTLY UNDER CONTROL."[79] And shortly thereafter a similar note was radioed to Manuel Enterprises. Visibly relieved, the vessel's owners immediately sent word of their great appreciation and gratitude to Oko and his men for their performance.

All in the nick of time, because "thirteen minutes later the radio receiver and transmitter were out of order due to blown fuses." Replacing them was the least of Oko's troubles.[80]

During the fire other equipment had also malfunctioned: Forbes had problems with the starboard lifeboat; when Oko grabbed a hose, his "fingers went through the rotten fabric"; and the "deck cut-off valve to the engine room fuel line" had been disconnected. Oko was to learn this last fact directly from Captain Bonicos, the former owner–captain, who at the time had frantically yelled out (Oko, more pejoratively, says he "squealed") "get the lifeboats out! Get the lifeboats in the water!"[81] Oko could take it no more, telling Bonicos "you son-of-a-bitch, I'm giving orders on this ship now [...], and don't come mid-ship or you'll be a dead pig!"[82] As matters were brought under control, tension gradually eased, especially after Ilves, Apaolaza, and Blanco completed "emergency repairs in the engine room and were able to get steam up in the boilers." In short, the vessel has regained a semblance of working order. On the bright side, the fire had cost no lives or serious injuries, and the damage was relatively light ($2,000). As Oko put it, "We got off easy." But many instruments "were out of commission," and the ship clearly was not in seaworthy shape for a long voyage.

Ironically, the vessel had been saved in large part "because the poor condition of the two lifeboats prevented the crew from carrying out the orders to abandon ship." According to Captain Perry, the pilot, too much paint around the bell system prevented the handle from moving to sound the alarm, and, more seriously, the riggings would not operate to lower the boats.[83] In other words, had the crew evacuated the *Kefalos* successfully, there is no telling what would have happened to the ship and to its projected mission. The *Kefalos* pulled into Erie Basin off Brooklyn at Todd Shipyards on Sunday, 6 June, at 6 p.m. Shalit and Recanati met the ship at its arrival. Manuel Enterprises had arranged for the vessel to go directly into dry dock. Nobody was more aware than Oko that substantial work lay ahead for the following week. He also knew that he had to act quickly.

Problems arose immediately after the *Kefalos* dry-docked at Todd Shipyards. In an interview with the FBI, William Monahan of the general manager's office at Todd, related that the vessel had indeed arrived at the shipyards on 6 June at the time given by Oko.

The next day the ship was placed in dry dock number three, and on 9 June the freighter was moved to pier number three, where work on the ship would be done. After all work was completed, the *Kefalos* left the shipyards for sea on 13 June.[84] Why had work on the vessel not begun immediately after its arrival, given the haste at hand? Why had it taken nearly three full days for the repairs to start? The main sticking points appear to have been twofold: uncertainty about the ownership of the *Kefalos*, and who was authorized to order the repairs. According to Monahan, of the Compañía Marítima Trans-oceánica, Bonicos — unclear if it was Michael or Gerassimos, though in all likelihood the former — had originally contacted him to request that the freighter be placed in dry dock "for examination and survey." Monahan soon learned, however, that Bonicos had sold the ship, and so he refused to order repairs "from anyone other than the present owners." Monahan informed the FBI that he was also contacted by George C. Stern of Shipowners Agency, who "guaranteed payment for the repairs," but had withdrawn the offer "two days later." It was at this point that Oko stepped in and gave authorization "for the nature and extent of the repairs," explaining that a fire had broken out on the ship he captained, and that a survey was carried out by a company to determine the extent of the fire damage. To make sure he was dealing with legitimate ownership and associates, Monahan then conferred with Arar of Manuel Enterprises, Recanati (perhaps mistakenly identified as belonging to Shipowners Agency), and Ilves (chief engineer of the vessel) "relative to the work done on the ship." Monahan's caution and doubts suggest that when the *Kefalos* arrived at Todd, the sale of the vessel had not been entirely finalized and that prospective new buyers were still in the process of assessing the total cost of the purchase, including the necessary repairs at the shipyards. Perhaps Manuel Enterprises had given the Bonicos a kind of advance or down payment at Portland, with the balance to be paid upon arrival in New York.[85] Admittedly a conjecture — though one based on bona fide, if fragmentary, evidence — it would help to explain much of the incertitude surrounding the ownership of the *Kefalos* during its first days at Todd.[86] One only has to examine the copious work orders and records of the repairs at Todd to get an idea of the confusion that reigned at the outset over who, or which company, had actual possession of the ship. As late as 13 June, the day the *Kefalos* departed from New York, according to a preliminary handwritten work order, the vessel was owned by the Compañía Marítima Transoceánica and its representative was Mr. Bonicos.[87]

Once the inspection of the ship was completed — one that had almost led to a bloody denouement — and Oko and his men had carefully gone over the entire ship, repairs began at breakneck speed two days later. Monahan found "unusual" Oko's "request to expedite all repair work, to have employees [...] work overtime, and the feeling that the amount of money spent for these repairs was no object to Captain Oko or his associates."[88] Vincent Taggart, superintendent of repairs at Todd and someone for whom Oko had great respect and sympathy, pointedly stated that he was suspicious of Oko and the purpose for which the ship was to be used ("for taking a tub like this and pouring money into repair"). He also noted that Oko had said he was in a hurry to leave to make cargo commitments to South America.[89] Oko and Manuel Enterprises did indeed pour money into the ship — to the tune of over $54,000, a bill that with "allowances as agreed" was settled for $50,000.[90] Factoring in the $190,000 paid for the vessel, Haganah had spent close to $250,000 on the *Kefalos* — a sizeable sum under the circumstances in 1948. And this amount did not include other monies that would be spent on wages, supplies, and other matters during the long journeys ahead.[91]

All in all, Oko had achieved much of what he wanted in substantially refurbishing the ship inside and out. The captain had used the necessary repairs as an excuse to achieve more ambitious results. With much more than minor fixes on existing problems, the *Kefalos* acquired a noticeable upgrade from its previous condition. Even the normally demanding captain admitted that "much that was essential did get done that week. An incredible number of details were attended to satisfactorily."[92] Had it been easy? Of course not; Oko had had to assert his considerable maritime expertise to secure results. The process at Todd from start to finish had been far from smooth. In a memorable passage in "And It Was So," the veteran captain, who never missed an opportunity to take a shot at Manuel Enterprises, deriding them as the "cloak and dagger boys," critically recounted how "Recanati and Shalit, and a young newcomer [...] Arrar were bustling all over the ship second-guessing engineers, handing us money for purchases with one hand, taking it back with the other, and keeping things in a happy state of enthusiastic youthful confusion."[93] Oko also notes that the repairs at Todd had been quite an experience because Shalit and Recanati were "busy all over the ship speaking Hebrew to each other, and this was all supposed to be greatly secretive."[94]

In addition to the tensions that grew out of the dry docking at Todd, Oko's conflicts with Manuel Enterprises would continue during the week of 6–13 June over a host of other issues: money, supplies, recruitment of new crew members, insurance, and secrecy. Funds were a constant source of friction; Oko complained that Manuel Enterprises personnel "were inconsistent as hell."[95] While claiming that money was no object, the captain chafed at accusations that he was "a spendthrift" when he insisted on buying good food. The new owners "haggled over expenditures for supplies necessary to morale on shipboard." In Oko's view, Shalit and company "had little idea of how important food is at sea, or how much good feeding offsets discomforts and hard labor on board." Even his "estimates for cigarette and tobacco stores were questioned," as were his demands for wine rations. Not a big drinker himself, Oko was aware that "wine served on board and served from big casks would be taken as a sign that [the sailors] were trusted." He also battled with Manuel Enterprises over "reconstruction of the galley and furnishings of adequate cooking and refrigeration equipment." The *Kefalos* would not lack basic food and drink during its entire journeys. Oko noted with satisfaction that "the only requisitions that went through without a hitch were Gladys's lists of medical and hospital supplies." As a trained nurse, she insisted on taking drugs, instruments, and hospital requisites. In sum, the ship's more-than-adequate provisioning was something that Oko and the crew would be "deeply grateful for many times during the voyage," and far outweighed being tagged as a "good but extravagant skipper."

In recruiting a new crew, Oko relied heavily on trusted stalwarts from his skeleton crew, specifically Manresa, Apaolaza, and Sánchez. In a complete Hollywoodesque scene, some of the new crew was conscripted "at a small Basque restaurant near the waterfront [...], a hole-in-the-wall place, called 'Nan Abe' or some such name."[96] After word had been passed around that "a captain of a Panamanian registry was ready to conscript crew," sailors were interviewed and screened there. Oko checked his impressions with his officers and perhaps even with Gladys, who had come along, much to Apaolaza's surprise and displeasure. Some were approved and hired, and others were not. Curiously, while Oko complained about the insistence of secrecy by Manuel Enterprises, he, too, was more than a bit concerned about the "infiltration of Blue Legion fascists, which would mean real trouble in a predominantly Spanish-speaking crew." Most likely on 9 or 10 June, those who were chosen to serve as crew were signed before the Panamanian Consulate.[97] Oko asserts that "eyebrows were raised in the office at the place and manner" of recruitment. Manuel Enterprises even offered to run a security check of the new hires. Oko, however, objected, and this made the "cloak and dagger lads cry into their cocktails." He was satisfied with the new crew: it was multi-national and an "unlikely mixture," but totally understandable from a maritime viewpoint. The captain felt that he had picked the right men. Proof of this, Oko proudly observed later, was that "most of the men [who] signed on in New York stayed with the ship throughout the voyage." Further, "Only fifty-seven men passed through the ship in the full eight months [of its voyages] [...]." Oko added that "the ship's complement of men varied from 37 to 43 during the voyage[s]."[98] Apparently, the only exception in recruitment at New York in which Oko did not participate regarded Jack Rothman, the new radio operator, who was brought in by the new owners. Oko became particularly fond of Rothman, noting at various points how much he had contributed to the ship's success. With admiration, the captain wrote that Jack, an older World War II veteran in his late 30s, "was not the dewy-eyed cabin-boy type with a kit of good intentions romantically slung over his shoulder. Such as those the *Kefalos* could not afford to carry. She needed seamen whose guts knew the meaning of 'able.'"[99]

The question of insurance proved to be one of the most nagging sticking points. Oko claims that he brought up the issue time and again with Manuel Enterprises, was promised that it would be taken care of, and was told not to worry about it. After the new crew was signed on, Oko "went to bat again on insurance," and Manuel Enterprises "broke down this time and confessed that the ship itself was uninsurable, and had been on the list of uninsurables for some time."[100] Much against his better judgment, Oko gave in on the matter when assured by the management that although the ship would sail without insurance, the crew would be covered. In this way, "the men and their families would be afforded at least that much financial security."[101] But within an hour of leaving port, "Shalit and Recanati came onto the ship" and handed him "the God-damndest package." They swore him to "absolute secrecy. No word was to reach the officers or men, not even Gladys." Oko was not prepared for what came next. His words are eloquent: "I alone was to know they had failed on insurance. *We sailed without a dollar's worth of insurance coverage on any life or limb on board.*"[102]

Finally, on the question of secrecy, it is difficult to know who among the crew beyond Oko and Gladys knew for certain of the ship's true mission. Perhaps some of his closest and most trusted officers, such as Forbes, Manresa, Apaolaza, and one or two others were aware of the purpose and destination of the *Kefalos* [Forbes's *Kefalos* papers in Photograph 9]. Although Oko understood all too well that the voyage's objective "needed to be kept under wraps," he derided the "Operation Secrecy" of Manuel Enterprises. His ideas and theirs were different. "Theirs," said Oko, "was the romantic pitch of storybook spies and counterspies with all the trimmings."[103] While the captain knew that the ship would by necessity "have to declare misleading destinations," he was particularly critical of a "fanciful document of 'secret orders'" that was given to him when the ship left New York. Oko characterized it as "way below spy-fiction standards and completely unrealistic — as was their whole approach to security." (More on this important piece shortly.) The day before sailing, "two handsome chaps" (possibly Shalit and Recanati) came to his cabin late in the day to give him and Gladys "a sample of the hush-hush treatment." Sarcastically, Oko remarks that he and Gladys entertained their obvious explanations and listened like children hearing about Santa Claus.[104] A hard-boiled realist, Oko might well have regarded their work as amateurish, but the shadowy Manuel Enterprises and their partners at Shipowners Agency were adept at disseminating misinformation. Thanks to the efforts of Shipowners Agency, the *Kefalos* was cleared to leave for Buenos Aires "in ballast."[105] And on 15 June 1948, *The New York Times* dutifully reported that the vessel was headed for Montevideo.[106] Time and again, in time-honored underground and conspiratorial traditions, Haganah and its associates generated confusion through false papers and leads to throw off national governments, international organizations, and outright enemies.

After numerous last-minute details and basic matters were resolved, the *Kefalos* left the Brooklyn pier on 13 June at 3:26 in the afternoon, as noted by the ever-precise Oko. Five hours later, the vessel left its pilot and "headed out to sea past Ambrose Lightship." Perhaps the captain had been too busy tending to basic matters and profoundly worried about the insurance issue to pay much attention to a three-page, typewritten yellow document titled "Instructions to Master," dated 12 June 1948 at New York, and from all appearances given to him just prior to departure. (See Appendix 1.) The instructions were in effect the "secret orders by which [Oko] was supposed to abide."[107] In other words, they were the operational manual for the mission. Who drafted the instructions is unknown to this writer; however, whether written by the personnel for Manuel Enterprises, or by some other entity, the instructions clearly had to be approved at the highest levels of the Israeli representation in New York, quite probably by Teddy Kollek himself.[108] Kollek headed the Haganah mission in New York beginning in mid-May 1948. Now that the ship was finally at sea, Oko finally examined the document. It did not take long for him to explode: "Of all the damnably unrealistic documents I have ever seen, this topped them for sheer idiocy and playful childishness. [...] [T]hey read like a fairy tale mixed up with kindergarten [sic] maxims of seamanship plus puerile rulings for a game of 'I Spy.'" After sharing them with his wife, Oko wrote, "Gladys and I had hysterics over all three pages of those instructions."[109] The Okos may have found them hilarious, but they were Oko's marching orders, and he could not avoid them; should he wish to continue the operation, which he certainly did, he was stuck with them whether he liked them or not.

So what exactly were the instructions? Divided into nine relatively short sections, the document instructed Oko how to proceed on the following matters: (1) destination; (2) ports of call; (3) cables; (4) agents; (5) crew; (6) finances; (7) name of vessel; (8) special supplies; and (9) general [matters]. (It probably did not escape Oko that the instructions had been so hastily written that the sections on cables and agents both carried the number three.) The question of destination (no. 1) was a key; the instructions ordered Buenos Aires (spelled "B.A.") as the designated terminus of the voyage. Its first port of call, however, would be Tampico, Mexico, "for bunkering purposes" (in effect, to pick up arms). From Buenos Aires, the ship's destination would be China. If entering Tampico posed problems, Oko was instructed to cruise the Gulf of Mexico until advised to go to Tampico or another port.

On ports of call (no. 2), the document surmised that in all probability the ship's papers would not be examined. (Why this was thought is not explained.)[110] The captain was to meet a certain David Gritzewsky in Tampico; Gritzewsky, in turn, was to call a fictitious Hyman Padover in New York. Then, Oko was to talk to Hyman Padover (no reasons were given for the sequence). While in Tampico, the captain was to prevent harmful behavior from local persons against the ship and crew and not permit unauthorized persons to come on board. Also in Tampico, Oko would be given his next port of call. Finally, in Tampico the ship would load with sufficient oil to reach its final destination plus 2,000 miles.

On cables (no. 3), those sent from the ship should be addressed to "'JACKSON' [at] SHIPSAGE, signed by 'KAY.'" (Shipsage was the cable address of Shipowners Agency.) The captain was to cable every twenty-four hours on oil consumption and speed, and two days before reaching Tampico he was to cable "ETA 48." All cables from New York were to be signed "JACKSON," and cables sent from Mexico were to be signed "HYMAN PADOVER." If problems of "machinery and the like" occurred, the captain was to cable using specific words.

On agents at ports (no. 4, though numbered as 3), Oko was to use the services of appointed agents. Their names would be communicated to him before arrival at port. On crew (no. 5), the New York office was to be advised of any changes. In case of discharge before completion of voyage, or at its end, crew was to be paid wages due plus air travel to New York. The captain was to develop teamwork with crew. If on the way south too much talk developed, the captain was to write cables with suggested specific wording. And at first port of call, the crew was to be kept on board working.

On finances (no. 6), the crew, as noted, was to be paid upon termination of voyage; advances to crew would be made according to captain's judgment; the captain would cover all expenditures by vouchers; the accounts would be kept by the purser and mailed from every port; and in the event that the vessel traded in Europe after the first journey, all financial matters would remain "centralized in N.Y., unless otherwise stated."

On the name of the vessel (no. 7), the instructions made clear that the ship's name would be changed through a complicated series of coded messages. One of the prospective new names was *Pinzon*. On the matter of special supplies (no. 8), the document cryptically stated without details that the captain would be supplied with "protective instruments" at the first port of call. Finally, on general matters (no. 9), the instructions made a number of disparate points, some of which might appear commonsense, even trivial, while others were far more consequential. The ship was to be conducted as a "normal commercial venture," belonging to a commercial company; the captain had full responsibility and command of the vessel; the instructions at sea were to be "received only from N.Y. unless otherwise stated"; the ship might be escorted from Italy, but the captain would be advised of it; the captain was "holder of 50% of the company's shares. D.S. [possibly Diane Schweitzer] holds other 50% and is the representative of people of Switzerland." (More on the ramifications of this important question below.[111]) If any changes of plan occurred, the instructions were to be executed carefully. And, finally, if the ship was "intercepted in mid-ocean," the captain was to explain the nature of the vessel and give the destination as stipulated in the opening section of the instructions (Buenos Aires).

Oko and Gladys may have found the "Instructions to Master" laughable, even farcical, but here they were, in an old cargo ship, headed out to sea with a crew heavily staffed with Spanish officers and men, to carry out what was a complex and dangerous mission. During the next eight months, the couple would be partners in an unlikely odyssey of events. Would they be prepared for everything that lay ahead? Probably not, but they knew each other all too well, having spent the previous fifteen years together under often difficult circumstances, including the Depression and World War II. As partners in every respect, their lives had been closely intertwined and would remain so until the early 1960s. Who were these two intriguing — and perhaps remarkable — individuals?

2

Oko and Gladys

Two Lives Intertwined

Certainly Gladys saw Oko clearly from the start. Asked for one word summing him up, [she replied]: "Crusader."

— *Marin Independent Journal,*
22 April 1961

Now mostly forgotten except to friends, remaining crew members, refugees, Israeli personnel on board the *Kefalos*, and a few historians of the vessel, the lives of A. S. Oko Jr. and his wife, Gladys, nonetheless deserve considerable attention. Unfortunately, as it so often happens in history, what is known about them is vastly unequal because of the gulf that separated their backgrounds, social conditions, and other considerations, such as gender and how success is achieved and measured. In effect, a great deal is known about Oko and very little about Gladys, who sometimes appears cast as a stereotypical silent woman, as Oko's appendix. The disparity in what is known about them individually is perhaps with good reason; Oko came from a prominent intellectual family with important national and international connections, while Gladys's origins and roots were vastly more modest, indeed obscure. However undeniable, the realities of class and gender are highly misleading. Significantly, Oko's notoriety and reputation would not derive primarily from family privilege or influence, but from what he was able to achieve through much hard work and determination — both reinforced by intelligence, ambition, and a fair amount of rebelliousness. And, interestingly, while Gladys secured a solid position as a nurse and also achieved a position of responsibility as a superintendent of nurses in a hospital, Oko did not attain a respectable occupation until late in life when he became a ship captain in the mid-1940s, and then eventually becoming a businessman, explorer–scholar, and prominent citizen in local civic affairs. More to the point, the first forty years of Oko's life, which leap-frogged from one troubled venture to another, could be regarded as a failure until World War II, the *Kefalos* odyssey, and beyond. An almost entirely self-taught individual, the captain would not attain complete respectability and standing in the community until the mid-1950s. Yet these two persons, one a Jew of Russian–Austrian ancestry, the other a Christian of Norwegian Lutheran descent, spent thirty years together as an inseparable, loving couple through good times and bad. One might never be able to discern completely the reasons for the unshakeable bond between them, but a review of their lives, separately and together, provides valuable clues for their shared values and ideals.

Adolph S. Oko Jr. was born on 12 December 1904 in New York to Adolph Sigmund Oko (b. 5 January 1883) and Rose Susan Weisinger (b. April 1886), an unmarried young Jewish immigrant couple.[1] Oko Jr.'s father was born in Russia in 1883, and after studying in Germany, had immigrated to the United States in the spring of 1903.[2] Rose and her parents, Bernhard Weisinger and Kate Scharp, were Austrian.[3] Significantly, Rose's slightly older sister, Etta (b. 12 May 1884), had given birth on 20 November 1904 to a daughter, Pearl, and A. S. Oko was also the father.[4] Oko Sr. would eventually marry Etta, and at some point soon thereafter Rose left New York, headed for California with her young son, and eventually married Peter Isaak, a Russian who had immigrated to the United States in 1891.[5] By 1910, Oko Jr., age five, was living in San Francisco with his parents and his half-sister Mildred, age two.[6] Little is known for certain about the young Oko during the following decade. According to a later account, in which he appeared to complain somewhat, Oko was "shuttled between two families," or as he put it, "I was a ping-pong ball," spending time initially with his father and later joining his mother, now Rose Isaak, in Calistoga and then in Marin County, including Mill Valley.[7] The latter area made quite an impression on Oko: "From the time I first saw Marin in 1915, I was in love with it."[8] At some point during the late 1910s, Oko returned to Cincinnati, Ohio, where he attended the Cincinnati Academy of Art with his sister, Pearl, for drawing lessons, as well as the University Prep School, where, by his own admission, "he was kicked out by teachers poorly adjusted" to him.[9] One might well imagine that it was quite the other way around. Despite his failure in art school, Oko would preserve a life-long interest in, and appreciation for, fine art. According to the 1920 U.S. Census, the young Oko was living in Cincinnati with his biological father, his aunt, and now stepmother, Etta, and his half-sister, Pearl.[10] After working in the Astor Library in New York City in 1905 and 1906, the elder Oko became librarian of the Hebrew Union College in Cincinnati, Ohio.[11] Under his stewardship the library expanded. An authority on Spinoza and on numerous Jewish topics, Oko Sr. was given freehand to purchase books. During his twenty-five-year tenure at the college, he was reputed to have bought some 600,000 books for the library.[12] The younger Oko lived surrounded by books; although he liked them well, in a way they would also lead to his departure from Cincinnati and his family there. As he would later admit, Oko Jr. had become "full of Moby Dick and Conrad," and this played into a "youthful revolt and a restless inability to adjust himself."[13] A good case can be made that Oko's life was more than a bit unsettled during the next two decades.

Most likely against his father's wishes and hopes, the younger Oko set out to sea in 1922 at the age of eighteen. During the next four years, Oko served as an ordinary (OS) and as an able-bodied seaman (AB) on at least eleven different ships on the Pacific and Atlantic.[14] These voyages enabled Oko to see the world, and he described them movingly: "I avoided ships on the milk routes and coastal lines [...] [E]ven in tough times I found foreign voyages. Out of it all, I got the adventure youth seeks with a training that later let me *serve my country and my tradition*."[15] That training, of course, included hard work and discipline. Oko appears to have been more at ease at sea than on land. Equally important, the voyages instilled in Oko a life-long love of the sea: "I still consider it one of the greatest joys of life to be on night watch in the darkness with silence all around."[16] And yet, in 1926 Oko abandoned the sea and briefly stayed in New York before returning to the West Coast for reasons that are not entirely clear, but that may be explained by events that occurred shortly thereafter. That same year, Oko married Doris Madge Reniff in San Francisco on 29 June 1926.[17] Little is known about this young eighteen-year-old woman who commonly went by the name Madge and was listed in the marriage license as a resident of Reno, Nevada. Where and how the couple met is equally unknown. At the time of their marriage, Oko was working as a salesman at S & G Gump. Virtually nothing is known about their marriage, except that on 7 August 1927, Madge gave birth to a son named Adolph S. Oko, exactly like his father and grandfather.[18] To avoid confusion, and because of tensions with Oko Jr., and since father and son served at the same time in the Merchant Marine, Adolph S. Oko III eventually changed his name to Aaron Steffins Oko, which he used for the rest of his life.[19] After working at Gump's, it is not clear what Oko Jr. did next; however, in August 1928 he became the editor of a glossy magazine titled *San Francisco Bay Yachtsman*, of which only a few issues exist.[20] Incidentally, in October of that year Oko had a brief run-in with the law and was arrested after a minor scuffle involving a U.S. Customs guard on Pier 37 in San Francisco.[21]

According to the 1930 U.S. Census, Oko was living in San Francisco at the time with Madge and their son, Adolph Jr., and his occupation was listed as an advertiser for a journal.[22] During the 1930s times were tough for Oko, as indeed they were for many during the Depression. He would hold a number of jobs, and his marriage to Madge would fall apart. In 1932–1933, Oko was employed for a year as a salesman on a commission basis for the Parker Printing Company in San Francisco.[23] In February–March 1933, Madge filed for divorce from Oko on the grounds of "willful desertion."[24] The divorce would not be entirely settled until 23 August 1934. In the meantime, Oko had begun to work as an advertising salesman for the *San Francisco Call Bulletin*, a position that he held from August 1933 until May 1936.[25] The advertising director of the newspaper, R. L. Lichtfield, in an interview with the FBI, "stated that the subject was so outspoken in his support of Communism that he made himself obnoxious to his fellow employees and that some of the customers had complained [...] [H]owever, [Oko] was not fired but did resign at about this time [...] due to the unpleasant conditions he had created."[26] But something far more important had occurred during Oko's employment at the *Call Bulletin:* he had met and married Gladys Zemple in 1933 or 1934.[27] Had Oko met Gladys while still married to Madge? The answer is unknown, as is whether meeting Gladys had contributed to the demise of Oko's marriage to Madge, even though it seems safe to assume that she had. Also unknown are the effects of the divorce on Madge, who remained single and died shortly thereafter on 16 August 1936, at the young age of twenty-eight, from acute infectious endocarditis (an infection of the lining of the heart) and septicemia.[28] A few months later, in January 1937, Oko is listed as the publisher of another magazine, the *Pacific Skipper*, though from all appearances this was an ill-fated venture.[29] In July 1937, Oko finally hit rock bottom, going into bankruptcy after accumulating a mountain of debts.[30] If the harsh 1930s had been tough on Oko, he seemed to have maintained a measure of generosity and good humor. As Gladys recalls, Oko "gave a party at the depth of the Depression, [and] the friends he invited saw him destroy $1,500 worth of their IOUs, which he'd thrown into a salad bowl."[31]

Despite the many difficulties, an undeterred Oko launched a new venture in the late 1930s: Oko Public Relations, which was based in the Monadnock Building in San Francisco.[32] Although this may have been a troubled period for many, one would not have thought so of the Okos based on the photographs, notes, and newspaper articles about Oko, and even about Gladys. For instance, the 2 June 1938 issue of the *San Francisco Chronicle* carried a photograph of Oko with Helen Hayes. That same year there are two brief letters from dancer Sally Rand and playwright Ben Hecht to Oko, probably in connection with the staging of Hecht's *Front Page* by the San Francisco Press Club, for which, at least for a while, Oko served as secretary until he stopped paying dues and became a delinquent member. And a 7 June 1938 caption under a photograph in the *Chronicle* blithely noted, "Mr. S. Oko and Mrs. Oko [...] never seem to have first names."[33] Even if at times the Okos were portrayed as the life of the party, Oko took his work in public relations quite seriously. From 1939 on, he compiled voluminous oversize albums of newspaper clippings meant in all probability for the clients he represented.[34] The personal interests Oko focused on through his public relations venture were as varied as the parties he threw and the company he kept. He advocated for entertainment establishments, such as the Shalimar Bowl; health concerns (teeth, dentists, and milk); and possibly as well for the 1939 Golden Gate International Exposition.[35] Of course, he had good reason to follow the exposition closely because Rose Isaak, his mother, was reputedly in charge of the Russian exhibit on Treasure Island.[36] Despite Oko's best efforts, his public relations firm was not successful, and if the FBI's records are accurate, by February 1941 Oko had been relegated to work as the agent and manager of a ventriloquist at the Fairmont Hotel under a 12-week contract.[37] Luckily for the Oko household, Gladys was gainfully employed and had a steady income; their economic situation might well have been dire otherwise.

The conflict of World War II gave Oko a renewed sense of purpose and also enabled him to return to an earlier love and what he knew best — the sea. During the next seven years, Oko would be profoundly involved in ocean-related matters in one form or another. According to an account that cannot be confirmed, and that on face value does not make much sense, when the war broke out Oko tried to enroll in the Canadian Royal Air Force as a navigator, but was denied because he was too old.[38] He was also said to have scored well in a civil service examination and offered a good job in Washington, D.C., but he turned it down. Instead, in April 1942, the thirty-seven-year-old Oko signed up for the U.S. Merchant Marine.[39] He enrolled at Alameda, California, as a seaman second class, and was assigned to the Maritime Service Training Station, Government Island, Alameda. After a battery of tests, Oko successfully completed "a period of three months probationary enrollment September, 1942, and was accepted for regular enrollment in the U.S. Maritime Service with grade of ensign."[40] After the intensive training, Oko began his service as third mate in October 1942. He served on six different ships, made nine voyages (October 1942–November 1945), and emerged from duty at war's end as chief mate, a rank he achieved in September 1944.[41] His rapid ascent in rank clearly demonstrates his familiarity with ships and their internal organization. The promotions also speak volumes about Oko's leadership skills and ambition. While some of the voyages were along the West and East coasts and short, others were in international waters and long (all of the latter in the Pacific). For his service, Oko received four commendations from the War Shipping Administration.[42]

While in the Merchant Marine, Oko and Gladys corresponded

regularly. Both avid writers, they exchanged numerous warm letters about everything that could pass the censor: home life, families, and stories about their everyday experiences. Gladys in particular always pleaded for more money to make ends meet. Oko, who had never lived in the South, was shocked to experience racism firsthand, particularly from some of the southern officers he served with briefly in the Gulf of Mexico. He was also taken aback at some of the conditions on board, and in a November 1942 letter to Gladys, he informed her that he was putting her on the mailing list of *The Pilot*, a paper of "the militant [...] National Maritime Union – C.I.O., which is quite 'left' & very informative of subjects pertaining to your husband's old & new profession. To sum it up – it's rugged!"[43] While in the Merchant Marine, Oko joined the National Organization of Masters, Mates, and Pilots of America in February 1943.[44] Safety and working conditions at sea were matters that Oko always took very seriously. (In early October 1944, while serving aboard the *S.S. Cape Elizabeth*, Oko received word of the death of his father.)

Oko's last voyage in the Merchant Marine proved to be extraordinarily fateful and have long-term consequences and repercussions. Oko was chief mate aboard the *S.S. George R. Holmes*, which left Los Angeles in June 1945 for a long journey to the South Pacific. In early November 1945, the vessel was docked in Ching Wan Tao (China).[45] The ship's captain, B.W. Dunton, in a statement dated 5 November 1945, said that two days earlier Oko had returned to the ship with a pass from local authorities giving permission to a ship's small party (four men and an interpreter) to visit the Great Wall. The next day, a jeep was provided, and "we left [...] on a picnic trip to the Great Wall [and] we were stopped by Nationalist Troops but allowed to proceed when they were informed of our destination." Their jeep advanced, but when crossing a river, "suddenly a burst of rifle fire came from the opposite side of the river. They raised an American flag, but the firing continued for fifteen minutes." Soon thereafter, fifteen men came and took the group into Communist territory. One of the group members was wounded: Oko. The troops informed Captain Dunton that the shooting had been accidental and that the group was taken by the Communists to the central bank of Manchuria in Changhai Kwan, held overnight, and released the next morning. What occurred next is not entirely clear, but it appears that Oko was kept in custody by the Communists for three days and given medical treatment. according to Captain Dutton, "The bullet entered [Oko's] left shoulder and came out his buttock." In a short while, Oko was apparently carried back to the ship, and after convalescing (possibly in Shanghai) for nearly three months, he was eventually flown back to the United States for medical care, arriving in San Francisco on 26 January 1946.[46] It is worth noting that Oko had been officially discharged from the *Cape Elizabeth* on 23 November 1945, a full two months before being flown back to the United States. He might well have used that time to acquaint himself with that part of China, make social and business connections, and most probably even buy a ship, the *S.S. Amur*, which was purchased on 28 December 1945.[47] (The important role that this vessel would play in Oko's life is discussed below.)

The fallout of the shooting incident was twofold: (1) Oko experienced persistent health problems in the area of the wound, and (2) there were unconfirmed rumors emanating from unknown sources, and which surfaced later, that Oko had "displayed a lapel pin bearing [...] a hammer and a sickle to Chinese Communists when he was captured by them." Moreover, after his release from custody, Oko is said to have remarked that "he felt like quitting Maritime Service and joining Chinese Communists against Chiang Kai Shek."[48] Captain Dutton pointedly asserted that he had never seen Oko display a lapel pin to the captors, nor did he hear him express "any opinions which would indicate that Oko was sympathetic to Communism." For good measure, the captain added that he was not aware that Oko had ever made statements that he would like to fight alongside the Communists. Finally, Dutton "regarded Oko as somewhat of a promoter, but that as far as he knew, Oko was completely loyal to the United States."[49] Because of this episode and other questions, the issue of Oko's allegiance to the United States greatly concerned the FBI throughout 1948.

After an apparently brief stay at Marine Hospital in San Francisco, Oko was quickly on the move again. On 2 April 1946, he picked up at Vancouver a shoal-draft ship, the *S.S. Amur*, now renamed *Far Eastern Carrier*, and sailed it to China under Panamanian registry.[50] Exactly what the vessel was carrying remains unknown, although almost certainly the cargo consisted of some type of contraband, perhaps even armament. Oko was proud of this venture, which he described vividly: "I pushed the rust-bucket across with my nose [...] [T]here was a derelict crew, some Chinese, one man went crazy now and then."[51] The *Far Eastern Carrier* arrived at Kowloon on 26 May 1946 and at Shanghai on 27 June. Whatever it was transporting, the voyage proved a huge financial success: "I had hit the jackpot [...] and for the first time in our twenty years of married life [Gladys and I] had a real lump sum."[52] Although the historical record is unclear, Oko may possibly have made one more trip to China in July 1946. On 2 August, he arrived in San Pedro, California, as a passenger aboard the *Mindoro* from Shanghai.[53] Whatever the precise chronology, Oko and Gladys now had reason to celebrate. Oko had not had much shore leave in previous years, and Gladys, whose wartime experience had been difficult, quit her job as a nursing supervisor at Green's Eye Hospital. The couple decided in October 1946 to take a vacation to New Orleans and New York. They also began to build a home in Inverness Park, California.[54] At age forty, Gladys had at last secured a measure of stability and satisfaction; getting there, however, had apparently not been easy.

Gladys Alice Zemple was born on 25 January 1906 in Oakland, California, to Otto G. Zemple and Belva Anderson, both recently transplanted Wisconsinites.[55] On Gladys's birth certificate, her father is listed as a mining engineer and her mother as a housewife. Gladys's parents were of Norwegian and German ancestry, and probably Lutheran, a fact that Oko liked to emphasize to show how different Gladys's ethnic and religious backgrounds were from his own.[56] In 1908, Otto Zemple is listed as an oil merchant.[57] Otto likely died shortly thereafter, because by 1910 Gladys was living in Oakland with her widowed mother, grandparents, brother, and other relatives.[58] In 1920, at the age thirteen, Gladys was living in San Francisco with only her mother.[59] Except for a couple insignificant social notices from 1925–1926 newspapers, nothing else is known about Gladys during these years. In 1928, Miss Gladys Zemple is listed in a voter roll in Oakland as a registered Republican.[60] According to the 1930 U.S. Census, Belva Zemple lived in Alameda, California, with her mother, Amalia, and an unidentified young man. Gladys was not living with them.[61] The next trace of Gladys comes from the 1933 San Francisco city directory where she's listed as a saleswoman.[62] And in the 1935 city directory, even though Gladys does not appear, her mother, Belva Zemple, is shown as living on the same street in close proximity to Oko.[63] By 1936, there appears to be confirmation that Oko and Gladys had married. In that year's city directory, Gladys, now a nurse, and Oko, still a salesman for the *Call Bulletin*, resided at the same address.[64] From that date on, the couple is always listed together in city directories.

Despite the scarcity of information on Gladys during the 1920s and 30s, there is fortunately an interesting 1961 description of how she met Oko.[65] While a nurse — perhaps at Green's Eye Hospital — Gladys recounted that she had artist friends, and that Oko was temporarily renting in a studio. She and her friends had been invited to the studio. There she joined her friends and Oko, who was carrying a bag of groceries. She had paused briefly at the entrance and wondered about the odd name on the door: "Oko? Japanese, maybe?" She remembers that he was wearing a sweatshirt and white ducks and needed a shave. Gladys had clearly made a huge impression on Oko, who called her the next day and announced that she would be having lunch with him. A dinner followed, and according to Gladys, they had been together ever since. They would both claim credit for the fortuitous turn of events. Still, it is not until World War II that information emerges about Gladys, and this in large part is because of the voluminous correspondence between her and Oko.[66] Her letters show her at her finest: sensitive, generous, strong-willed, determined, warm, loving, and generous. They also reveal her heavy work schedule and that she was having to take care of her frail mother; deal with Oko's mother, Rose, an argumentative and difficult individual; grapple with her troubled stepson, Aaron; and tend to other family members and matters as well. Continually short of money and missing a husband whom she loved profoundly, her life from 1942–1946 was anything but easy. While she was her family's financial and emotional compass at home, Gladys looked to Oko as her central support. The war had only tightened their bonds even more strongly, and their political ideas would also converge closely in the aftermath of the conflict.

During the 1930s and early 1940s, Oko was surrounded by leftists of different types. His mother, Rose, was in all likelihood a Communist, as was his half-sister, Mildred Steuwe.[67] Some of the lawyers who handled his divorce were closely associated with "anti-fascist" groups, and the record is full of left-leaning associates and acquaintances. When the FBI launched an investigation in January 1948 of Oko's activities during the previous years, the cover page pointedly referred to him as "A. S. Okovich, 'Igor.'"[68] It is interesting how he was given the nickname Igor. According to the manager of S & G. Gump's, Oko was called Igor while he worked there in the mid-1920s. After returning to land in 1926 after four years at sea, he had seen a good deal of the world and had become quite radicalized, often talking in extreme left terms. Some in Marin County, California, remembered Oko as someone who "spoke not only of the sea, but of the world of ideas, such as socialism."[69] And a woman living in Mill Valley (Marin County) noted that Oko seemed "like a meteor in our sky. The things he knew we hadn't heard of yet."[70] These positions, however, would temper considerably over time, and by the mid- to late 1940s, Oko had become increasingly moderate in his political opinions — and more likely to invoke Lafayette and Paine than the dictatorship of the proletariat — except for his growing interest in Israel, which he embraced with vigor and conviction. Gladys wholeheartedly shared her husband's views. In fact, she supported unconditionally all of his subsequent actions with respect to Israel, and became an ardent Zionist, perhaps even more so than her husband.

It is important to remember that Oko was Jewish, and, while not overly conscious of his Jewishness as a boy, according to friends, as years passed he became increasingly aware of his father's "monumental achievements on behalf of Jewish thought, feeling, and artistic expression."[71] And even though he lived for a short while in a hotbed of Reformed Judaism, which some Orthodox Jews viewed as a betrayal of hallowed traditions, Oko never lost sight of his Jewishness and that of his family. Years later Oko wrote that while he had "not kept to the orthodox traditions of my forebears [...] I have deep respect for my heritage."[72] To be sure, much to his father's dismay, Oko did not follow in his footsteps and instead opted for the sea. Also, neither one of his two wives was Jewish, and he prided himself in the friendship of Christians, such as Bartley C. Crum, author of the *Behind the Silken Curtain* (1947), and others who influenced him greatly. Moreover, his mother was much more political than religious or observant.[73] Yet, Oko was unmistakably Jewish: he spoke some Yiddish (notably with some of the refugees on one of the voyages from the Balkans to Israel); was fond of Jewish proverbs and expressions ("Nothing gripes me more than to find another member of *my minority* acting like a schlemiel."); quoted on occasion from Scriptures; and suggested that "God's chosen people" could be recognized in the Exodus saga in 1947 as well as in his own odyssey on the *Kefalos*.[74] Oko was also surrounded, especially in the 1940s, with Jewish friends, business associates, and acquaintances. Some, like the sculptor Jacob Epstein, the painter Abel Penn, and the writer Marvin Lowenthal, were friends of his father; it was precisely Lowenthal who put Oko in touch with the Israelis in 1946. Oko was also deeply aware of anti-Semitism, having experienced it firsthand in some business dealings and having been the recipient of offensive anti-Semitic screeds in the 1950s.[75] World War II and the struggle against fascism, as well as the Holocaust, were undoubtedly defining events that spurred Oko to action on Israel's behalf. In his own words, "The two years [1946–1948] spent back in California sharpened my urge to serve *fellow members of my minority in Israel*."[76] As noted in Chapter 1, during his meeting with Shind in New York in 1946, Shind questioned Oko about his interest in Israel, to which he replied testily: "But for the grace of God, with a name like Adolph Sigmund Oko, I'd be one of the refugees in Israel now — should I have survived."[77] Bringing up the horrors of the Holocaust, Oko added: "I meant it because both my parents were born in Old World spots that had been much more than decimated of Jews in the years since my parents were brought to America, where they grew up and married and had me."[78] Oko was "annoyed as hell" when Shind found Oko's reasons for helping Israel "purely emotional."

Returning to California after his last voyage as a Merchant Marine, Oko began to delve deeply into Jewish matters, and in the process Israel became an important cause. His friendship with lawyer and author Bartley Crum became especially significant; Oko increasingly gravitated toward Jewish issues. The struggles of "the remnants of Jewry seeking access to their home," fired Oko's imagination. He likened their fight to that of the American Colonists for "freedom and self-determination."[79] In a moving passage in "And It Was So," Oko noted, "Where is there a better answer to the question 'Why Israel?' than in one given to Bartley Crum by a cobbler in a

D.P. Camp: 'Six million of our dead tell me I am Jew.'"[80]

Oko's correspondence in October 1946 rapidly fused two important personal interests: maritime matters, an old one, and Israel, a more recent one.[81] He busied himself in the shipping business and began to explore the purchase of vessels (letters dated 31 October, 3 December, and 13 January 1947). In the letter dated 13 January, Oko, perhaps only half-seriously, asked Crum, "What do you think of our chances of establishing ourselves in the shipping and steamship business in Japan at this time?" Simultaneously, Oko attempted to learn as much — and as quickly — as he could about the situation in Palestine. He read Crum's *Palestine Diary* as well as Arthur Koestler's *Thieves in the Night,* including a review of the latter work by Lowenthal. In a poignant letter to Lowenthal, dated 26 November 1946, Oko commented that *Thieves in the Night* had left him baffled and confused because he "had expected [the novel] to sharpen my feelings toward *my people's struggle,*" but instead had left him "with a feeling of disgust at the minor compromises the author was willing to make with a sharp question, the question being, 'Were these disposed and beaten people to have a home?' [and] 'Were the British going to fulfill their pledge of the Balfour agreement?'"[82] After glossing over recent conflicting reports of the situation in Palestine, the ever-curious Oko asked Lowenthal a number of probing questions, among them whether "the Jews [were] united against the British in Palestine." Oko asserted that this was information he badly needed, and he pleaded with Lowenthal to give it to him "in a manner that I, as a sailor, can understand." Oko's correspondence with Lowenthal is also particularly noteworthy for a less obvious reason: it contains at both ends cryptic references to unnamed "friends" and unexplained "packages" — allusions undoubtedly to Israeli representatives in the United States and their communications to and from Oko. In effect, although turned down by Shind in 1946, Oko had never broken his ties to Haganah's operatives in the United States; they knew exactly how and where to contact him.

From everything that is known, however, there were no communications between Oko and the Israelis in New York until early May 1948 when Shalit flew to the West Coast to meet with him. The apparent long silence may well have been the reason why an impatient Oko decided to act on his own in early 1947 in purchasing (with several partners) a ship (the *Adelanto*) for the purpose of sailing to Israel by himself.[83] They paid $106,310 for the vessel on 21 March 1947, and Oko took control of it on 5 May 1947. In Oko's words: "Together with several associates I bought a sound cargo vessel, the *Adelanto*. I proposed to load it with a cargo of essential supplies — everything from radar to nuts and bolts — to be taken to Israel under my command as a private venture."[84] In a later account, Oko expanded upon the ship: "She was the ex-*U.S.S. Aries*. She was in beautiful condition, little laker type vessel [...] eminently sea worthy. [...] [S]he would have been the vessel that I would have liked to have seen gone to Israel" loaded with supplies from Lerner's Yard in Oakland.[85] In direct and indirect ways, the *Aries* would play an important role in the *Kefalos* saga. As noted in the previous chapter, Oko used the nucleus of officers from this vessel to staff the upper leadership of the ship.[86] All of this activity did not go unnoticed by the FBI, which launched a full-scale investigation in January 1948. The documents provide a wealth of valuable information about the *Aries/Adelanto* (price, transactions, and principals involved), Oko's business connections, and more significantly, the vessel's real or imagined future uses and purposes.[87] Edward T. Joste, assistant to the operations manager of the U.S. Maritime Commission in San Francisco, declared that Walter Haas, president of the city's Chamber of Commerce, was a member of the syndicate that had purchased the ship. Joste added that Oko "appeared to be well acquainted with a number of prominent Jews in San Francisco, and that it was rumored among shipping people that [Oko] was buying this ship for the purpose of running Jewish immigrants into Palestine."[88] Captain Leighton S. Robinson, a former Deputy Shipping Commissioner of San Francisco and a close friend of Oko, revealed to the FBI that Oko had recently sought his advice in buying the *Aries* as well as help in moving it from Suison Bay to the mooring off San Francisco.[89]

Incidentally, some of the FBI inquiries cast important light on Oko's changing political views. Captain Robinson, who had known Oko for many years and whom Oko greatly admired, citing him as a major influence in his life, recalled that Oko had criticized Harry Bridges as "Communist head of the International Longshoremen and Warehousemen's Union on the Pacific Coast, for the way he was damaging West Coast shipping."[90] Reflecting more about it, Robinson, possibly in an effort to protect his old friend, further "advised [that] he actually knew very little about [Oko's] family, activities, or political philosophy." In contrast, "Buzz" Powers, owner of the Parker Printing Company where Oko worked from 1932–1933, was considerably more forthcoming. Powers said that at the time Oko was his employee, "he was Communistically inclined, but did not appear to be actively engaged in Communistic activities." But when he last saw Oko some six months prior, Powers teased him about his "Communistic tendencies," but declared that Oko did not "seem so ardent a Communistic sympathizer as he formerly had." Powers added two interrelated significant points, namely that Oko was "primarily engaged in improving his financial position; that he [was] constantly engaged in some 'quick money deal' which generally [fell] through."[91] Powers's comments seem to confirm Oko's progressively moderate political stances, as has been underscored.

Koo Okamoto, Oko's secretary from February to June 1948, also provided significant information to the FBI regarding the use of the *Aries/Adelanto*. According to her testimony, Oko told her that there was a "cargo of half-tracks" in South America, and that "he might be able to ship them to Palestine" on a ship that he and his associates had purchased in April 1947 (the *Aries/Adelanto*).[92] When the plan fell through, the consortium that owned the ship had tried to sell the "vessel for profit, but [had] been unable to do so." Even though her facts were not entirely correct on a number of points, the substance of her testimony seems to agree largely with Oko's statements regarding the use of the ship. His proposal to transport a cargo of materials to Israel "was turned down by my associates for conventional business reasons. Then toward the end of May 1948, negotiations were well under way for the sale of the *Adelanto* to a Finnish company at a price that promised profit for all concerned."[93] In a revealing last-minute attempt to settle the issue, one of Oko's business associates, Philip S. Ehrlich, wrote to David R. Wahl, a potential New York buyer, on 20 May 1948. Without naming the price, information that may have been shared earlier, Ehrlich offered the *Aries/Adelanto* for immediate sale or time charter, and informed the would-be client that Oko was "particularly desirous of having [a] vessel made available to be transferred as the first vessel to carry [the] flag of Israel, and also desirous of commanding her himself."[94] Eh-

rlich wrote Oko two days later, informing him of Wahl's negative reply due to the short notice he had been given.[95] But it was already too
late; Oko had left San Francisco for New York on 21 May to inspect
the *Kefalos*. Time had run out on the *Aries/Adelanto*, in the coming
years the ship would cause nothing but headaches for Oko and his
associates at the Adelanto Steamship Co. Oko would even incur accusations of embezzlement in connection with the handling of the
vessel.[96] The *Adelanto* was eventually sold to two British subjects residing in Hong Kong in late 1949.[97]

   In late May 1948 time was also running out for Oko and Gladys
in the West Coast. After Oko's whirlwind tour to the East Coast, he
returned to San Francisco on 28 May, gathered his crew, and three
days later, with Gladys and eight crewmen from the *Adelanto*, departed for Portland, Maine. Gladys had needed no persuasion; she was
eager to go, despite the fact that she and Oko had spent only three
nights in the house they had just completed building at Inverness
Park.[98] Events moved swiftly thereafter. Two weeks later the couple
headed out of New York for Tampico, Mexico, on the rust bucket *Kefalos*. They were served by a loyal Spanish Republican core crew and
armed with a wealth of good intentions and a mutual understanding that they had accumulated over nearly two decades. They would
sorely need all these assets during the trying next eight months.

   In conclusion, although a persuasive case can be made that Oko
had failed at nearly every endeavor he had undertaken before taking
helm of the *Kefalos*, especially during the period 1926–1942, he was
certainly intelligent and an excellent sailor, more disciplined at sea
than on land. And in Gladys, Oko had found an equally capable individual, who, if anything, was far more stable and even-keeled than
he, and someone whose unwavering love and support would sustain
and nourish Oko through difficult times. Far more than his wife,
Gladys was Oko's better half and soul mate.[99]

3
Tampico and Arms

"Everything is in order in Tampico. . . . It's in the bag. . . . Our agent will be there to meet you. . . . All you need to do is enter and work our winches. That is what I was told in New York."

— Oko, "And It Was So" (p. 52)

So wrote Oko in 1958 in an unpublished memoir about events a decade earlier. He remained bewildered at the time of these recollections: "It is still a mystery to me today how I ever got out of there alive, let alone in command of the ship with a full cargo aboard."[1] And he pointedly added that it was "impossible to sort the memories of Tampico into anything like a reasonable sequence. Everything came at once." The captain can perhaps be excused if "nothing fitted into neat pigeonholes to be dated with tidy labels."[2] Perhaps Oko's puzzlement and faulty memory are somewhat understandable given the events that unfolded with dizzying speed in Tampico, Mexico, during the next forty days. From the moment the *Kefalos* arrived at this port under false pretenses on 24 June 1948, nothing would go according to plan. For nearly six weeks Oko would experience communications snags and conflicts with Haganah's operatives in New York; problems with port authorities and the ship being moved several times; delays in getting the arms and in loading them after they arrived in Tampico; continual money shortages (Oko estimated the cost at around $4,000 each day the ship was delayed at port[3]); public scandals when the secrecy surrounding the operation was exposed by local and national newspapers; intrigue on the part of foreign agents about the ship's mission and surveillance by U.S. personnel; the loss of the port agent assigned to the vessel, forcing him to act as both agent and owner; changes in crew, including the loss of two of his most valued officers (Manresa and Ilves); being forced to deal with Hank Greenspun and his group, who were illegally exporting armaments to Israel on behalf of Haganah; and suffering from dysentery and high fever a good deal of the time while at port. And all this in the midst of Tampico's humid, sweltering heat. While Haganah's men in Mexico viewed Tampico, in Oko's words, as "small potatoes," it was little wonder that the captain regarded the time there as a nightmare.

The journey of the *Kefalos* down the eastern seaboard was slow and uneventful. According to Oko, the "men on board began to feel like a crew."[4] [An excellent picture of Gladys and Manresa engaged in pleasant conversation can be found in photograph 4.] Although Oko began to relax somewhat, he was not entirely at ease. While reviewing the instructions he had been given, he began to work on some type of excuse for putting the vessel into Tampico, because strangely, the orders provided absolutely *no* reason to enter that port.[5] Had he perhaps verbally been given in New York some grounds for arriving in Tampico? If he had, Oko surely would have mentioned the reason in his unpublished works and it would be known. Instead, based on all of the evidence available, Oko was left to his own devices on this matter; it was up to him to find a reasonable rationale for docking in Tampico. After much thought, the captain settled on a "*cause majeur* [sic] that would at least get us into the port and give us a chance to stick around a few days if the crates of arms and munitions were not on the dock ready to thumb a ride [...] as I had been assured they would be."[6] Clearly, Oko needed "some degree of legal cover."[7] The captain conferred with the chief engineer, Ilves, and inquired whether "he had anything to offer in the nature of an emergency in the engine room." "Hell, yes," replied the Estonian, "the engines are gulping oil," and he then listed other problems as well. Oko asked him for a list of issues that could be sent to New York, and instructed Ilves to make plans to put the vessel into Tampico. Troubles began shortly thereafter. Oko "sent daily wireless reports to Shipowners Agency" concerning the "alarming figure of average daily consumption of fuel oil," but no answer was returned. The captain angrily recalled that "They maintained complete radio silence."[8]

It was then that Oko changed course on 19 June, off the coast of Miami, Florida. In identical radio messages to Manuel Enterprises and Shipowners Agency, dated the same day, Oko filed a "notice of protest," stating that fuel requirements and radio repairs "necessitated decision to enter Tampico." The communication also requested a number of additional documents and clearance papers to allow the ship to put into Tampico instead of Buenos Aires. Oko also asked for a berth — presumably to be arranged through New York — to await "the necessary papers and to undergo repairs."[9] Whether of their own volition, or because Oko had asked them (perhaps ordered them?) to do so, the communication was countersigned by Ilves, Forbes (chief mate), and Apaolaza (first assistant engineer). A fig leaf perhaps, though one that Oko felt would allow him a measure of cover. Although the subterfuge would work in the short term, it would cause countless complications later. As the ship neared the port, Oko admitted that he was "apprehensive of what might occur in Tampico." He decided to gauge the level of support among the crew for the operation. Just outside port Oko gathered them all in the mess hall and addressed them. The captain's significant remarks were as such:

> You have heard a lot of talk as to the nature of the voyage. You know now that we plan to enter Tampico. [...] [W]e will take on cargo. You may have guessed as much, but I wanted to tell you myself. Other than that, the only thing I can tell you is that when you see the cargo, and if you decide you don't wish to sail, sign out. You will be repatriated to New York, first class, with wages paid until arrival. In the interest of your shipmates, however, I must ask you to stand by until we get port clearance. If you decide you want out, let me know at once. [...] But stay aboard until then, and observe the security that your shipmates are entitled to. That is all I ask. I have told you as much as I can. I want you aboard[,] but only if you want to go along. Is there anyone, now, who wants out?[10]

To Oko's satisfaction, not a hand showed. The captain then had the ship's whistle blown to signal the ship's arrival, and a pilot's launch came to meet the *Kefalos* to escort it to port. The pilot was clearly surprised and told Oko, "I had not been advised of your arrival, so I took the liberty of bringing out an agent." The person in question turned out to be a representative of López Hermanos, a local shipping agency. All of them then proceeded together to Tampico. The *Kefalos* entered port on an emergency basis; the contrived *cause majeure*, or *arribada forzosa*, had worked.[11] Oko would admit years later that these actions were far from honorable. But on the day of the vessel's arrival, he only wanted to get to shore as quickly as possibly to find out what arrangements, if any, had been made.

Oko did not have much to go on at that point, only the instruction to contact a certain David Gritzewsky in Tampico. Gritzewsky, in turn, was to place a call to New York to a fictional Hyman Padover, who would then talk to Oko. Barely arrived at port, however, and now accompanied by the agent of López Hermanos, Oko had not had time to find Gritzewsky. Instead, he was led to the shipping agency's office to place a call to New York. Upon arriving there, Oko noticed that the building also held the offices of the British and Dutch consuls, something that immediately caused him alarm. In effect, by being led to López Hermanos, Oko sensed that he would place himself in the hands of the British, who would be "well informed of all [his] shipping movements."[12] The captain had little choice if he wanted to contact New York quickly; he called Shalit from López Hermanos's office. The former was furious, yelling, "You shouldn't have done this." Oko was far from pleased, sensing that Shalit was angry because of the inconvenience he was causing him. In the heated exchange that ensued, Oko pointed out that he had received no answers to his radio communications, particularly one that requested the name of an agent in Tampico. Oko also advised Shalit that at least for now they could use López Hermanos. The captain's words proved counterproductive: "That really blew the lid in New York."[13] Patently frustrated, Oko then signed off and hung up the phone. His first hours at port were hardly auspicious.

The next day Oko received official permission from the Panamanian consul, Dr. Fernando Matienzo, to carry out the necessary repairs on the ship.[14] That same day, Oko wrote a lengthy letter to the captain of the port explaining the many reasons behind the ship's forced entry into Tampico. He not only cited the excessive consumption of fuel, but also added interesting details not found elsewhere.[15]

Like so much else in this record, it is impossible to know how much
of the account was true, but Oko's explanation suggests some degree
of carelessness on the part of Manuel Enterprises (e.g., a shortage of
fuel on board when the ship was bought), as well as the haste with
which the *Kefalos* had left New York without taking care of all that
needed to be repaired (e.g., potable water boilers had not been properly cleaned, there were ventilation problems in the engine room,
and the radio needed to be fixed). It stands to reason that these matters should have been taken care of at Todd's Dry Dock after Manuel
Enterprises had paid the company $50,000 to get the ship ready to
sail. Oko's request for permission to stay at Tampico to make repairs
would prove to be a double-edged sword. While it gained him time
until the arms arrived, especially since Oko made it clear that he
needed specific *imported* parts to carry out the repairs, the longer it
took for the equipment to arrive, and the longer the *Kefalos* stayed at
port without any repairs, the greater the likelihood that suspicions
would grow that Oko's explanations were simply delaying tactics to
cover ulterior motives.

According to Oko, López Hermanos was interested in handling
the ship since "they stood to make something on the repairs or whatever else was done in port."[16] The agents in New York, however, had
different ideas. On 26 June, Oko received a strange-looking telegram
from Shipowners Agency urgently asking him to call New York informing him that Manuel Enterprises requested that he abstain from
making decisions, that work was being done on a shipment of 1,000
tons of sugar, and that Gritzewsky was returning to Tampico the
next day.[17] On 26 or 27 June, Oko, accompanied by Manresa, went
to look for David Gritzewsky. However, Gritzewsky's wife and his
brother, Luis, informed Oko that he had left for New York to receive
instructions and money. Gritzewsky returned to Tampico the next
day. Much to Oko's dismay, however, he returned without money for
the ship's disbursements. Moreover, Gritzewsky was instructed to go
to Mexico City for the funds, which did not materialize there either.
To Oko's wry amusement, Gritzewsky inexplicably had been given
an expensive gold cigarette lighter in New York, something that had
embarrassed him because he did not smoke.[18] The ship's financial
situation was dire; according to Oko, at that point there was $4 in
the vessel's safe.[19] Exactly when the coffers of the *Kefalos* were replen-

ished is not entirely clear; through "trick and subterfuge," however, Oko managed to secure sufficient cash to "take care of things and [leave] $10,000 in the ship's safe to meet future contingencies."[20] By Oko's own admission, he sheepishly added that he had "cut corners in ways not favored by copybook maxims." While the sum was hardly a fortune, Oko appears to have kept the ship solvent during the rest of his lengthy stay in Tampico. It is probably not accurate, however, to attribute the success of the black on the balance sheet entirely to Oko. It should not be forgotten that Gladys, the purser, kept a close eye on all financial matters and handled day-to-day monetary transactions with the crew. In fact, an important general pattern emerged during the course of the voyage, one that engendered trust among Oko, Gladys, and the crewmen. When a sailor would ask for money, the following dialogue would typically occur:

> Oko: Did you ask the purser?
> Crewman: She said to ask you.
> Oko: Have you got it coming?
> Crew man: I think so.
> Oko: Check with the purser, and if it is correct you can have it.[21]

In essence, Gladys should also be given credit for maintaining the vessel's successful monetary situation.

Meanwhile, on 23 June, the ever-efficient Diane Schweitzer, on behalf of Manuel Enterprises, had sent Oko several documents he had apparently requested en route to Tampico and assured the captain that he would get everything he needed. Unfortunately, of the ten documents on Schweitzer's list, only three are found in Oko's papers.[22] While most of the missing documents seem fairly routine and their content easily surmised, it is regrettable that one document in particular cannot be found: a provisional patent "in connection with the change of name to S/S PINZON."[23] While there is no concrete evidence that on 23 June the men in New York had decided on the name change for the ship, such a conclusion appears inevitable, especially since it was specifically entertained in the instructions penned eleven days earlier. As for Oko, he would spend the next few days from late June through mid-July tending mostly to personnel matters.

Changes — some voluntary, others not — were in store for the crew. The captain was most concerned about Ilves and Manresa: The former was visibly nervous about becoming a father for the first time (his wife was in Philadelphia), and the fact that he had just obtained his U.S. citizenship papers, and the latter was increasingly ill with throat problems that soon turned into a serious and ultimately incurable cancer. Under different circumstances and for different reasons, neither would leave sail on the *Kefalos*. By mid-July, Oko realized that "we should not take Peter Ilves on with us" since he was worried about his wife, and, in turn, was also "keenly aware that, because he had only first citizenship papers, the operations of the ship might put his whole future in jeopardy."[24] Oko claims he offered him out, but Ilves protested. Ultimately he relented and left the ship just prior to sailing and under suspicious circumstances.[25] As for Manresa, the vessel's second mate, his case was at once more clear-cut, yet also more complicated. Manresa's condition had worsened rapidly, as Gladys had noticed, and Oko gave him leave to travel to Mexico City. Although not well, Manresa quickly returned to Tampico with a nephew and a brother-in-law. The latter begged Oko not to allow Manresa to set sail because of his poor health. After a conference with the brother-in-law and Gladys, and despite the fact that Manresa "was eager to continue the voyage," Oko informed his second mate that he should not go with them. Manresa admitted to them that he knew that their decision would be negative, and that was the reason why he had brought his nephew, explaining that he "wanted to have some personal stake in the voyage." It was a blatant lie, because the supposed nephew was Carlos Blanco Aguinaga, my father, who was taken on at Tampico as a mess man.[26] According to Oko, the young Blanco "was fired by the idea of carrying on for his uncle, who was a hero not only to Carlos but to all sympathizers with Loyalist Spain who knew Manresa as the one responsible for getting Loyalist funds to Mexico."[27] Oko's words at seeing his old friend leave are eloquent: "Another body blow [...] [H]is proven idealism, in addition to seamanship [...] were factors I had counted on to help get us through."[28] After returning to Mexico City, Manresa sent a moving parting letter to Oko, requesting not money but a certificate explaining why he had left the ship to enable him to travel to the Mayo Clinic for an operation. Manresa closed by expressing his desire to be able to sail with Oko again.[29] It was not to be; Manresa died of throat cancer on 8 December 1948 in Mexico City.[30] His presence in Tampico, however, as will be discussed shortly, had not gone unnoticed and had proven quite unfavorable in many ways.

Oko quickly was forced to make adjustments in the crew. Apaolaza was promoted to chief engineer, but the captain still needed an experienced first assistant in the engine room, as well as someone to serve as second mate. According to Oko, Shipowners Agency "responded immediately and sent down two good men, Nathaniel Ratner as engineer and Bernard Marks to replace Manresa."[31] But no sooner had Marks settled in that Manuel Enterprises changed its mind and informed Oko that Marks was needed for another vessel in Veracruz. Oko was dismayed because Marks had sailed on the *Exodus* and knew the waters ahead.[32] On 13 July, Oko was notified that Marks was to leave the ship immediately and would be replaced by Louis Markovitz, an individual who clearly disappointed the captain: "He was an unstable type, scared silly, a man I dared not take on board."[33]

Trouble was brewing elsewhere as well, and it was beginning to creep up on Oko. On 28 June, Manuel Enterprises had notified him that it was "diverting one of [its] other vessels [to] Buenos Aires, enabling [him to] change course. Purpose lifting thousand tons [of] sugar [at] Tampico; also additional sugar [at] Havana. Both parcels for Italy."[34] A clever stratagem, no doubt — two ships, different destinations and cargos — but one that would put Oko in a bind because now he was forced to maintain the fiction of waiting to pick up cargo, something that was conveyed to several crew members.[35] In an attempt to buy time, on 9 July Oko informed port authorities that he was moving the ship (apparently anchored in the middle of the river Pánuco) to a more convenient place in order to free up port traffic and facilitate repairs on board.[36] [Photograph 5] This unilateral action, apparently taken without consultation with the interested parties, probably ruffled the feathers of port authorities. In response, on 14 July the port captain of Tampico notified Oko that he was commissioning an employee to inspect the repairs that were being carried out on board the *Kefalos*.[37] Three weeks after putting into port, Oko was clearly in a bind, noting, "There was no cargo in sight, not even sugar [and] the atomizer tips and Dahl burners [...] ordered a month earlier [...] had not arrived either."[38] Already backed into a corner, things would get much worse for Oko in the coming days.

On 17 July, Oko received word that López Hermanos was withdrawing from their handling of the ship.[39] That same day, Oko received a curt note from the port captain that because López Hermanos was no longer managing the vessel, he should, according to law, name another consignee (*consignatario*) or agent to deal with the ship's business. Otherwise, the port captain added ominously, Oko would not be permitted to carry out any operation at port.[40] Quite possibly in reply to this ultimatum, Ilves drew up — at Oko's direction, no doubt — a detailed list of parts and repairs required "before the vessel [was] ready for sea."[41] Two additional developments around the same time further aggravated Oko's situation: Gritzewsky had a cryptic note delivered to the ship, essentially bidding him farewell, and by 17 July "the dysentery hooks bugs really had their hooks" into the captain. Gritzewsky's message in part begged Oko to be careful before ending with an abrupt "It was nice to meet you."[42] Gritzewsky's unexplained departure meant that Oko was losing his "most direct means of contact with Manuel Enterprises [...] since Gritzewsky's telephone had been [the] most direct line to New York [and] the only one not suspect of tapping or [...] eavesdropping."[43] In addition, both Oko and Gladys liked David and felt that he was on their side. As for the stomach condition, it would only worsen; Oko's temperature climbed to 106 degrees and he felt "like hell inside." During most of his remaining stay in Tampico, Oko would suffer enormous discomfort and was forced to station himself as close as possible to a bathroom at all times.[44] At one point a doctor was sent by Spanish Republicans in Mexico City to tend to him. Hospitalization was considered, but Oko declared it out of the question. Instead, the doctor prescribed a steady regimen of injections (presumably antibiotics), and he left Gladys a supply of medications and a hypodermic needle, which, Oko jokingly complained, she "jabbed into a soft spot every time he looked at her." Although he was miserable being forced to sit upright and speak as little as possible, Oko earned the sobriquet "Man of Steel." If there was a silver lining to all of this, Oko would find it in the "diabolically uncertain and feverish circumstances." In effect, he felt that recent developments had "freed [him] completely" from important ties and commitments that had constrained his actions (i.e., New York and López Hermanos). Perhaps the captain was hallucinating, but by accepting his fate, and assuming full responsibility for all actions, Oko now sensed that he had "a new lease on hope." Ill as he was, and while New York was still trying to send him the requested materials,[45] by sometime in mid-July Oko decided to act.

Because word had reached Tampico that the "major cargo was in Mexico City," Oko "dispatched Chief Mate Forbes to go look it over, so the loading plan would be ready" when the shipment reached port.[46] Parts of Forbes's trip to Mexico City are extremely comical, but the visit proved fruitful. When ordered to fly to the capital, Forbes, who had been working in Tampico's steamy, sweltering climate, grabbed a "white silk shirt, white pants, and a Panama hat." Apparently no one had informed him about the weather in Mexico City's plateau. So not only did he nearly freeze to death, Forbes also felt out of place, in Oko's words, "dressed like a damned planter from Yucatán on his first visit to the big city."[47] The *Kefalos*'s first mate, and Oko's most trusted right-hand officer in the foreseeable future, was finally called to the hotel where the persons in charge of procuring the arms were lodging. What he found was not pretty; Forbes encountered men "dressed like [...] Esquire dummies, lolling around [...] putting in long-distance calls to Rome and Naples, just to look impressive."[48] Forbes quickly got down to business, demanded to see the cargo, and insisted that the men "get off their asses and see that [the shipment] got to the ship." Returning hastily to Tampico, Forbes brought back useful information: the largest pieces that the vessel would carry were French 75 mm canons, and, regrettably, the heavier equipment, such as MSTs, that "we had been led to expect, were not included in the shipment."[49] (A detailed discussion of the arms occurs later in this chapter.) Still, Forbes's visit produced results. Shortly after his return, a long cargo train from Mexico City "pulled into Tampico and shunted twenty-five boxcars on sidings along the dock." From a variety of sources, the arms arrived at port on 16 July. The train had been escorted by the Mexican military. The desired moment had finally come; it was now important to load the arms as fast as possible. According to Oko, "Forbes stripped for action [...] and worked the crew like clockwork. We started to load first thing Monday morning."[50] Oko even wrote the head of the customs office the same day (19 July) to request permission to leave Tampico with merchandise for its next port of destination (Shanghai).[51] In turn, the administrator of the customs office endorsed Oko's petition and gave orders to several of the parties involved to facilitate the operation; however, he also made it a point to make sure that the process be observed.[52] As Oko lay sick with an elevated fever confined to his cabin bed, he felt he could relax a bit with "the welcome sound of working winches." This made Gladys happy because she had been extremely worried about Oko's condition. Her joy and Oko's repose, however, were extremely short-lived. In Oko's words, "The winches were little more than well warmed up when suddenly they stopped, and the whole noise and clanger of loading went dead." Oko was quickly on his feet yelling for Forbes, who "was on the dock arguing with some officials with papers to stop loading operations."

What caused this sudden and unwelcome turn of events? The catalyst for these and subsequent events was a lengthy article in the 19 July issue of the local daily *El Mundo*.[53] A blaring headline in bold type across the entire top page of the second section read "A Suspicious Ship Came to Tampico to Load an Arms Cargo." The alarmist exposé about the *Kefalos* — a mixture of fact and fiction — noted that "a train loaded with canons and other arms has also arrived." In another caption in bold letters, the piece asserted that the vessel had "almost the same crew as the famous yacht *Vita*." Additional captions before the article proper mixed fact and innuendo: (1) "The 'Kefalos' or 'Larranga' came in under [the pretext] of a forced entry, alleging damages that it doesn't have, to await the arms train"; (2) "Twenty-five boxcars loaded with artillery pieces and other war materiel"; and (3) "It appears that difficulties have arisen to load those materials because the train is under military custody." The piece elaborated on these matters, while adding in heated terms a number of serious accusations. The article labeled the *Kefalos* "a pirate ship" and asserted that its cargo was "a considerable and scandalous contraband of national armament for export." It also noted that numerous soldiers guarded the train convoy and that its boxcars were closed, sealed, and carried labels indicating that they contained minerals for export with government permission. However, some curious observers had been able to peer inside a hole in one of the wooden cars, and had seen that the metal objects inside were shaped like canons. According to reports from bystanders, other boxcars contained munitions, bombs, rifles, military backpacks, and helmets. When the train cars were about to be opened by stevedores to load the ship under the direction of a port agent, ship leaders, and some "Jewish-looking foreigners," armed personnel of the port intervened and interrupted the unloading of the train to the angry protests of those interested in carrying out the operation. Despite repeated objections, the stevedores refused to unload the train, asserting that proper documentation was needed from the customs office. Significantly, the influential Mexico City daily *Excelsior* reported the same information the same day on its front page, citing *El Mundo* as its source.[54] The next day (20 July) *Excelsior* reported that another train with 14 boxcars had arrived in Tampico the previous day.[55] This meant that between 16 and 19 July, a total of 39 boxcars with arms had arrived in Tampico, some of which had been loaded aboard the ship but most of which had not. And so, for the time being at least, a standoff developed at port.

As the scandal surrounding the ship exploded, it blew the cover off what was already at best an open secret at port. For the next two weeks until its departure, the vessel would be the object of heated controversy in local and national Mexican newspapers.[56] One of the first casualties of the episode was the ship's location. On 21 July, the port captain ordered the *Kefalos* to leave its berth and return upstream to mid-river.[57] This would not be the last time the vessel was moved. Its movements in Tampico were a reflection of the larger political game, as Oko aptly put it, "played across the board of Mexican officialdom."[58] The Mexican Ministry of Defense in the first days of the affair provided contradictory explanations for the cargo that had arrived in Tampico. While vehemently denying that any sort of smuggling or illicit activity was involved, two leading members of the ministry offered different explanations. The Mexican Secretary of Defense, General Gilberto R. Limón, declared that the matérial in question was armament no longer needed by the national army and that it had been sold to foreign armed forces. However, the ministry chief of staff, General Antonio Sánchez Acevedo, asserted that these were old arms that had been sold as scrap [*chatarra*] to a private concern. He added that the arms "were totally unserviceable and useless [...], only caused storage costs, and [...] their sale brought a good sum to the national treasury."[59] *El Mundo* had a field day with the assertion that the arms were in fact scrap. A cartoon on the editorial page of the daily's 22 July issue shows two men standing on the dock, one, holding his nose, asking the other, "Is there something here that smells funny to me?" The other replies, "It must be the scrap of the Kefalos."[60] More seriously, a strong editorial on the same page urged clarifications from the highest levels of the government regarding the "scandalous case of the 'Kefalos.'" Keeping up the pressure, on 23 July another strongly-worded opinion piece on the editorial page demanded explanations regarding the "big scandal" from the administration of President Alemán to safeguard the "government's decorum and the nation's prestige."[61]

At least one Tampico newspaper came to the defense of the *Kefalos*. On 20 July on its front page, *La Tribuna*, a left-leaning afternoon daily, refuted the accusation that the cargo that had arrived by train consisted of smuggled war materiel.[62] *La Tribuna* also took to task the "yellow journalism" of *El Mundo* — without naming it — and denied that there were crew members of the yacht *Vita* aboard the *Kefalos*, an assertion that was literally, if disingenuously, true inasmuch as Manresa had left for Mexico City. In general, *La Tribuna* readily accepted the government's explanations concerning the arms. However, in its haste to agree with the Mexican authorities, *La Tribuna* erroneously reported that the arms were headed for Mexico's southeast, based on unofficial information from the Ministry of Defense that allegedly had not previously been disseminated because of security considerations. The front page of *La Tribuna*'s contained a suggestive short item that might well have been of considerable relevance: the visit to Tampico of Carl V. Strom, the U.S. General Consul to Mexico, who was accompanied by Harold B. Quarton, U.S. Consul at Tampico, and other dignitaries. Announced as a courtesy call with local authorities, Strom's presence *might* have had other objectives, especially since Quarton had been keeping a close eye on the *Kefalos* and was reporting intelligence to higher-ups in the U.S. State Department.[63] In other words, while there is no tangible proof, it is not far-fetched to surmise that Strom was in Tampico to persuade the local authorities to relent on their "siege" on the vessel. Whatever may have been the reasons behind Strom's visit, Oko was generally pleased with the article in *La Tribuna*. The daily had given the *Kefalos* "a clean bill of health [...] as an honest ship trying to make an honest living."[64] On

20 July, another newspaper, *El Universal* of Mexico City, in its front page also came to the government's assistance — and, in passing, to that of the vessel — by reporting that the shipment authorized for the *Kefalos* "was composed of worn-out arms and ammunition [...], hence legally sold for its iron and steel."[65] Oko assessed the piece as a "face-saving deal all the way around," but not as one that proved helpful to his immediate situation. As noted earlier, the ship was ordered out to the mouth of the river Pánuco, where "during the war German and Italian ships had been interned." The captain could do little but plead his case before the port authorities and wait for something to happen in the capital. But Oko was also faced with another problem, one closer to home: he had to tell his crew the truth about the arms, something that from all appearances he had only done in the vaguest and most general terms just prior to entering Tampico.

My father, Carlos Blanco Aguinaga, relates that more than a week after his arrival in Tampico, the crew learned of the imminent arrival of a train that purportedly was bringing sugar.[66] Orders were quickly given to lift anchor and move the vessel from its position in the middle of the river Pánuco to the dock. When the long train arrived around mid-day — 16 or 18 July — the ship's sailors were surprised to see that it was escorted by fully armed soldiers from the Mexican Army. Blanco Aguinaga also notes that the train cars were sealed (*precintados*). Shortly thereafter the story broke out in the local newspapers concerning the supposed "pirate ship," and, as noted, the scandal quickly spread to the national press. According to Blanco Aguinaga, Oko was forced to inform the entire crew that the destination of the arms was Israel. The captain told them that he understood "perfectly" that they had not signed up for a voyage on board a vessel that was carrying arms to a region at war — and to an area long controlled at sea by Great Britain. He also expressed to them that he understood if anyone wanted to leave the ship, and in the event that any should leave, there would be no hard feelings and he would pay them what they were due. All of this information was relayed to the crew primarily in Spanish by young Blanco Aguinaga, who was one of the only sailors aboard who was fully bilingual. (Keep in mind that half of the sailors were Spaniards. More on this question and on the rest of the crew in Chapter 4.) Crew members then began to form small groups to discuss the situation and what decisions to make. A good number of them were Spanish Republican exiles and sailing without proper papers. Leaving the ship in Mexico would have presented significant legal problems for them, especially if they wished to return to the United States to sign up to serve as crew aboard other ships. Most, therefore, opted to remain with the *Kefalos,* for political reasons and/or expediency, except for a handful who decided to leave. Mindful of the dangers that awaited them, particularly in the Mediterranean, whose waters were said to still contain numerous mines, the captain announced that he would double their salaries after entering the *mare nostrum.*[67] This appears to have settled the question; there was nothing left for the crew to do but wait for the ship to load. Blanco Aguinaga asserts that it would be a few more days before the seals on the boxcars were broken and the crew could fill the cargo holds of the *Kefalos.*

Meanwhile, *El Mundo* continued on 21 July its campaign against the national government's "vagueness and contradictions in the embarkation of arms" while "waiting for President Alemán to tell the truth to the Mexican people." Oko wrote the head of the customs office on 23 July to restate his positions and appeal for consideration from the administrator.[68] The captain complained of the hardship upon the crew as a result of the *Kefalos* being anchored in a position that was unsafe and that allowed "heavy silt [and] much mud through our pumps." He also reminded the port authority that it was tropical season, and that all delays increased the dangers to the ship. Oko also cited his own illness, recent developments, and "inaccurate news stories" as having left him, in his own words, in a "rather confused state," which was quite probably a way of pleading for time and assistance. In response to an apparent question from the chief of the customs administration, Oko informed him that there were thirteen nationalities represented among the crew and that "Spanish [was] the predominant language aboard our vessel." Whether any of Oko's entreaties were successful remains unknown.[69] What appears more certain is that direct orders from the highest levels of the Mexican government had a far more effective result.

Oko wrote that since the ship's arrival in Tampico, he had been asking his contacts how things were being handled on the local level. "Don't worry about the local angle [...] [E]verything is being taken care of at the top in Mexico City. Tampico is small potatoes," he was told.[70] Isolated and dejected, Oko had apparently informed those involved in the operation in Mexico that he was fed up and about ready to leave port. The *Kefalos* had been at port for a month, enduring interminable delays in the tropical heat, and the money was running dangerously low.[71] Suddenly, however, on 24 July, "permits to resume loading operations came through." What had caused this important turn of events? Unquestionably, directives from the Mexican government. While the concrete details of internal debates and decisions may never be known, by 23–24 July the Mexican government had concluded that the *Kefalos* should be allowed to load all of the arms in Tampico. On 22 July, *Excelsior* reported that agents of the President Alemán were investigating the embarkation of arms on the vessel, presumably in Tampico proper.[72] More significantly, on 24 July the same daily informed that "the loading operations coincided with the return to Tampico of the agents of the Presidency and of the Attorney General who had come to investigate the reasons for the suspension of the loading."[73] And the previous day, *El Mundo* reported that the Eighth Military Zone had received orders to allow the embarkation of the arms sold by the national government.[74] The newspaper *La Tribuna* also noted that the port captain had issued permits allowing the *Kefalos* to return to its original berth as a result of a new order he had received.[75] After these decisions, events moved quickly in Tampico.

During 24–28 July, the *Kefalos* loaded the rest of the arms (recall that some had already been loaded before the operation had been interrupted). A detailed report of unknown origin, but countersigned by Eric Forbes, the ship's first mate, provides an accurate picture of the work done, days carried out, and total cargo loaded on the vessel.[76] Teams (*cuadrillas*) of stevedores carried out the loading operations, working four days and nights, and were assisted and supervised by the ship's crew. The total cargo consisted of 754 tons of war materiel; 30 tons of radar (also labeled as radio in some documents) and helmets; 1,020 tons of sugar; and 589 drums, barrels, and cases of water and/or fuel.[77] [Photograph 6] The war materiel had arrived on 35 train cars, and the sugar (possibly along with the radar and helmets) on 21 train cars. Oko's receipt for the arms is significant; it states that he had received the content of 35 train cars from an officer of the "Almacenes de Armamento y Municiones de la Ciudad de

México, D.F."[78] In effect, the armament had come directly from one of the Mexican government's armories in the capital. The helmets and radar/radio were shipped under the name of David Gritzewski and were divided as 72 boxes of miners' helmets and 18 boxes of radio parts. The manifest for this cargo listed the destination as Genoa, Italy, for delivery to "China and American Export and Import Co.," and identified the cargo as being aboard "[the] *PINZON EX-KE-FALOS*."[79] As for the sugar, according to the manifest for the cargo it was allegedly being shipped by the Unión Nacional de Productores de Azúcar, S.A., bound for the same destination and in the same ship.[80] Oko was elated by the "cargo winches roaring day and night; gear being dragged across the decks, longshoremen and gang bosses shouting, plus the shunting of cars and clangor of handling on the dock. It's an infernal roar, but more welcome to my ears than the quieter hours" of previous days.[81] Despite the sweltering heat and soggy climate, the captain was also starting to recover from the dysentery that had afflicted him. He was happy to be able to see Gladys clearly again: "She looked as cool-headed and composed as ever, and I was almighty grateful that she was there with me." This tender moment made him recall one of the love letters he had written to her from the South Pacific during the war.[82] Oko soon realized, however, that this was no time to linger with reminiscences; with the cargo on board, the *Kefalos* became more vulnerable, and he took extra precautions to guard the ship against the dangers of accidents and sabotage. The captain was particularly concerned that the vessel was docked next to what he called "the Arab village and marketplace," a heavily transited area in the immediate vicinity of the ship. He was desperate to leave what *El Mundo* a few days earlier had gleefully described as the mousetrap (*ratonera*) he was caught in.

Having successfully weathered a barrage of problems and setbacks for nearly forty days, the ship was finally ready to sail. In fact, nearly all of the crew had been on board for several days awaiting departure.[83] On 2 August, the port captain instructed Oko to have the vessel ready by 17:00 in front of the *Muelle de Alijadores* so that it could be tugged out of port.[84] Oko was all too happy to oblige and immediately replied affirmatively. He also took the opportunity to tend to some last-minute paperwork, discharging officially from the *Kefalos* two officers: August Karjus, a second engineer aboard the vessel since 11 June 1948, and Peeter Ilves, chief engineer since 1 June 1948.[85] On 3 August, port authorities gave clearance papers for the *Kefalos* to sail for Shanghai.[86] That very day the port captain also issued exit permit number 271 for the "Panamanian steamer '*Kefalos*'" to leave port for Shanghai via Genoa. According to the document, it had a crew of thirty-six, carried two passengers, and a cargo of 1,250 tons.[87] Already out to sea, Oko surely would have appreciated the news item in the 4 August issue of *Excelsior* with the headline "The *Kefalos* Left for Shanghai."[88] Like so much of the paperwork and other matters surrounding the ship, most of this was pure fabrication, fiction quite probably secured through generous payments to port officials. An angry Oko would later learn that $36,000 had been the "pay-off" to port authorities to obtain the necessary documentation, an excessive amount in the opinion of ship officers. The captain wrote, "My Spaniards in the crew, who knew the language well, and who did a very good job of keeping me informed in the port, know that this was a matter that could have been settled with the Port Director, Dr. Gómez Soriol, for a matter of between $3,000 and $10,000."[89] All parties were likely pleased by the final outcome of the previous weeks' fluctuations, and for different reasons: Oko because he had left with the arms, port officials because they had gotten rid of a pesky problem and made a little money in the process, the government of President Alemán because an embarrassing international issue had been made to disappear, and Haganah because much-needed armament was finally on its way.

But where had these arms come from, how had they been procured and by whom, and, more important, exactly what arms did the cargo holds of the *Pinzon*, ex-*Kefalos*, carry? The origin of the arms was twofold. A small portion of the armament came from Hawaii, via Los Angeles and Acapulco. But by far the largest portion of the arms was purchased from the Mexican government in Mexico proper by operatives acting on behalf of Haganah. The broad outlines of the Hawaiian operation to secure arms are well known.[90] Hank Greenspun and a member of his group, Willie Sosnow, took the arms some time between January and March 1948 from the Universal Airplane Salvage Company at Iroquois Point, which was owned by Nathan Liff, a pro-Israel sympathizer, as well as from an adjoining Navy "dump" of arms that, in Leonard Slater's words, "had not been declared surplus and still belonged to the Navy." While Greenspun is not very precise with dates and other facts, it appears that he arrived in Hawaii in late December 1947 or early 1948 and was joined shortly thereafter by Sosnow.[91] Working feverishly for two to three weeks, Greenspun and Sosnow, operating with local ad-hoc monetary and physical assistance, packed several dozens of crates with airplane engines, spare parts, and machine guns. After the work was completed, in all there were a total of ninety-five crates of war materiel.[92] Greenspun and Sosnow then returned to the United States on 24 January and 25 February 1948, respectively, having made arrangements before leaving Hawaii for the airplane engines and arms to be shipped aboard the *S.S. Lane Victory* for Wilmington, California, as its destination.[93] According to the FBI, the vessel, owned by American President Lines, left Hawaii on 19 March and arrived in Los Angeles on 25 March 1948 at 8:50 p.m. From all appearances the operation had been enormously cheap and successful: the materiel had been procured entirely free of charge, the only costs incurred were for labor and freight, and the shipment had arrived safely.[94] An unidentified FBI source asserted that Greenspun had paid him $4,000 in cash in Hawaii for "the labor and freight charges on the shipment of the 95 cases to Los Angeles."[95] There had been other reasonably small charges involved in the shipment. For example, when the cargo was picked up in Los Angeles, Abraham J. Levin, one of Greenspun's associates, had paid $4,647.53 for the shipment — $2,700 by check and $1,947.53 in cash.[96] It appears that the amount paid in cash was for demurrage charges that had accumulated because the shipment had been picked up late.[97] In essence, if the Los Angeles district attorney's figures during the 1950 trial of Greenspun and his associates are to be believed, for less than $10,000 Greenspun and Sosnow had procured close to $2 million worth of arms in Hawaii.[98]

After their arrival in Los Angeles, events started to go wrong very quickly for Greenspun and his associates. Between 31 March and 2 April, the Nelson Trucking Company hauled ninety-fives cases from the American President Lines berth at Wilmington to Maxwell Associates. It is worth noting that the shipment was paid for by John L. Westland and Sons, brokers for Service Airways, Al Schwimmer's and Reynold Selk's company. (Recall that they were the two individuals who had persuaded Greenspun to go to Hawaii.[99]) It soon became clear that someone had tipped off U.S. authorities — the U.S. Customs Bureau and the FBI — about the armament, and now Greenspun was forced to scramble to find places to hide the cargo. In the next days, the boxes were moved several times to different Los Angeles locations to keep them from falling into the hands of the authorities.[100] Despite Greenspun's frantic efforts, eventually, on 14 April, the U.S. Customs Service seized all of the boxes containing the airplane engines and components but failed to confiscate sixteen crates that held machine guns.[101] Staying one step ahead of the pursuers, according to Greenspun, "We managed to jockey sixteen crates of arms" onto a truck, and then stored them in the warehouse of a "sympathetic [...] surplus dealer."[102] Through a stroke of luck and/ or incompetence on the part of the U.S. authorities, Greenspun and a motley group of volunteers had prevented some 500–600 machine guns (approximately 15 tons) from falling into the government's hands. By mid- to late-May 1948, Greenspun had to find a way to get the arms out of hiding and transport them down the West Coast by sea to Mexico. There was little margin for error because the FBI and customs officials were closing in rapidly. If procuring the armament in Hawaii had been a relatively simple action, its aftermath, by contrast, would prove to be a far more complicated Hollywood movie production, complete with colorful characters, revolvers, and drama galore. Fortunately for historians, what might be labeled the *Idalia* affair left a wealth of primary and secondary sources, including several first-hand testimonies.[103]

According to Greenspun, the ringleader of the operation, he searched for a week for a suitable boat to transport the arms, but his efforts were not easy because a relatively large vessel was required. After several unsuccessful attempts to secure a yacht through Jewish owners ("the first half-dozen begged off," wrote a disappointed Greenspun), he was introduced to Leland Robert Lewis, a young twenty-five-year-old veteran of the Merchant Marine, a seasoned sailor who had worked in San Diego's tuna fishing fleet, and owner of the schooner *Idalia*.[104] The 75- foot, 34-ton, double-masted schooner/yacht had a long and distinguished history as the property of the noted dentist Painless Parker. Built by George Lawley and Son Shipbuilding Company of Boston in 1906, Painless Parker had paid $86,000 cash for the vessel (Official No. 202991). Arriving in the

West Coast in 1923, in the years that followed the *Idalia* had been involved in numerous long-distance competitions in the Pacific Ocean,
including the celebrated San Francisco to Tahiti voyage in 1925.
Painless had modernized the schooner with electrical equipment and
radio-telephone connections to land. He had also equipped it with a
100-horsepower motor and carried out other modifications and im-
provements, making it possible for the *Idalia* to travel at 11 knots
under auxiliary power. On February 1946, Painless Parker sold the
Idalia to Lewis for $8,000. With great care the new owner gradually
and lovingly restored the yacht to a semblance of its former grandeur
and used it to charter cruises and fishing trips. When Greenspun met
Lewis in May 1948 at San Pedro/Wilmington, California, the *Idalia*
had just returned from a three-month cruise to Mexico with a group
of passengers that included artists, photographers, film cameramen,
and writers.[105] A complex drama would unfold aboard the *Idalia*
during the next two weeks.

When approached by Greenspun to make a trip to Acapulco
with a cargo for $3,000, Lewis was reluctant to accept. For one thing,
Lewis had not yet been informed of the contents of the shipment:
around 150 bags, each weighing about 200 pounds and containing
four machine-guns per sack (estimates of the total weight of the
arms vary between 15 to 18 tons).[106] Greenspun was insistent on using Lewis's vessel. In fact, according to Lewis, Greenspun "said he
was going to have the guns loaded aboard the yacht whether I liked it
or not [...] [W]hile brandishing the revolver, [Greenspun] stated that
they had to get the guns to Palestine. He said that the transaction
was bigger than any of us."[107] Matters got off to an even rougher start
when Greenspun and his group of "amateur stevedores," as he called
them, broke the schooner's gangway and one of the guard-rails while
loading the vessel. They also threw down some of the heavy sacks
into the well below, causing additional damage.[108] Greenspun admitted that the *Idalia* was "sluggishly riding" under "a far heavier
load than her builders had ever intended." Lewis at that point appears to have changed his mind, informed Greenspun that he was
not going, and ordered him to remove the bags from the boat. Several tense exchanges followed between them, and Lewis eventually
offered to sell the *Idalia* to Greenspun for $17,000, so that he could
sail the yacht himself. After the initial tensions subsided somewhat,

and a temporary understanding was reached on the cost of the trip, Greenspun requested additional help from Bernie Fineman, one of his main contacts, in recommending a cook, a navigator, and an engineer to bring on board. The three were Jacob Fuchs, Alvin Ellis, and Nathaniel Ratner, respectively. Together with Greenspun and Lewis, the five would make the trip to Acapulco. It would not be an easy voyage. During the long trip (more than 1,400 nautical miles), the crew of the *Idalia* encountered problems with the motor; navigation was carried out without the aid of proper instruments; there was a shortage of gasoline and food; bad weather occurred off Mazatlán (gale winds, rain, and high seas); and the men had to sleep on deck because the vessel's cabins were full of armament. (At one point the *Idalia* was forced to enlist the assistance of a tuna boat to repair its failing engine.) Ratner recalled that the schooner was riding so low in the water that he could actually hear a seal breathing next to him while he rode in the back of the deck.[109]

Given the volatility of the situation, conflicts continually erupted, especially between Greenspun and Lewis. The former brandished his Mauser pistol, which he carried in his pocket at all times, and threatened to blow Lewis's brains out and throw him over the side. According to Greenspun himself, he put the "muzzle up to Lewis's temple" and asked him "Will you take us to Acapulco, Lee? You have five seconds to answer. Yes or no?" Greenspun then began to count down the seconds. Eventually, Lewis assented.[110] It is impossible to know for certain whether this was cheap bravado or serious intimidation to keep everyone in line; two additional incidents, however, suggest that Greenspun meant business. Shortly after leaving port, he handed Ratner a gun and exclaimed, "We have to take over the ship!" Ratner was, in his words, "totally confused," and asked him from whom they were taking over the ship. Greenspun explained that Lewis did not want to go along with the pre-arranged deal. He then told Lewis that if he cooperated, he would get his promised money, but if not, Ratner, "an Irgun terrorist," would kill him. Poor Nathaniel admits to have been "ill prepared for this drama."[111] An equally telling moment occurred when it appeared that the *Idalia* was about to founder in the midst of a storm. Lewis suggested lightening up the ship by disposing of at least half the machine guns, with which Fuchs, the overweight cook, agreed. Greenspun told the latter to shut up, adding "Right now I'd be willing to dump you if it would save a dozen guns."[112]

Greenspun also was not above deception and outright fabrication to ensure that the *Idalia* reached its destination. He had originally told Lewis that the boat would only go to Catalina Island, where another boat was waiting for them. There, the arms would be transferred to the other vessel. Once at sea, however, Greenspun informed him that there was no other ship and that the Idalia was going all the way to Acapulco. Of course, Lewis was furious, but there was little he could do about it. *His* vessel was under Greenspun's control, and the situation created a number of dilemmas for Lewis. For example, he could try to escape by swimming ashore or by running away when the *Idalia* was put into Ensenada, Mexico, for gasoline and supplies, but this would have meant abandoning the ship altogether and perhaps not seeing it again (in effect, losing the *Idalia*). This consideration, along with money-related matters, probably accounted for Lewis's numerous equivocations, hesitancies, and changes of heart, and ultimately, for his reluctant assent and decision to stay with the schooner. Yet, this interpretation has to be considerably nuanced and weighed in light of certain contradictions that surfaced during the voyage itself (i.e., Lewis's desire for adventure, as well as his on-again, off-again desire to assist the Jewish people).[113] As a young Jew, although not particularly a Zionist one, Lewis was somehow aware that he was involved in an operation to help a beleaguered people halfway across the world. Greenspun was quick to sense this, and he played on Lewis's Jewish background. "Just what kind of Jew are you?" he would ask him. And when Greenspun thought that Lewis was attempting to "shake" him down, he would dress him down: "You're Jewish and I'm Jewish, but there's one big difference between us. I got into this thing because I felt a sense of duty. You did it for money." Greenspun also brought up Israel and its cause several times, a fact that undoubtedly resonated with the all-Jewish crew.[114] In the course of these discussions, underpinned by appeals to ethnic solidarity and politics, if not a complete meeting of the minds, a tenuous détente appears to have gradually developed between them — enough to neutralize Lewis and keep him from bolting or interfering with the operation. This does not mean, however, that Lewis afterward did not continue to harbor deep resentment against Greenspun for commandeering

his vessel and damaging it in the process, depriving him of his livelihood. Lewis made this abundantly clear in many declarations to U.S.
authorities in subsequent times.[115]

If the *Idalia*'s voyage was fraught with physical dangers, it was
equally replete with a panoply of legal problems because the transportation of arms violated a number of U.S. export laws. As such, the
crew members associated with Haganah (in effect, all except Lewis),
as well as their confederates on land, would soon find themselves entangled in extensive U.S. government investigations, indicted, and in
several instances tried in federal courts in 1949 and 1950.[116] In other
words, because Mexico was now involved, the legal stakes surrounding the *Idalia* saga were far higher than in the previous shipment of
arms from Hawaii (a U.S. territory) to California. Even without yet
having most of the details of the schooner's voyage, the legal attaché
at the U.S. Embassy in Mexico, shortly after the ship's arrival in Acapulco, asserted that "it is felt there is substantial evidence to warrant
the belief that the operators of the vessel 'Idalia' may have violated a
Federal law, either in the acquisition or the exportation, or both, of
machine guns."[117]

While Greenspun failed to record the date of the schooner's
arrival in Acapulco, the FBI's legal attaché in Mexico City reported
that the vessel had reached port "on or around June 15th."[118] (Recall that only nine days later the *Kefalos* would arrive at Tampico.)
In effect, even with a brief stop at Ensenada, the *Idalia* had covered slightly more than 1,400 nautical miles in approximately two
weeks. Greenspun and his associates had made plans to have a Mexican confederate, Tito Rivera, a mysterious individual about whom
little is known, meet the *Idalia* in Acapulco to make arrangements
to unload the weapons. There is abundant evidence that the Mexican Navy was heavily involved in offering assistance and support
to remove the arms from the *Idalia*, an important point on which
different testimonies coincide. Lewis, for instance, unequivocally
asserted that, "All the guns were unloaded and placed on the dock
by Mexican sailors. While the unloading operations were in progress, two Mexican officers in uniform came to the docks [...] from the
presidential yacht 'Sota Venta,' [sic] which is the Mexican Presidential yacht, and observed the operations."[119] Ratner corroborated the
account and wrote that arrangements "were made with the Mexican

government to have the Mexican Navy unload the 600 heavy machine guns we were carrying."[120] With the armament safely secured in the hands of the Mexican Navy, the *Idalia* crew started to disperse, and Greenspun quickly headed for Mexico to make arrangements for the shipment of the machine guns to Tampico and to continue work on a separate arms deal with the Mexican government. Lewis contacted U.S. authorities in Mexico, and then made the first of several round-trip voyages to the United States. His main concern was the repair of the *Idalia* with the monies agreed upon and promised by Greenspun. Ellis and Ratner traveled to Mexico City. Both would play important roles in assisting Greenspun in procuring arms in the capital and then escorting several train convoys with armament to Tampico. Along with Greenspun and some Haganah associates in Mexico, Ellis and Ratner were the most direct links between the *Idalia* and the *Kefalos*—both of them sailed on the *Kefalos* from Tampico. Finally, after a brief two-week stay in Mexico City, Fuchs was given $200 by Greenspun and told to return home, which he did by bus. Apparently not an upstanding citizen, Fuchs would eventually run afoul of the law. His declaration about the *Idalia* affair before FBI agents took place at California State Prison, San Quentin, in October 1949, where he was serving a sentence for burglary.[121] And for all of Greenspun's purported heroic efforts aboard the *Idalia*, he had only managed to ship 15 to 18 tons of machine guns from California to Mexico, a minute fraction of the 754 tons of war materiel loaded onto the *Kefalos*. In the weeks that followed after arriving in Acapulco, and working in close cooperation with Mexican government officials, Greenspun and his confederates would speed up their efforts to secure the rest of the arms that would leave on the *Kefalos* on 3 August 1948.

For a variety of diplomatic, political, and military reasons, Israel's interest in Latin America had grown in 1947. Accordingly, Israeli officials had begun to devote more attention and resources to this region's possibilities.[122] These efforts accelerated during the course of 1948. It is, therefore, important to underscore the fact that Greenspun's arms-buying spree in June and July 1948 did not start from scratch; he and his close associates had benefitted from numerous advantages that were already in place when they arrived on the scene. Among the most significant were the following:

- Prior contacts between Israeli representatives and Mexican government officials dating back to 1947
- Negotiations already in place for the purchase of arms by Israel in Mexico
- Complicity on the part of Mexican government personnel, both civilian and military
- Assistance from private Mexican sympathizers of the Israeli cause, ranging from relatively low-level modest individuals to some who were wealthy and highly placed
- Substantial funds that were funneled to Mexican banks from foreign sources for use in the purchase of arms from the Mexican government[123]
- A relatively efficient, tightly-knit association of North American citizens, acting on behalf of Haganah, who had cultivated wide-ranging local contacts for several months prior to Greenspun's arrival in Mexico (Larry C. Ives, Rosenblum, Gladstone, and so forth) and who he had come to rely on

This latter group was bolstered with the arrival of Eliyahu Sacharov, sent by Teddy Kollek to assist Greenspun in the spring of 1948, and with the incorporation of Ratner and Ellis, both of whom came on the *Idalia*, and then were instrumental in Mexico in the summer of 1948.

Even before Greenspun emerged on the scene in Mexico, negotiations between Israeli and Mexican officials were well advanced. In April 1948, Sacharov and Arazi reported to Shaul Avigor on an important "Mexican arms offer" worth more than $1.5 million.[124] The deal was important because it included three B-25 bombers, nine 16-ton tanks, and three LSTs. In May 1948, U.S. intelligence reports from Mexico also echoed the rumor that the Mexican government had purchased twenty-five P-51 planes and that they were to be shipped to the Haganah along with several "P-47s belonging to the 201st Squadron of the Mexican Air Force."[125] A check of the P-47s accounted for all of them; as for the P-51s, none were possessed by the Mexican Air Force. Nor were any tanks sold by Mexico to arms dealers acting on Israel's behalf.[126] The same proved to be true regarding the B-25s, P-51s, and P-47s, despite intensive efforts by the Israelis and their Mexican intermediaries.[127]

A host of Mexican accomplices from the highest levels of government on down proved invaluable in securing the armament sought by Greenspun. Starting with General Gilberto R. Limón, the Minister of National Defense, his chief of staff, General Ramón Familiar, and an engineer of unknown rank, Alejandro Paredes, who according to Greenspun was "appointed by the government to handle all transactions," Mexican military personnel facilitated the procurement and transportation of the arms.[128] Other Mexican political personalities emerged during the course of the arms deals, including Senator Carlos I. Serrano, who the FBI said was acting "as a front for President Alemán in private business."[129] While Serrano's role was most likely minor, his presence and actions on behalf of the president points to the essential fact that nothing could have been implemented or achieved without the tacit or explicit approval of Alemán. This key conclusion was articulated in a number of ways by John N. Speakes, legal attaché for the U.S. Embassy. For instance, in his 11 August 1948 report to FBI Director Herbert Hoover, Speakes hinted that the arms aboard the *Idalia* involved persons "high in the government, probably including the President himself."[130] A little over a year later, with much more information on hand, Speakes was harsh and unsparing in his assessment of the Alemán administration's role in the *Idalia* affair. When Assistant District Attorney Herschel Champlin requested that witnesses be brought from Mexico to Los Angeles to testify at the upcoming trial of Greenspun and his associates in connection with the illegal export of arms on the *Idalia*, Speakes pointedly wrote the FBI Director Hoover on 27 October 1949:

> The Alemán regime in Mexico is regarded by many experienced observers as the most corrupt regime which Mexico has had in recent history. . . . In this Palestine matter, it will be recalled that there was considerable evidence tending to reflect that the Palestine group settled a large amount of money on President Alemán or some individual acting for him so Mexico could be used as a concentration point for the shipment of arms to Palestine. The deal involved Mexico's giving the Palestine group all possible cooperation, such as the sale of arms of the Mexican government [...] on an off-the-record and hence dishonest basis, the returns not going to the

Mexican Government, but to the Mexican Army officers
handling the deal; the use of Mexican ports for shipping;
the use of Mexican railways for necessary transportation
to the ports, and even the faked purchase of arms in the
United States by the Mexican Government with subsequent disposition of the arms to the Palestine group in
Mexico.[131]

In yet another report, the FBI Director was notified "that high officials of the Mexican Department of Defense, including Minister
of Defense General Limón and General Ignacio Beteta, dishonestly
participated in the unloading of this cargo [of the *Idalia*]." Conse-
quently, participation of any Mexican official in Greenspun's trial
and that of his associates "would no doubt adversely affect the prestige of the Alemán administration."[132] Although Greenspun would
claim that the arms had been procured legally, it is clear that their
purchase could not have been carried out without considerable payments to numerous Mexican officials.[133]

Greenspun and his group of arms buyers enjoyed the assistance
of notable Jewish sympathizers in Mexico, notably Elías Sourasky,
Aryeh Dulzin, and Abraham Z. Phillips, as well as lesser-known
individuals, such as the previously mentioned David Gritzewsky.
Sourasky in particular, an important banker, was at the heart of
the financial side of the operation. He assured Greenspun that "the
needed funds were pouring in [...] from banks in Geneva, Paris, and
elsewhere as friends of Israel collected from world Jewry on behalf of
the homeland."[134] According to Greenspun, Sourasky handed him
a "thick envelope" with *pesos* "for small emergencies," and added
"here in Mexico, there's always the question of *mordida*." The finan-
cier would handle important funds on Greenspun's behalf. Sacharov
called Sourasky a "central participant" in the operation and asserted
that "the deal could not have been made without him."[135] Phillips,
born in Poland and a naturalized Mexican citizen since 1927, was
involved in import–export activities and was reputed to have had a
hand in smuggling. He had traveled several times in the past to the
United States, and according the FBI sources, was a friend of President Alemán, for whom he had handled many deals in Tampico.[136]
David Gritzewsky was a key link in Haganah's Mexican operation,
especially in Tampico, where, as noted before, he played a significant

role in facilitating the arms shipment.[137]

Greenspun and his associates had access to substantial amounts of money to pay for the arms. According to a 10 September 1956 confidential letter from the Chairman of the Federal Communications Commission to the U.S. Attorney General, "In July, 1948, three payments totaling $1,300,000 were made to Herman Greenspun through the Banco del Ahorro Nacional, Mexico City, by cabled order of one Dr. Erwin Hayman, Geneva, Switzerland [...] Heyman [sic] [...] was reportedly an officer of a firm which procured war materials for Israel."[138] (Recall that this was the same individual involved in the purchase of the *Kefalos* [see Chapter 1].) Greenspun then wrote a check to the Tresorio [sic] de la República de México in the amount of $1,165,000 to cover the purchase of the arms that he had selected in Mexican armories in previous days.[139] Anxious to know how the Mexican arms deal had been financed, the U.S. government heavily audited the accounts and transfers of some of the principals involved; Larry C. Ives's books in particular were closely scrutinized.[140] He, too, received large sums in addition to those given to Greenspun. As early as July 1948, the U.S. Government was aware that some of "the arms and ammunition being loaded aboard the Kefalos has [sic] been sold by the Mexican Government to the 'Western Ordnance Corporation'" — a company owned by Ives.[141] During his 1950 trial, Greenspun continually was forced to defend his monetary transactions in Mexico, especially given their sizeable scope and the fact that the arms purchases had been carried out without any accounting and with no paper trail left. When confronted by the judge with the fact that he had received $1,300,000 "in connection with this venture, and that it extended over some period of time," both Greenspun and his attorney, William Strong, vigorously denied any wrongdoing. Addressing the court, Greenspun replied, "The $1,300,000 was spent in Mexico legally, everything was purchased from the Mexican government, and every nickel that I procured down there for some purchases was spent for the Israeli government, and it was a perfectly legal transaction, your Honor."[142] To underscore these points, Greenspun's attorney informed the court that "Mr. Greenspun did not go into this for profit and made no profit whatsoever."[143] The totality of the evidence was not on Greenspun's side on this score, as well as on the more serious charges of violations of the Neutrality Act and other restrictions on the unlawful export of armament from the United States. And although Judge Peirson M. Hall gave Greenspun a stern talking to, calling him "the ringleader, in so far as the shipment of arms and ammunition to Mexico was concerned," the sentence that the magistrate imposed upon him in July 1950 was relatively light. The fine of $10,000 without jail time was hardly commensurate with the numerous and serious transgressions charged in the indictment.[144]

Finally, it is important to keep in mind that Greenspun had substantial support in Mexico from a cast of North American associates who were closely aligned with Haganah's objectives. Some were major players (Ives, the arms dealer), others were less so (Rosenblum, who worked for Ives), and the precise roles of some remain relatively uncertain (Gladstone). This core nucleus was enlarged with the eventual incorporation of Sacharov, Ellis, and Ratner. The FBI kept close watch on their movements and communications. Their phone calls to each other in Mexico, as well as to contacts in the United States, strongly suggest a high degree of coordination of the organization as a whole.[145] While in Mexico City in June and August 1948, the main group (Greenspun, Ives, Rosenblum, and Gladstone) was reported to be "in contact with elements in Acapulco and Tampico."[146]

Flush with cash, Greenspun, accompanied by his "'aide-de-camp" Tito Rivera, launched, in his revealing words, into a "*mordida*-punctuated shopping spree through a series of Mexican arsenals."[147] But he was not alone in these endeavors; Sacharov, Ratner, and Ellis participated as well in the selection and purchase of armaments. Sacharov insisted on the three accompanying Greenspun on a visit to an arsenal to see for themselves what they were buying. In the process, Sacharov bargained for lower prices and claimed he had secured two new 155-caliber cannons.[148] Ratner's testimony is especially telling on a number of points. After "a deal was worked out with the Mexican government to purchase heavy arms," Ratner writes that he and Ellis "went to the arsenal outside Mexico City to count and supervise the freight car loading" of a considerable amount of armament.[149] Ratner also claims that while counting the arms at the arsenal, the Mexican soldiers lost track of the agreed upon numbers, and they took Ratner's word for the amount.[150] With a mixture of satisfaction and guilt, Ratner admitted that "considerably more than was agreed upon was shipped [on the *Kefalos*]. After the deed was done and the cars loaded, it worried me that perhaps I was risking the whole shipment by being greedy, and therefore, never mentioned it to anyone."[151] After the arms were procured, they were loaded onto special trains — in an arrangement made, according to Greenspun, by his constant assistant Rivera — and shipped to Tampico.[152] Ratner and Ellis rode the trains to Tampico as "guards" to keep an eye on the much-coveted cargo.[153] Oko was well aware that the arms had come "from the armory in Mexico City."[154] Nevertheless, the captain was dismissive of their quality: "I can also state that I have never seen such a low grade of arms."[155]

In light of all of this, when the rust bucket left Tampico, what war matèriel and equipment did its cargo holds carry? Fortunately there are a number of overlapping accounts concerning the content of the cargo that, while not entirely consistent and difficult to reconcile, provide a reasonably accurate estimate of the contents of the thirty-five to thirty-nine train cars of arms and equipment that were loaded onto the ship. In effect, the 784 tons of armament and radar attested to by first mate Forbes when they were loaded onto the *Kefalos* (soon to be the *Pinzon*) included 32 75 mm cannons with 16,000 shells; 2 75 mm American mountain cannons with 4,000 shells; 170 air bombs (each 50 kg); 500 6-Browning machine guns (0.3"); 10,000.000 bullets; 4 sets of marine radar; 60 heavy Vickers machine guns (with an unknown number of bullets); 24 heavy American machine guns; 15,000 steel helmets; and an unknown quantity of high-octane aviation fuel.[156] While hardly amounting to what Greenspun proudly christened "Israel's new arsenal,"[157] undoubtedly because of his important role in the operation, the armament transported by the old freighter, arriving as it did at a crucial juncture, proved significant in Israel's war with the Arab states.

In conclusion, Tampico had been a nightmare. Little, if anything, had gone according to plan, and the contretemps seem to have vastly outweighed the achievements at port. And yet Oko and his officers had managed by hook and crook to muddle through until the long-awaited arms arrived. For their part, Greenspun and his confederates had also successfully, if somewhat improbably, acting in concert with highly-placed Mexican officials and local sympathizers of the Israeli cause, secured the war matériel and transported it safely to Tampico. It had cost a good deal of money to purchase the arms and pay off government military and civilian personnel, and legal corners, both in the United States and Mexico, had continually been side-stepped or cut altogether. Understandably, there was elation and relief in numerous quarters when the *Kefalos* finally sailed on 3 August 1948, just after noon, for its long voyage to Tel Aviv.

Significantly, having arrived in Tampico under false pretenses, the ship would also leave port under questionable circumstances. Even though there was not the slightest doubt in anyone's mind as to where the vessel was headed, Greenspun and Sacharov had obtained documents from the Chinese embassy in Mexico City that were used to falsify the vessel's ultimate destination.[158] Not only would the *Kefalos not* proceed to Buenos Aires as originally stipulated, the exit certificate for the ship explicitly stated that the freighter was headed for Shanghai via Genoa.[159] On 4 August, in a wonderful bit of unintentional misinformation, the authoritative daily *Excelsior* dutifully reported, "*El 'Kefalos' Salió Hacia Shanghai.*" ["The '*Kefalos*' left for Shanghai."]

4

The Crew and the
Long Voyage

Most of the crew of the Kefalos were Spanish Republicans who could
not return to Spain because of Franco.
— Ratner to Greenspun, 11 April 1967

Another worry was that the Spaniards on board might try to take over
the ship and weapons to use against Franco. (I slept with my gun until
we were well passed [sic] Gibraltar.) I continued to worry that the Spaniards might abandon ship if we were attacked by British or Egyptian
warships as we neared Israel. Instead, these Spaniards turned out to be a
tough, competent, and loyal bunch.
— Nathaniel (Nat) Ratner, American Veteran of Israel, 1946–1949[1]

Shortly before leaving Tampico, Oko drafted a typewritten list of the
crew and "passengers." The document carries the heading "CREW
LIST of the Panamanian s/s 'PINZON' ex 'Kefalos," Captain A.S.
Oko, Jr." and carries Oko's signature. (Is it reproduced in its original form as Appendix 2.) Remarkably, it is the only extant list of
the thirty-eight individuals who made the voyage from Mexico to
Israel in August–September 1948. There is little doubt that the list
was compiled at the very last minute since it contains Oko's handwritten deletions of those who bowed out for one reason or another
just prior to the ship's departure, as well as notations of late additions. The list details each individual's name, nationality, and occupation on board. At the top of the list are the officers: (Captain, A.

S. Oko Jr.; first mate, Eric. E. Forbes [both U.S. citizens]; third mate, Carlos Sánchez, Uruguayan; first assistant engineer, Félix Apaolaza, Spanish (although traveling with a Costa Rican passport); third assistant engineer, José Blanco, Spanish; radio operator, Jack Rothman, U.S. citizen; purser (and nurse), Gladys Z. Oko, U.S. citizen; and bos'n, Julio Larrauri, Spanish).[2] Below them came the carpenter, Francisco Corino, Spanish; and below him eight individuals who were simply identified as sailors: William Wolders, Dutch; Lorenzo Aldalur, Spanish; Joaquín Torrealday, Spanish; Florentino Ferreira, Spanish; Harald Kalte, Finnish; Honorio Fernández, Cuban; Perfecto Piñeiro, Spanish; and Hector Pineda, Honduran. The next three were greasers: José Cacheiro, Spanish; Evaristo de Medisos, Portuguese; and Joao de Almeidas, Portuguese. Below them are three firemen: Miguel Urriolabeitia, Spanish; Calixto Díaz, Spanish, and Avaro Rufino Nuñez, Portuguese. Next are three wipers: Emilio Suarez, Spanish; Vicent Estrada, Spanish; and José Oliva Mateos, Spanish. And below them the steward, Ernesto Borrego, Spanish, and two cooks, Daniel Dewitt, U.S. citizen, and José Luiz, Portuguese. Next, there is another sailor "(O.S.)," who may be out of place, Jaime Rivera, Peruvian,[3] and three messmen: Ricardo Gutiérrez, Chilean; Carlos Blanco [Aguinaga], Mexican (although he was actually Spanish); and Casiano Totoricagüena, Spanish. Finally, on this list there is yet another fireman, José Rivera, Mexican.

Below Oko's signature there appear four handwritten names, with their corresponding nationalities and occupations. They are first assistant engineer, Nathaniel Ratner, U.S. citizen, (now clearly promoted to Apaolaza's former position); second mate, Robert Keller, U.S. citizen, (promoted to the position that would have been Mariano Manresa's had he been able to make the voyage); second radio operator, Arye Kesselman, Palestinian (i.e., Israeli); and supercargo, Abraham Elazaroff, U.S. citizen.[4] The last two individuals may well be the "passengers" alluded to in the ship's departure permit issued by port authorities. In sum, upon leaving Tampico, on board the vessel were seventeen Spaniards (eight of them Basques), eight U.S. citizens, six Latin Americans, four Portuguese, one Dutch, one Finn, and one Israeli.

From the top to bottom, with few exceptions, the ship's crew had considerable sailing experience (see Appendix 3 for the age of each crew member and length of service at sea). The selection of such a seasoned personnel for the delicate and potentially dangerous mission was hardly accidental. Oko had enlisted trusted officers and sailors from the *Aries/Adelanto* (Forbes, Sánchez, Apaolaza, Blanco, Larrauri, and Corino)[5], and Manresa, Apaolaza, and Sánchez, as noted in Chapter 1, had also assisted the captain in picking and screening crew members in a Basque restaurant in New York. Mature sailors who were profoundly familiar with ships and the ways of the sea held numerous positions on board. Including the young U.S. volunteers, along with Arieh Kesselman, Jaime Rivera, and Carlos Blanco Aguinaga, the average age of the thirty-three individuals whose ages are known with some certainty was around thirty-five.[6] And a rough estimate of the average length of service at sea for crew members hovered around twelve years.[7] That some of the vessel's officers had served together in the past aboard another ship is highly significant. They knew each other well, had already worked alongside one another, and were keenly knowledgeable of their positions, functions, and tasks within a vessel's hierarchy and organization. In addition to the leadership nucleus transferred from the *Aries/Adelanto* to the *Kefalos/Pinzon*, other sailors who made the voyage from Tampico to Tel Aviv had also served together in pairs aboard other vessels at other times.[8] These facts undoubtedly assisted in fostering cohesion on board the *Kefalos* during the long trip to Israel. Similarly, the solidarity among the Basque contingent cannot be underestimated as having been a significant unifying factor. (Significantly, the Jewish group would also enjoy considerable cohesion on board.) Even though communication problems naturally existed aboard this multilingual, multinational ship, many of the barriers were overcome by a mixture of gestures, shouts, swearing, and most importantly, by the crew's deep knowledge of their respective duties and responsibilities. (Moreover, having sailed earlier aboard Panamanian and/or North American vessels for lengthy periods, most of the sailors were familiar with basic ship terminology, which enabled them to carry out their tasks.) And so despite their many differences, as my father, Blanco Aguinaga, vividly and lucidly explains in the only extant account of the voyage, with rare exceptions, there was a good deal of camaraderie and common understanding among the crew.[9]

Although normally extremely demanding of himself as well as those he commanded, Captain Oko heaped praise time and again upon several crew members. First mate Forbes (b. 1912) in particular received kudos from the skipper, and justifiably so. If a task needed to be performed, no matter how important or menial, "Red," as he was often called, could be counted on to carry it out. Whether dispatched from Tampico to Mexico City to speed up matters upon delivery of the arms cargo, or painting the new name of the ship while hanging overboard on a make-shift seat made of wooden planks and ropes, Forbes was Oko's trusted right-hand and best man for nearly any job. [Photograph 10] Oko had nothing but admiration for his "hard-slugging, hard-drinking, marlin-spike seaman of a First Mate."[10] The captain was likewise extremely fond of Félix Apaolaza (b. 1914), whom he described as a "Spanish guerrilla with a weakness for Lorca's poetry."[11] (At one point in Tampico, Oko received word that there was a tall, fair American man in a *cantina* [bar] reciting the poetry of Lorca with Apaolaza, already an improbable scene, but all the more so when it turned out that the individual in question was an intelligence officer, probably from the State Department, who had been assigned to keep an eye on two Soviet ships and had taken advantage of the situation to also keep the *Kefalos* under surveillance.[12]) Oko was undoubtedly grateful when Apaolaza, without missing a beat, stepped in and assumed the duties of chief engineer upon the sudden and unexpected departures of Ilves and Karjus in Tampico, which left the ship without important personnel in the engine room. The captain lavishly praised the "crackerjack engineering crew on board" and its "terrific competence" — accolades meant not only for Apaolaza, but as well for Nathaniel Ratner and José Blanco, who were also promoted into the vacated positions.[13]

Oko also had very kind words for Francisco Corino (b. ca. 1913), the ship's carpenter, remarking that he was "illiterate but completely trustworthy."[14] And an indefatigable worker to boot! Corino completely rebuilt and refashioned the deck to change its appearance.[15] (More about the *Pinzon* stratagem later in this chapter.) Mindful of the political realities of the era, while in route to Israel, Corino also built "a little Mediterranean type sailing vessel," which was later given to the Sea Scouts in Haifa as a memorial to Bill Bernstein.[16] [Photograph 33 shows the carpenter at work on the vessel.] Nor were other sailors, seemingly somewhat lower in the ship's social scale, overlooked by Oko. For example, the captain had much good to say about the vessel's steward, Ernesto Borrego (b. ca. 1901–1902), a man from Málaga. A veteran of the sea who had started sailing at the age of fourteen, Borrego, now with some thirty years of experience, played a key role in the ship's successful voyage. He had been largely responsible for provisioning the ship in New York and Tampico. As Oko was aware, "maintaining a decent happy ship [...], as any master knows, is good food."[17] The provisioning was done wonderfully, according to Blanco Aguinaga, who recalls that the crew enjoyed excellent food and drink throughout the trip. This, however, was not achieved without some tussles between the captain and Borrego (as well as with the men from Manuel Enterprises, Inc.), because the steward, in Oko's words, was used to sailing in a "hungry ship." Borrego had originally signed on as a second cook, but had been eventually promoted to steward, a task he performed admirably throughout the journey. The captain recalled him as round and fat and as one who wore glasses and "ran around in skivvy." If not universally liked by the crew because of his fastidious manners, Oko nevertheless praised Borrego as a "wonderful shipmate."[18]

There were other important sailors on board about whom Oko wrote little or nothing. Fortunately, Blanco Aguinaga recalls them well and had a good deal to say about them. One of the most significant was Julio Larrauri (b. 1918), the vessel's bos'n (or boatswain, in charge of hull maintenance). Generally called "Bermeo," after his birthplace in that Basque port, Larrauri worked closely on board with Forbes.[19] A fisherman in his native region, Larrauri had been exiled during or after the Spanish Civil War, most probably after fighting on the Republican side. Exactly what he did during World War II is unknown, although in the mid-1940s Larrauri found himself devoid of identification papers, indigent, and in a French jail. While in exile, through the offices of the Basque government he was eventually offered employment in a *chantier* (shipyard) in southern France in late 1946.[20] At some point in 1947, Larrauri traveled to the West Coast of the United States, where he came into contact with Oko, who hired him to work on the *Aries/Adelanto*. Characterized by Blanco Aguinaga as a "superb sailor," Bermeo, who spoke primarily Castilian and Basque, was ubiquitous on the ship, giving orders and ensuring that a seemingly endless array of tasks got done in a timely fashion.

Despite obvious language limitations on both sides, for example, Bermeo was able to communicate fully through countless gestures, signals, and shouts with Harald Kalte (b. 1916), known on the ship as "Finland."[21] An experienced sailor, the Finn, according to Blanco Aguinaga, was blond, tall, very strong, and always in a good mood. Finland could always be counted on to perform cheerily the most onerous tasks — lifting, pulling, and moving materials, among other arduous assignments. For all of these reasons, my father fondly recalls Finland as an important member of the crew. Another valuable crew member, if hardly acknowledged by Oko, was Joaquin Torrealday (b. ca. 1915), who was one of the most experienced helmsmen on board. Born in Guernica, Torrealday had sailed extensively in the Caribbean, primarily between Cuba and the eastern coast of the United States, serving in various capacities.[22] Because of their growing friendship, Torrealday took it upon himself, going well beyond his duties, to instruct my father gradually on how to take the helm, allowing him to try his hand at steering the ship, a fact unknown to the captain. This gave the lowly mess boy a sense of empowerment and awe, although it also resulted in an incident that very much angered Oko (the captain eventually relented somewhat, conceding that one has to learn to steer a ship through actual practice).[23]

Bermeo, Torrealday, and my father were accomplices in a wonderful episode that added a new crew member to the ship. One night in Tampico, while paying for their drinks, a young man about my father's age approached the group, and addressing Bermeo in Basque, informed him that he was from Guernica, that his name was Totoricagüena, and that he had arrived in a Spanish ship but wished to escape from the jurisdiction of Franco's Spain. Would they be able to take him on the *Kefalos*? Bermeo consulted with Torrealday and agreed that it would be possible to do so. The question was how to smuggle "Totori," as he came to be called, on board given that a ship officer and a Mexican policeman were on guard to prevent unauthorized access. Bermeo, Torrealday, my father, and Totori waited patiently until the ship officer was distracted and out of view. They then enticed the policeman away with the pretext of offering a gift (possibly a carton of cigarettes), and took advantage of their respective distractions to quietly bring Totori aboard and place him on the only empty bed available — my father's. Everything was going well until the next morning when the steward, Borrego, discovered a new person in the room he shared with the mess boys. Borrego started shouting and asking who the hell was this individual. Torrealday and Bermeo decided that it was impossible to keep the matter a secret, and my father was chosen to break the news to Oko, who, instead of reacting negatively, responded enthusiastically because this was an excellent opportunity to save a sailor "from Franco's claws."[24] The captain ordered Totori to stay on the ship and then fixed his papers (with a bribe). Totori began to work as a mess boy. While my father was the officers' mess boy, Totori served in the same capacity for the rest of the crew, earning, incidentally, nearly twice my father's salary. The two, however, became best friends during the course of the voyage.

Haganah made certain that there was a strong Jewish presence on board. Five crew members and/or travelers were Jews (not counting Oko): four North Americans (Jack Rothman, Nathaniel Ratner, Abraham Elazaroff, and Robert Keller) and one Israeli who had lived in the United States (Arieh Kesselman). Jack Rothman, the radio operator, was the oldest of the group. Born in 1911 into a large family, Rothman attended primary and secondary school in New York and then attended Upsala College in New Jersey.[25] A small institution of higher learning, Upsala had Swedish Christian roots.[26] It was there that Rothman apparently "tasted anti-Semitism for the first time [and was] told that Jewish students were not accepted in college fraternities." His reaction was to start a Jewish fraternity of which he became president. The college yearbook for 1934 lists him as the tennis team captain, a person of serious demeanor, and destined for a career in medicine.[27] During World War II, Rothman served in the U.S. Merchant Marine and at some point became the chief radio operator on a munitions ship. After the war, he went to work at a factory as a draftman (*possibly* the same one where he had worked earlier). He then became a lecturer in mechanics at Columbia University. It was during the mid-1940s that Rothman started to become inspired by the Jewish people's struggle to attain independence. How he came into contact with Haganah's "procurement" section is unknown; however, in June 1948 he sailed on the *Kefalos* from New York as radio operator, a position he would hold until the vessel's arrival in Tel

Aviv in September of that year. By the time he shipped out of New York, Rothman was married and had a daughter. As noted in Chapter 1, well-liked and respected on board, Rothman became a kind of father figure to the younger Jewish shipmates. Alvin Ellis, the navigator aboard the *Idalia*, in particular spoke of him admiringly and credited him with being a positive influence on Oko.[28] According to Ellis, Rothman was "the only member of the Haganah that the captain was prepared to hear what he had to say."

Upon arriving in Israel, Rothman decided to stay, volunteered for the Israeli Air Force, and was killed in an airplane crash in Italy on 31 December 1948.[29] Of all of the crew members' identity cards given to Oko in Tampico, Rothman's was the only one to be found among the captain's papers. Not normally a nostalgic individual, clearly Oko felt an enormous fondness for Rothman. In fact, as part of a speech he gave in 1950 at a Jewish Welfare Fund Campaign, Oko movingly eulogized Rothman as someone who had given up his professional career to serve as a radio operator in the arms-running operation.[30]

Much more is known about the first assistant engineer, Nathaniel M. Ratner, in large part because, unlike Rothman, he left important written recollections of the *Kefalos/Pinzon* odyssey. In addition, Ratner was aboard the *Kefalos* during its entire travels, including the two trips to the Balkans to rescue Jewish refugees. Born in Chicago in 1922, he enrolled at the newly-established Illinois Institute of Technology (IIT), which was formed through the merger of older and smaller institutions. IIT was one of the first American universities to host a Navy V-12 program during World War II.[31] Sometime in 1942, Ratner passed a physical examination "of the navy's engineering volunteer probationary program."[32] During World War II, he served as chief engineer "on a destroyer escort in both the Atlantic and Pacific oceans."[33] After the war, Ratner was approached in December 1946 by someone in the Jewish underground who was looking for volunteers to run weapons to Jews in Palestine. He was clearly a person with the experience needed at the time. Uncharacteristically blunt for someone of extraordinary modesty, Ratner recalled later, "I knew how to run ships [...] I was recruited because I knew what I was doing."[34]

It came to pass that an unidentified man, who was working for playwright Ben Hecht as a fund-raiser, learned about Ratner's World War II service in the U.S. Navy and approached him to assess the condition of a vessel as well as its possible use in overseas service. The ship in question was none other than the sadly-celebrated *Altalena*.[35] Much effort was put into making the former landing ship tank *USS LST-138* "sea worthy again and to train the crew." According to Ratner, "side trips were made to Prince Edward Island and Cuba before we sailed to Europe."[36] After reaching Italy, the crew learned that the United Nations had voted in favor of the Jewish state of Israel. It was then decided to wait for independence "rather than immediately risk a blockade run." While biding their time, the crew took the ship out for trial runs, and during one of these exercises a boiler exploded, injuring both of Ratner's legs (he was wearing shorts and suffered burns). Unwilling to wait for a long period before Israeli independence was declared, Ratner returned to the United States from Italy in February 1948.[37] If fortuitously saved from the eventual disaster of the *Altalena*, Nathaniel did not have to wait long to be embroiled in another important adventure. Upon reaching the United States, he volunteered "to both the Irgun and Haganah." In his own revealing words, "I was non-political."[38] While staying with his sister in California, a call came saying that he was needed. Although Ratner thought he was headed for a position as chief engineer on a ship in New Orleans, as he had been led to believe by Haganah, he instead was told, without explanation, that he would be picked up on a street corner at midnight and driven to San Pedro Harbor, where he "was introduced to the man in charge of the operation — Hank Greenspun."[39] Shortly thereafter, as related in Chapter 3, he sailed on the *Idalia* and some weeks later eventually arrived in Tampico, where he enlisted on the *Kefalos*. Needing another engineer, Oko named him first assistant engineer, and Ratner, an excellent fit, rose to chief engineer in Naples when Apaolaza left the vessel there for reasons that remain unclear. His services to the *Kefalos/Pinzon* proved invaluable.

Al Ellis (purportedly born Abraham Elazaroff in Los Angeles in 1926), was raised in Vista del Mar, a Jewish orphanage in Southern California.[40] Ellis's father, Isidore Elazaroff, was of Russian ancestry, and his mother, Savia, was apparently of Middle Eastern descent.[41] Eventually, Abraham anglicized his name, calling himself Alvin Ellis or Al Allis. After life in the orphanage, he completed four years of

high school, enlisted in the armed forces in July 1944 and served in
World War II, and earned a Purple Heart at the Battle of Okinawa.[42]
Although little is known about his post-war activities, Ellis served
on at least two vessels in 1947–1948: the Liberty ship *H.H. Raymond*
and the Victory ship *Iran Victory*.[43] The date of the latter ship's arrival
in the United States (15 May 1948) is interesting because no more
than two weeks later, Ellis found himself on the *Idalia*, with Ratner,
headed for Acapulco. By mid-July, the two had arrived in Tampico
with the first trainload of arms. It is significant that Ellis had no specifically assigned duties as a crew member on the ship (he is not listed in the official crew list [see Appendix 2]). Quite possibly this was
because Eliyahu Sacharov (part of the group, along with Ratner and
Ellis, that had assisted Greenspun during the spring of 1948) had assigned him the task of acting as an "escort to keep an eye on the ship's
captain. [Oko's] behavior and hints that we picked up from his wife
[...] gave us the impression that he was not very stable."[44] Perhaps this
also helps to explain why, in this poisoned atmosphere, Ellis claimed
that the Jewish volunteers aboard the *Kefalos* considered Oko to be
their "enemy."[45] Equally troubling are Ellis's wildly fanciful assertions that Rothman and Kesselman "were actually in controll [sic]
of the ship, as they were the ones who sent and received the coded
messages from our stations along the way."[46] Upon arrival in Israel,
Ellis, Rothman, and Kesselman quickly enlisted in the Israeli armed
forces: Ellis in a "brand new unit in the para-troops," Rothman in an
air force engineering unit, and Kesselman in an intelligence unit.[47]

Another of the Jewish volunteers was Robert Keller (b. 1924).
According to Leonard Slater, Keller was a graduate of the U.S. Merchant Academy and had served as an officer in the U.S. Merchant
Marine during World War II.[48] Keller's name appears on several ship
manifests, in positions ranging from deck cadet (1943) to second
and third mate (1944–1945).[49] Little is known to this author about
Keller's activities in the post-war period; however, his name surfaced
with particular prominence in January 1948 in connection with the
celebrated episodes of the *S.S. Executor/Pier F*, which involved considerable amounts of TNT, some of which had been discovered accidentally when a wooden case split open.[50] Although dangerously
messy, well-publicized incidents, according to Slater, Keller "mirac-
ulously had escaped involvement with the law."[51] Keller and his wife,

Miriam, were also participants in the saga of the *S.S. Marine Carp*, an American flag liner, some of whose passengers were detained by Lebanese authorities in May 1948 on the grounds that some of them "were joining Zionist groups in Palestine to disturb the peace of the Holy Land."[52] After internment for more than a month, the *Marine Carp* was allowed to depart for the United States on 28 June and arrived in New York on 13 July.[53] Although what happened next remains unclear, including what orders or instructions were given to Keller in New York, he quickly left for Mexico and arrived in Tampico in time to sail with the *Kefalos/Pinzon* as second mate on 3 August.

The last Haganah representative on board was Arieh Kesselman (b. 1925), an Israeli who had lived for some stretches of time in the United States. Unfortunately, of the Jewish volunteers, the least is known about Kesselman. Moreover, nearly everything that we are able to glean of his painfully short life comes from a limited source — his memorial, whose accuracy cannot be verified independently.[54] Born in Tel Aviv, according to his tribute, at the age of six he was taken to the United States (possibly Columbus, Ohio, where he had family), and completed elementary studies there. He returned to Israel to study at the Herzliya Gymnasium, where he was an excellent student. Kesselman reportedly joined the Haganah at a young age and attempted to enlist in the Palmach, but his parents opposed it. While working in a kibbutz for a year, he is said to have learned about irrigation and land preservation. Kesselman then studied at the Haifa Technion for two years, and in his leisure time took groups of younger students on tours of the area, including trips to Arab villages. The information he gathered was allegedly used to sabotage a radar station on the Carmel, and for his participation in the operation he was arrested. Almost at the same time, one of his cousins, also named Arieh Kesselman, was killed in an attack. Given the growing dangers that his involvement entailed, the Jewish Agency is said to have spirited Kesselman out of the country, sending him to Columbus, Ohio, to continue his studies in agricultural engineering. While at Ohio State University, he continued to be active in political movements close to Habonim, and at an unknown time, learned to fly with the assistance of the local Jewish community. Significantly, however, Kesselman was contacted in July 1947 by Ralph Goldman, a recruiter for Haganah, who emphasized a different direction for him as well as the group's primary need "for experienced licensed officers and qualified seamen."[55] Although Kesselman at the time needed only one more semester to graduate from Ohio State University, after the United Nations General Assembly vote in November 1947 for Palestine to be partitioned between Arabs and Jews, allowing for the formation of a Jewish state, he forewent completion of his studies and decided to return to Israel. He did so by way of Mexico, sailing on the *Kefalos/Pinzon* as second radio operator and assistant to Rothman.[56] Shortly after arriving in Israel, Kesselman joined an intelligence unit, and on 21 November 1948, the jeep he was riding in hit a mine near Imara, and he died soon thereafter.

Barely a few days out of Tampico, the crew started to change the ship's name to the *S.S. M.A. Pinzon* as well as transform the vessel's appearance.[57] Oko called it "the most important change in the ship on the way to Gibraltar."[58] It was a major undertaking that required a good number of hands on deck — and even overside. As noted earlier, Forbes swung from ropes overboard and, with assistance of others, including Bermeo, painted the new name on the ship.[59] The name was prominently stenciled on the lifeboats and lifesavers as well. (Just as the ship still had the name *Larranga* displayed on some of its lifeboats upon arriving in Tampico, the name *Pinzon* remained on some of the lifeboats and lifesavers well after arriving in Israel with its valuable cargo.) Oko claimed credit for an additional flourish in the stenciling process. According to the captain, he "gambled that by spacing the initials [closely] with the name," the ship would be "picked up as MAPINZON," thereby preventing an accurate reading and eluding the British, who might be looking for a ship simply named *Pinzon*.[60] More important, the deck's appearance was significantly changed, thanks in large part to Corino's work and imagination. Oko explained: "[W]ooden wings to replace the canvas wings to the bridge had been built. Then the metal on the pilot house had been painted the same color as the wing dodgers to give a continuous horizontal that had the effect of making the ship look broader and less high."[61] Added the captain: "[T]he vessel, instead of looking tall and narrow, took on a stouter line. These were not complete subterfuges, although they did physically change the vessel considerably."[62] The before and after photographs of the bridge plainly attest to the extraordinary amount of work carried out by Corino and others to alter the vessel's visual aspect in an attempt to resemble the real *Pinzon* — efforts that, ironically, were all for naught. After twenty-six days at sea of continual cleanup, painting, chipping, wire-brushing, and the general tedium of work, and having disguised the ship's appearance, cruising at a leisurely 8.5 miles an hour in calm waters, the ship was about to face what many crew members considered its severest test: crossing Gibraltar.

Oko confesses that he was "more scared than I had been in Tampico or anywhere else in the forty-three years of ups and downs I had had up to then."[63] Added the captain: "[H]ow to sail scot free through the channel into the Mediterranean under even routine observation at Gibraltar and not be recognized for exactly what we were would have been a problem even if we had felt certain we were wraps of secrecy."[64] Assessing the high stakes that were involved, Oko admitted that Gibraltar was "one place where the voyage could have ended in failure."[65] In the looming tug of uneven forces, the skipper seemed obliged to use a mixture of subterfuge, wits, and, if necessary, force; no contingency was apparently left to chance. First, the vessel flew no flag on its stern. Second, Oko asserts he placed "the darkest Spaniards where they could best give character to the ship." His rationale for this action seems to have been to have the two officers in question (Sánchez and Apaolaza) resemble Arabs in appearance.[66] How or why this would have been beneficial to the operation was never adequately explained by Oko. Third, the captain removed the blinker from the bridge so the crew would not be able to return any blinker signals from shore. According to Oko, he placed stock in the fact that "the average merchant ship does not hold tight to protocol and skippers are not generally regardful of navy procedures." And when the *Kefalos/Pinzon* was blinked *four times* and asked "what ship?," the skipper related that "no notice was given [...] and the two Spanish officers were told to stand there and bat the breeze."[67] It helped that at the time of the crossing (10:50 in the morning), "there was fairly heavy traffic going in and out of Gibraltar and [...] about five vessels within our view."[68] Finally, Oko made plans for a desperate last stand in the event hostilities broke out: sidearms were issued to all officers; six 55-gallon drums of gasoline were placed on deck (three on each side) to be set on fire to anything that came alongside; the chief engineer was in position to scuttle the ship; lifeboats were readied to evacuate the crew; and machine guns were taken out of cargo and placed "inside the passageway at the break of the fore-deck (midship house). They had been tested at sea and were ready for action if unavoidable or needed."[69] Far more realistically, Oko remarked at another point that "we hadn't enough of anything on board to stand a chance of fighting it out on any other basis. Not even if we had been foolish enough to break into cargo and armed both hands of everyone on board."[70] Luckily for the ship and crew, none of the preparations proved necessary, and the vessel sailed through unimpeded. (Significantly, as the *Kefalos/Pinzon* crossed Gibraltar, the real *MV Pinzon* was on its way from Liverpool to Bilbao.) However, there is more to the episode than Oko's account. Crew member Blanco Aguinaga's narrative of the crossing of Gibraltar, while confirming some parts of the captain's story, deviates in significant parts and adds important and moving details.

After nearly three weeks at sea, at dawn one day some crew members began to see some lights on land at a distance. The ship was nearing Tarifa, and according to Blanco Aguinaga, the entire crew knew that they would soon get a glimpse of the Spanish mainland. It was, in my father's words, "a moment of unforgettable emotion."[71] All the more so for the Spanish crew members, most of whom had not seen or visited the country they had left after the Spanish Civil War. Breakfast had been served at breakneck speed, well before 7:00, and numerous crew members were on deck, leaning on the railing, standing still, smoking, and observing in dead silence the Spanish coast. But Gibraltar was approaching, and preparations had to be made. Suddenly, all of the officers disappeared from the bridge, except the one on watch. The steward barked out orders to the mess boys to get to work clearing the tables and doing the dishes. When these tasks were finished, several crew members returned to the bridge, and they were startled to see the *entire* officer corps dressed in their best summer white uniforms.[72] Upon seeing this, there was laughter among the crew but also some concern, given that a few sailors sensed that perhaps the showy demonstration was designed to suggest that in case the ship was stopped by the English, the captain had ordered the officers to assume their detention with a maximum of dignity. All of this was a far cry from Oko's assertions that sidearms had been issued to officers, and that other preparations had been made to scuttle the ship, if necessary.

However, as Oko asserted, directly in front of Gibraltar, a powerful British blinker began to signal the ship, requesting identification and other information: Who are you? Where are you coming from? Where are you going? The captain had given strict orders to the vessel's radio operator to not reply to the questions. But then a small torpedo boat suddenly approached at great speed (possibly at 20–25 knots per hour), and appeared headed straight for the *Kefalos/Pinzon*. After a brief moment of uncertainty, the fast boat passed in front of the cargo and continued directly toward North Africa. Following the incident and alarm, everyone returned to their normal tasks, but with the indelible image of the Spanish coast in their memory, according to Blanco Aguinaga.

Although the crossing of Gibraltar had been virtually incident-free, a serious navigational error by the second mate shortly thereafter nearly caused a disaster and scuttled the entire operation. Four or five days after entering the Mediterranean — possibly on 2 or 3 September — as the ship was passing at night between Sicily and Tunisia, near the island of Pantelleria, the vessel veered slightly off course and headed straight for some shoals. As Oko's notes indicate, "the good eyes of the 3rd mate [Sánchez]" saved the day. Sánchez called Oko to the bridge, and they discovered that a "light bobbing" in the distance was not a ship or a fisherman, but in fact a "man waving [a] light from shore."[73] A quick adjustment was made, and the ship regained its proper course. Oko remarked bluntly that "to pile up there would have destroyed cargo [and resulted in] the failure to fulfill [the] delivery of arms."[74] Blanco Aguinaga's recollection of the incident is more detailed and vivid. He relates that "one fairly dark night, around nine or ten, we almost crashed onto the rocks [at Pantelleria]. Luckily we had extra watchmen on duty on bow."[75] The danger was narrowly avoided and matters returned to a calm state for a few more days. However, a mysterious episode soon had the entire crew on edge for three days.

As Blanco Aguinaga recounts the incident, one night several crew members were chatting and smoking atop the canvas that covered cargo hold number two when a large warship (traveling without lights) appeared about one hundred meters from the right side of the *Kefalos/Pinzon*, cruising at the same very slow speed. The officer on watch had spotted the ship at almost exactly the same time as the crew members. The officer ran to alert the captain, who immediately came up to the deck and started giving orders.[76] Everyone assumed that the warship in question was a British vessel and that it was going to board the cargo. According to Blanco Aguinaga, the skipper ordered two machine guns brought up from cargo; these were placed on deck. [Photograph 15] Those who carried them up did so with a mixture of trepidation and concern for the captain's sanity. After all, what chances did two machine guns have against a heavily armed war vessel? Yet nothing happened, and the warship continued to shadow the *Kefalos/Pinzon* while making no radio contact or giving any signals. Exactly the same event occurred three nights in a row. Blanco Aguinaga recalls discussing the episode with the captain and with the first officer, both of whom had arrived at the reassuring conclusion that the warship was American and not British (perhaps part of the Sixth Fleet), and that its intentions were protective rather than hostile. There was no factual basis for this determination; however, it was communicated as such to the entire crew, which calmed down immensely, and, according to Blanco Aguinaga, it again became evident to all that the ship would reach Tel Aviv without any problems.[77]

Oko explains that once in the Mediterranean, "[I]nstead of taking a course directly for Tel Aviv, we came under Crete on a course for Beirut. I felt that being tracked by radar by any British patrol, the sympathy would have been toward the Arab nations rather than toward Israel at the time. And it wasn't until we got under Cyprus that we started straight toward the canal."[78] The cautious approach worked well, but a serious problem dogged the ship after 29 August: the vessel lost all radio contact with land stations.[79] The unforeseen development caused extraordinary consternation among all interested parties. According to Yehuda Ben-Tzur, "[T]he lack of radio contact with the ship in the middle of a cease-fire caused quite an uproar, which even reached as far as Ben-Gurion."[80] Referred to as the "Dromit" in internal frantic communications, vigorous efforts were made by Israeli officials to locate the vessel, none of which bore fruit, and the ship suddenly turned up in Tel Aviv on 8 September (more on this later in the chapter). Oko, clearly angry, complained some months later: "I am still without knowledge why Israel failed to contact us or what happened that would not enable us to reach them on the wavelengths they had given to my radio operator. This could have been serious — fortunately it wasn't."[81] Long after the events in question, Oko resentfully recalled the episode in his "1960 Account."[82] Ben-Tzur observes that there was something of a silver lining to the unplanned "communications blackout," because it saved many bureaucratic headaches, including economic and perhaps also political ones. "More important," he remarks, "it saved a great waste of time, and some vital arms and the airplanes [sic] fuel arrived quicker than they would have otherwise."[83]

The decision to enter Tel Aviv without proper notice or advanced warning was not taken lightly. It is clear, however, that Oko and the crew had little choice. Both water supplies and fuel were running dangerously low. According to the captain, "[O]n arrival in Tel Aviv we had exactly one hours [sic] water for the boilers. We had 190 barrels of fuel, and we were burning 180 barrels of fuel a day."[84] Ratner's account is more explicit, and quite probably more accurate, inasmuch as he was in the engine room: "[L]ack of water for the boilers almost did what the enemy failed to do. If we would have had to steam for 6 hours more to reach Israel, we would have been adrift without power. In a Hollywood finish, the lights of Tel Aviv became visible just as the water dropped out of sight in the boilers."[85] In fact, Ratner relates that they had run out of fresh water long before reaching Israel, and the crew was rationed to one glass of water per day. The water level was so low that engine room personnel were about to add sea water to the boilers.[86]

There was little margin for error, but Oko was reassured by his proximity to Tel Aviv: "I checked water and oil and saw that we still had leeway of an hour of water and almost a day's supply of fuel. We had made it. We were in Israel waters, soon to go on shore and shake hands with the people we had thought about so long."[87] There was nothing left to do but enter the harbor: "When we came directly abeam of Tel Aviv, I felt we could make a straight run for Tel Aviv and if need be, call for patrol planes to protect us from Israel."[88] The vessel entered Tel Aviv flying an Israeli flag that had been made by Gladys out of her husband's blue pajamas and cloth from a mattress.[89] Blanco Aguinaga's account adds important details to the ship's arrival on 8 September. According to my father, the *Kefalos/Pinzon* entered the harbor very slowly, and when it had advanced only about

3 to 4 miles toward shore, a motor boat with military personnel on board approached at full speed, stopping on the starboard side. They asked for permission to board, and the captain granted the request. The stairway was quickly lowered, and the Israeli officers came on board. After they exchanged military salutes with Oko, the group then retired to the officers' mess hall to confer.[90] Although there is no foolproof evidence, this advance party may well have brought false papers for the ship to facilitate and/or clear U.N. inspection the following day. (More on this later in the chapter). Shortly thereafter the Israeli personnel left for shore, and about half an hour later the ship's radio officer received the order to enter and was informed where to anchor. Around an hour later, another motor boat appeared, and Israeli military personnel boarded the vessel and established surveillance (perhaps even control?) throughout the ship. In short order yet another small vessel arrived from land with about fifteen men, and with the assistance of Forbes and Larrauri, who were preparing all of the ship's winches, they began to unload almost immediately. Sugar would be unloaded slowly during the day, and arms very rapidly at night; the process would last three days.[91] Blanco Aguinaga underscores the significant point that as soon as it became dark, three or four small boats, with forty to fifty men each, would approach the ship and then unload the armament with extraordinary speed. My father would learn that these were not ordinary stevedores, but, in fact, Israeli soldiers who had volunteered for the task.[92] [There's no doubt the ship arrived in Tel Aviv as the *S.S. M.A. Pinzon*; see photograph 16].

The Israelis appear to have been taken by surprise by the ship's sudden arrival. On 10 September, Shaul Avigor, an important official, telegraphed Haganah's procurement office in Geneva: "Without our knowing beforehand and without succeeding to establish contact, the 'Dromit' arrived at Tel Aviv. She is being unloaded, and we can hope for a successful end [...] [L]et Teddy [Kollek] know."[93] And the previous day, Ben-Gurion wrote in his diary, "The Mexican ship has arrived. It was checked by U.N. observers and authorised to unload [the sugar]. They will start tonight."[94] One of the first top Israeli aides to visit the ship was Levi Skolnik (the future Levi Eshkol). He wrote a gracious handwritten note to Oko (perhaps also addressed to Gladys) that read, "To the true guides who have brought the boat safely ashore."[95] Not only that, they had done so in clear violation of provisions of the Second Truce (18 July–15 October 1948).[96]

The ship's arrival and its rapid unloading had been enormously assisted by lax and sloppy procedures on the part of U.N. observers, who had barely bothered to inspect the vessel's cargo. For instance, on 8 September, the daily report from Commander Akerblom in Tel Aviv to the Chief of Staff in Haifa informed that, "at 1430 hours the Panamanian steamer 'Mapison' [sic] arrives from Venice."[97] The next day, 9 September, Commandant Fleury wrote the following report: "At 0830 hours: inspected Panamanian ship 'Mapinson.' Cargo: Ammonium, Sulphate, Farm machinery and General Cargo."[98] (More on this matter later in the chapter). Finally, a laconic, unsigned report, apparently written on 11 September, simply affirmed, "At 1800 hours 'MAPISON' departs. U.N. Report Negative."[99] There is ample reason to believe that the last document was patently wrong regarding at what time the ship departed. For example, Oko, a fastidious record keeper, wrote in his log that the ship left Tel Aviv on the morning of 12 September at 6:15.[100] The vessel was not in Tel Aviv long, but important developments occurred during its four-day stay.

While Oko and Gladys were invited to go ashore to tend to business and socialize, the crew was forbidden to follow suit. According to the captain, "[W]e kept the crew aboard so that there would be no break in our security, but we were promised the following day of having the opportunity of giving the crew liberty because we had discharged all the arms."[101] On the evening outing in Tel Aviv, the port captain took the Okos to "a very attractive open air night spot," where there was an orchestra and dancing. Oko observed that "you didn't have a feeling that you were in a country that was in a state of high tension."[102] Understandably, the restless crew had grown increasingly bitter in its confinement, especially since they were eager to visit the city, eat out, and interact with the opposite sex. It did not help matters that some Tel Aviv residents, including young, attractive women, approached the ship in small rowing boats. Blanco Aguinaga remarks that most sailors had become resigned to their fate. However, the ship's carpenter, Corino, came up with a seemingly clever idea to get to shore: he hit his thumb with a hammer, and after Gladys was unable to treat him because of the severe injury, a call was put in to shore to have Corino taken to land and given medical assis-

tance. A motor boat quickly arrived, and two armed men took the
elated carpenter away. Two hours later Corino was back, bandaged
up and profoundly embarrassed; he had been held a virtual prisoner
and had not been able to approach any of the many presumably attractive women in Tel Aviv.[103]

Although all of the arms (and sugar) had been unloaded by 10
or 11 September, there apparently remained substantial problems
with the ship's papers. Unfortunately, Oko is not specific on the exact
nature of the sticking points; there is, however, sufficient evidence
to suggest that perhaps a second U.N. inspection of the ship would
prove troublesome. As the captain related, "[W]e were told that word
was coming through for a ship investigation. This the vessel couldn't
stand. [...] *The papers were in perfect order and had been presented to us
on arrival. They were beautiful pieces of forged fiction and of necessity at
the time. [...] Manifests and everything else were beautifully written and
pure fiction.*"[104] Adding a comical touch — if also a highly problematic
element — to the situation, Oko and Gladys had dubbed themselves
Captain Gino Martino/Martini and Olivia Martino upon arriving in
Tel Aviv.[105] Two United Nations representatives, a Frenchman and
a Belgian, came to inspect the ship around lunchtime on 10 or 11
September (Oko fails to provide the date). The Okos proved perfect hosts ("never more charming socially"), in particular plying the
Frenchman with a bottle of vintage pernod bought in Tampico.[106]
It remains entirely unclear whether the U.N. observers were indeed
convinced by the gracious hospitality of the Okos, although Oko
offers the tantalizing hint that "they had closed one eye," implying
that perhaps they had only carried out a half-hearted and incomplete
inspection.

On the surface at least, all major hurdles appear to have been
overcome. Arms had been safely delivered past U.N. observers, and
much-needed armament was quickly making its way to the battle
fronts, chiefly in the Negev.[107] Oko had even had time during his
brief stay in Tel Aviv to confer with Skolnik about the ship's next
mission. According to Oko, Skolnik had asked, "if we would continue our service to Israel and carry refugees from Bakar, up at the head
of the Adriatic, into Haifa, and I acceded, recognizing the need and
feeling a great feeling of devotion to Israel's spirit and to her cause."[108]
This was not a decision arrived at lightly. Ben-Tzur writes that "while

the ship was being unloaded, there were numerous discussions in the Procurement Headquarters about what the 'Dromit' should do next."[109] Ultimately, Israeli officials decided to use the ship for humanitarian purposes. To start this process, the memory of the *Pinzon* had to be erased. Avigor wrote in a cable, "the name Pinzon will not be mentioned again."[110]

Blanco Aguinaga eloquently narrates some of the final moments after the unloading had been completed. The ship's cargo holds emptied, at dawn he looked out from the railing to glimpse the last small boat (*barcaza*) headed toward the storerooms where the arms had been deposited. One of the men in the launch waved good-bye to him, and, smiling, shouted to him in Castilian, "*Adiós, paisano!*" ("Good-bye, fellow countryman!").[111] My father admits to being very moved by this gesture.

Despite the façade of tranquility and order, there lurked unexplained forces that had pushed the vessel to leave Tel Aviv as rapidly as possible. How to account, then, for the sudden and unexpected departure of the ship on 12 September? The sailing was so frantic and rushed that the freighter had not even had time to load fresh water or fuel. Lacking a firm and undisputable basis for the hurried leave that had caught the crew by surprise, it is necessary to entertain a mixture of fact and speculation. For example, had the ship "sailed toward Italy to avoid seizure by the U.N.," as Ratner suggests?[112] If so, did the surprising flight have anything to do with the cargo's shady manifest papers? Had U.N. observers figured out at last that they had been fooled, and that the arms — to use Ben-Tzur's nice phrase — had been unloaded "under their noses"? Or, more seriously still, had Israeli authorities possibly received information of a possible attempt on the life of Count Folke Bernadotte of Sweden (the United Nations choice as mediator to seek peace in the Arab–Jewish conflict), and urged the ship to leave immediately?[113] (On 17 September, Count Bernadotte was assassinated.) As of now, there is no convincing, or even adequate explanation, for the sailing of 12 September.

Despite the less than graceful exit from Tel Aviv — parallel in some ways to the hasty departure from Tampico — the voyage had been an unqualified success, and the crew could be justifiably proud of what they had achieved. They had defied long odds, performed admirably under pressure, and delivered an important arms cargo to the nascent state of Israel. If admittedly a demanding, difficult, and nervous individual, Captain Oko had nevertheless galvanized a multinational, multicultural, and multilingual crew to sail the rust-bucket *Kefalos/Pinzon* some 7,096 miles in 35 days from Tampico to Tel Aviv without stops.[114] (See Appendix 5.)

5

Neapolitan Interlude

Preparing for a New Mission

Many times in recent weeks, due to the wasteful incompetence on the part of those engaged in the "management" of converting my vessel, the temptation to turn in my resignation appeared to be the only alternative. . . . The type of work going forward represents improper planning and great unnecessary expense. It is a complete revelation to myself and to my officers. It is the most unshipwise wasteful us of labor and material I have ever witnessed.

— Oko to Skolnik, 31 October 1948

The departure of the *Kefalos* from Tel Aviv on the early morning of 12 September was as hurried as it was disorganized: So suddenly had the exit been ordered that the vessel left without fuel, and angry engine room personnel had been forced to fill the boilers with salt water.[1] The crew was somewhat mollified when informed that in two days the ship would be met by an oil tanker to refuel at sea. Be that as it may, the *Kefalos* left Tel Aviv hastily, and at its usual pace of 8.5 knots per hour, headed for a rendezvous with the tanker. Trouble would soon ensue. The *Kefalos* ran into a storm, which not only slowed down its speed considerably, but also made the vessel lurch every which way ("like an empty nut shell"), because the vessel was now totally empty of cargo.[2] It was under these conditions that the ship eventually met with a small Greek tanker off of Haifa. What followed next was a harrowing episode of danger, fear, and cowardice. The crux of the situation was the implicit peril of refueling at sea under these circumstances; the ships could not get too close to one another or risk crashing in unsteady seas and high waves, and the crews, therefore, had to be extraordinarily adept in connecting the fuel lines. To achieve this, the best thick new chords of the *Kefalos* were tied between the vessels to bring them into proximity with one another to link the oil lines to the ship's fuel tanks. Once this was achieved, during the entire refueling the Greek captain and his crew were extremely nervous, running up and down the vessel and yelling at the top of their lungs as if a disaster was about to occur. After about an hour, the Greek captain signaled that the operation was over, and some of his sailors, eager to get out of the relatively dangerous situation, began to cut down the cables with axes instead of waiting for them to be pulled back to the *Kefalos* and tied properly. At this point, tempers boiled over, and Larrauri, the bos'n, at the top of his lungs, began to insult the Greek crew members (both in Basque and Castilian), calling them every name in the book, and even making an apparent effort to board the Greek vessel. Meanwhile, Captain Oko, as equally enraged as Larrauri at the behavior of the Greek crew, took out his pistol and was about to fire on the tanker's captain, but was restrained by Forbes, who grabbed Oko's arm, and the latter was only able to get off one shot into the air. Undaunted, the tanker's sailors cut down all of the *Kefalos*'s cables and left hurriedly, with the ropes still dangling behind their ship.[3] In contrast to Blanco Aguinaga's detailed description of the episode, Oko, in remarkably understated fashion, observed that they "had taken oil on that night from a little Greek vessel at sea off the port of Haifi [sic], and that was a rather dangerous procedure because safety precautions were not carefully kept."[4] The *Kefalos*, now refueled, but with salt water in its boilers, left Haifa for Naples on 13 September at 10 p.m. Despite another strong storm in the Messina Straits, the *Kefalos* put into Naples on 19 or 20 September, with Torrealday at the helm. The crew was about to experience life on land for the first time since Tampico. But to do so, the sailors had to look presentable. Gladys brought four barbers on board, placed chairs on the deck, and one after another of the crew were given haircuts before leaving the ship.[5] With minor exceptions, the *Kefalos* arrived in Naples with essentially the same crew as had reached Tel Aviv: Four of the five North American Jewish volunteers had remained in Israel (Ellis, Keller, Kesselman, and Rothman [the ship had no radio operator on the voyage to Naples]), and the only new addition was Aryeh Mambush, a Haganah member whose "duty was to arrange Kosher papers for the ship."[6]

Except for the frightful refueling incident and other poor weather, the seven-day voyage from Israel to Italy was generally uneventful. As the *Kefalos* was steaming toward Naples, a wonderful photograph captures the satisfaction of Oko and Gladys after completing the delivery of arms. Taken on deck, the photograph shows the Okos smiling, clearly pleased with their recent accomplishment. Significantly, the lifeboat behind them still bears the inscription "S.S. M.A. PINZON," an indication of the previous mission and of the fact that the crew perhaps had not had time to change the ship's name to its original name.[7] [Photograph 17] If the Okos and the ship's crew thought for certain they would now transport refugees from Bakar (modern day Croatia) to Israel, this assumption was apparently somewhat premature, because Israeli officials had not yet made a final decision regarding the vessel's next mission. More to the point: for several more weeks in September–October 1948 there were extensive discussions among high-ranking Israeli officials as to what use should be made of the *Kefalos* — even as the reconversion of the steamer to carry passengers was about to begin in Naples.[8] The debates revolved around distinctly different courses of action; the *Kefalos* could be used to carry refugees, arms, or even both. After considerable internal arguments among Israeli aides, the decision was reached to use the *Kefalos* to rescue thousands of Jews who were stranded in the Balkans.

Almost immediately after entering Naples, planning was started to recondition the ship to carry passengers, and repairs began simultaneously to clean the boilers.[9] (More on the latter task later in the chapter.) The reconversion of the *Kefalos* would be long, arduous, and costly. Oko, who oversaw and directed the operations, provides the best description of the complexity of the endeavors, explaining not only what work was carried out, but also the numerous technical and logistical hurdles that had to be overcome. For example, Israeli representatives in Italy "wanted to put gravel into the vessel for ballast because there would be no cargo carried other than food stuffs for the passengers (refugees)."[10] Oko insisted, and prevailed, on using fresh water as ballast: "Domestic water I insisted upon in sufficient

quantities, and when told that we would allow them only a liter a day
[...] they had me to fight, and that is one victory the local representatives didn't win [...] I felt that the only responsible thing to do would
be to put the [water] tanks in, insist upon it, and did secure tanks."[11]
Sleeping facilities, sewage disposal, and cooking installations also
posed substantial challenges to solve. Oko relates that "bunks were
made like on a slave ship, roughly about 30 inches between the bunks
and the break of the hatch to the cargo battons, which are the battons
which run along the skin of the ship on the inside."[12] The sheer numbers of refugees involved also raised daunting problems: "[T]o carry
4,300 people on a 6,000 ton vessel, to try and work out a program
where there would be adequate sewage [...] these may sound like un-
important things, but all of them required great care."[13] Food preparation for such a large number of people necessitated considerable
attention and special equipment: "To cook enough potatoes or rice,
or some similar stew [...] we worked out a program to use our steam
lines in the passage ways, and big copper kettles that were hand made
in Italy of tremendous size, standing about four or five feet, and running steam lines through for the cooking of food."[14] Finally, the disposal of waste was of paramount importance: "[W]e built out-houses
literally along the bulwarks of the ship and used the fire lines to keep
a constant flow of water through them, bringing an offset outside
the vessel and down, welded to the side, for sewage disposal. These
[out-houses] were half-round culverts with wood facing one edge."[15]

Oko provided precise written instructions for much of the work
and purchases involved in the time-consuming, difficult reconversion.[16] To get what he wanted — and, more importantly, needed —
Oko continually squabbled with Israeli representatives in Italy. The
captain was highly critical of their youth and inexperience, sarcastically observing that they "must have been chosen much in the same
way as Shind in N.Y. — knew opera but not ships."[17] One of Oko's
Israeli liaisons, for example, was a twenty-five-year old man whose
last name was Rosenberg. And another Israeli aide with whom Oko
worked was a veterinarian. The captain tempered these unfavorable
views by observing with hard-boiled realism that Israel "ha[d] to take
what she had and make do" with whatever personnel was available.[18]
More to the point, whatever failings individual Israeli representatives may have had in Oko's eyes, he never lost sight of the fact that

Israel was in dire straits and that he was its representative. A telling incident involving child laborers and minors underscored this point. Upon returning from a trip to Rome, Oko found some "apprentice 16-year-olds being used to clean out the boilers." Moreover, "due to malnutrition, they appeared about 7 to 9 years-old." Oko ordered the practice stopped and decreed "the lads were to be retained on the payroll to work on deck with Larrauri." He also directed that they be fed on the ship.[19] Had Oko made these decisions for moral and humanitarian reasons? Of course. But the captain also "felt that as long as he represented Israel the least he could do was to give an example of decent, ordinary consideration."[20] Even as he was battling what he considered an incompetent bureaucracy, there are numerous other examples of Oko's pride at serving as Israel's agent during this time.

Yet, as the conversion work on the *Kefalos* grew longer for a variety of reasons, Oko became increasingly impatient and eventually exploded in a scathing letter to Skolnik on 31 October.[21] By that date the vessel had been at Naples for nearly six weeks (longer than at Tampico). The skipper pulled no punches in the strongly-worded communication, which included more than a touch of exaggeration and considerable hyperbole, but also exposed — perhaps inadvertently — some of the internal debates among Israeli higher-ups as to the future purpose of the ship that had caused inordinate and costly delays in Naples. Highlights of the letter underscore Oko's frustrations, some justified, some not. The captain, for example, asserted that "since 30th May 1948 my 6,000 ton vessel has only carried 1,000 tons of cargo to purchase her and existence." (In reality, the figure was incorrect: the *Kefalos*, as noted earlier, had carried 784 tons of arms and a cargo of 1,020 tons of sugar.) In an over-the-top flight of fancy, Oko labeled this fact "an extravagance without parallel in the annals of shipping." On surer footing, Oko accurately noted that upon "our arrival in Naples, no cargo was awaiting us, nor was there any in prospect." More seriously still, Oko asserted that "after 23 days of constant pressure on our local representatives for either cargo or orders, the decision was reached to convert the vessel to a personnel carrier." If Oko's chronology is correct, work on the conversion of the *Kefalos* did not begin until around 12–14 October 1948. Oko continued: "'ten days' was the time quoted for completing the conversion. The 'ten days' should have seen the vessel ready on October 24th. Today is the 31st of October." The captain pessimistically observed that "the prospects of seeing another week pass before the ship is ready for sea are all too real." In a scathing indictment of what had occurred until then, the captain launched yet another powerful volley: "The type of work going forward represents improper planning and great unnecessary expense. It is a complete revelation to myself and to my officers. It is the most unshipwise [sic] wasteful use of labor and material I have ever witnessed." Oko gave no names, nor singled out those entities responsible for the situation, but in an important sense, this hardly mattered. His damaging bill of particulars — whether he was aware of it or not — was squarely aimed at the Israeli organization in Italy, and by extension, at its superiors elsewhere. And yet, short of resigning, Oko had little choice but to work with these associates who, after all, held the purse strings and approved all expenditures. The day before leaving Naples for the Balkans, Oko wrote a brief but telling note to Minieri, one of his local suppliers. In it Oko informed Minieri that "pursuant to our conference with Sr. Rosenberg yesterday, it is understood that all unpaid bills bearing my signature are unchallenged and to be paid in full by Sr. Rosenberg at the earliest possible date."[22] While apparently a straightforward proposition, the liquidation of outstanding bills would drag on for years, creating a good deal of ill-will on all sides, and earning the captain a reputation for extravagant spending.[23]

Compounding Oko's problems, he was faced with substantial changes in personnel at Naples. Several seasoned sailors left the ship and had to be replaced. The most significant departure was that of Félix Apaolaza, chief engineer, who had served on the *Aries/Adelanto* since 12 March 1948 and on the *Kefalos* since 11 June of the same year. The reasons for his leaving are unknown and subject to conjecture; had Apaolaza and Oko experienced a falling out, or had the chief engineer simply had enough? At any rate, his letter of separation from the ship written by Oko seems particularly tepid, even distant, for someone who had been a faithful officer and who was trusted enough to assist with recruitment in New York.[24] Also exiting the vessel at Naples were Joao de Almeidas, greaser; Avaro Rufino Nuñez, fireman; Daniel Dewitt, cook; Carlos Blanco Aguinaga, mess boy; Hector Pineda, seaman; an unidentified seaman; and in all likelihood other seamen as well.[25] While some internal reassignments were possible, and, in fact, carried out, Oko needed additional sailors. Interestingly, he did not have to go far to find them; some of them came from Campo Bagnoli, a camp for displaced persons in Naples run by the International Refugee Organization (IRO/OIR).[26]

Six new crew members came from Bagnoli, all of them Spanish, and, from all appearances, Republican refugees from the Civil War. Alfonso Álvarez (b. 1915), Benito Echeverría (b. 1915), Eleuterio Herrero Poza (b. 1920), Salvador Miralles (b. 1917), Francisco Morales (b. 1905), and Manuel Ramón Ruiz (b. 1914).[27] Two new sailors were taken on in Naples upon the recommendation of Captain Gad Hilb of the *Pan York*: Juan Alonso (cook/baker) and Gonzalo Salazar (unspecified position).[28] Unfortunately, it is not known how five other seamen found their way to the *Kefalos*: Vicenzo Castaldi, Manuel Díaz, Samuel Habuba, Miguel López, and Joaquín Martínez.[29] In all, thirteen new crew members served on the ship after its arrival to Naples; the preponderance of Spaniards among them is striking. A convincing case could be made that the crew as a whole acquired an even more pronounced Spanish character after departing Naples. Surely this was no accident; Oko at all times showed a marked preference for Spaniards, particularly those of Republican background.

While at port, Captain Oko read an undoubtedly intriguing item in the 30 September issue of the *Informatore Maritimo Di Napoli*, announcing the imminent arrival of an interesting vessel, the *M.V. Pinzon*, which put into port on 3 October.[30] In a somewhat surreal situation, for two days the real *Pinzon* and its former impersonator coexisted at Naples. Of much greater direct consequence was what Oko called "a small adventure," when at an unknown date two sailors working on the *Kefalos*, Wolders and Kalte, chipped through the side of the vessel and made a gaping hole on the side of the ship. Forbes immediately brought the accident to Oko's attention. According to Oko, Wolders despairingly apologized to the captain ("I didn't mean to do it"). To defuse the gravity of the situation, Oko reputedly told Wolders, "[W]hat the hell are you worrying about? It's above the water line." By his own admission, however, the skipper privately worried about the "thinness of the plates, and the possible serious tragedy that would ensue in the event that any disaster befell the vessel."[31] Especially, as Oko was aware, for a ship that probably would soon have thousands of refugees on board. The hole was rapidly repaired, and the *Kefalos* soon engaged in outings in the vicinity of Naples to test its seaworthiness. When Apaolaza arrived in New York City in mid-October, he reported to Shipowners Agency that the ship was performing well.[32]

It was during one of these short journeys that the *Kefalos* assisted another vessel in distress, the *M/N Scio*, a small 1,200-ton diesel ship used by the Israelis to transport arms. While the episode is far from being altogether clear, some of what purportedly transpired is known.[33] One of the assistant engineers aboard the *Scio* apparently sold some of the vessel's fuel on the black market; both he and his accomplices in the transaction were fired. Their replacements did not fare any better, and, in fact, burned out the ship's bearings close to the Island of Capri. What occurred next is somewhat confusing and subject to a degree of speculation. The *Scio* was not supposed to make direct radio contact with Israel, but it did so. The Israelis, in turn, communicated the *Scio*'s predicament to their representatives in Naples, who then instructed Oko to take the *Kefalos* out on a trial run. (Given the *Scio*'s cargo, the Israelis were naturally eager to avoid the use of local salvage tugs and the ensuing publicity.) Oko's crew eventually sighted the *Scio*, and the *Kefalos*, with the assistance of its officers and machinists, towed the small ship to Naples. In doing so, the *Kefalos* garnered the gratitude of the *Scio*'s captain as well as the Haganah's Ha'Mossad Le'Aliya organization in Italy, and earned some much-needed cash in the process.[34]

With such a prolonged stay in Naples, the crew had ample time to move around the city, sightsee in surrounding areas, visit nightspots, and engage in more high-brow activities, such as going to the opera. According to my father, the city resembled the Italian neo-realist films of the era: destroyed neighborhoods, poverty and unemployment, black markets, thefts and assaults, and women who approached sailors seeking cigarettes — cigarettes that had been bought with U.S. dollars and that were then exchanged for liras at favorable rates.[35] In this moral and social climate, female company was not hard to come by, and sailors quickly found an easy, carefree life. My father, for instance, along with Totoricagüena would eat during their free days in the fishermen's wharfs of Santa Lucia with their "girlfriends," enjoying fried fish and white wine while listening to trios of musicians who played and sang Neapolitan standards.[36] Their evenings were spent carousing on the town, in particular frequenting a low-down bar aptly named Il Lanternino Rosso, then returning to the ship at dawn to shower and prepare breakfast for the crew, as the mess boys that they were. My father recalls two memorable outings in particular. He, Totori (as he was known), and their girlfriends went on a picnic at Pompey, where a guide showed them some supposed pornographic frescos, which they were told regular tourists were not shown. Even more unforgettable was the evening that my father took Totori and Torrealday to the Theater San Carlo to hear and see *La Traviata*. They sat in the cheap seats while those around them ate peanuts and sang along to the opera, as my father suspects they knew Verdi by heart. Despite the less-than-dignified circumstances, as a sign of respect (perhaps for high culture?), Torrealday even took off his ever-present Basque beret (*txapela*).[37] First mate Forbes also made his way to San Carlo, afterward acidly remarking that "there was a vast display of bald heads and boiled shirts — of shaved armpits and shoulders coated with liquid powder."[38] Forbes may well have also accompanied the Okos and other crew members on an outing to the Trocadero nightclub. Gladys heard about the cabaret and wanted to go; Oko resisted: "All the sailors going there [...] not a place I would take you."[39] Unmoved, Gladys insisted: "[Y]ou as skipper can take me." When the establishment's staff tried to seat the Okos in a corner, the captain objected, saying that he wanted a big table because his crew would soon be there and he wanted them around him. Seven tables were placed together, and soon the crew members were joined by several women, who until then had been sitting alone. Champagne was ordered, and the party enjoyed itself while listening to music. Inevitably, "O Sole Mio" was sung by a young woman who was waiting for her sailor to return. When Gladys went to the ladies' room, many of the women followed. When she put on some lipstick, the women looked at it longingly. So Gladys reached into her purse, grabbed a handful of lipsticks, and passed them out to the women. A small gesture, to be sure, but one that exposed some of the needs that prevailed at the time. It may well have been on this occasion that Forbes danced with a woman named Piera; Oko did not think that Forbes danced well. He joked that his first mate was "cavorting with the grace of a Pegasus mounted by Nijinsky."[40] But surely Forbes had the last laugh, because he eventually married Piera. After an often-turbulent life, the *Kefalos*'s former first mate had finally settled down.[41]

Yet it was clear that these pleasures were coming to an end; the arrival of an Israeli delegation in Naples at the end of October suggested that the Neapolitan interlude was nearly over. The group included four *melavim*, a new radio operator, and two members of the Israeli Defense Forces.[42] [Photograph 19] These seven joined Arie Mambush-Ambash, a specialist in forging documents for Haganah, who, as noted earlier, had prepared "kosher papers" for the *Kefalos*, had traveled with the vessel from Tel Aviv on 12 September, and was already in Naples.[43] *Melavim* (the plural of *melave*) was the name given to Israeli ship commanders "who accompanied each load of refugees, taking command of the immigrants from the moment the ship left the European shore until they were landed in Palestine."[44] They acted as protectors and guardians of the Jewish refugees, and aboard the vessels used in transporting them as part of Aliya Bet (the illegal transport of Jews to Palestine between 1920 and 1948, when Great Britain controlled the area), the melavim did not have to take orders from the ship captains; in effect, they were technically above the skippers. According to Arie Mambush-Ambash, as soon as the melavim came to the ship in Naples, inevitably a substantial conflict arose as to their status on board. Oko expressed to them that they would be under his command, and they, in turn, replied that they would be responsible for the passengers and would not take orders from him. The captain warned them that he would arrest them if they disobeyed his orders. A parallel command structure on a ship was completely against Oko's maritime experience and way of thinking. Mambush-Ambash attempted to calm things down by explaining to the captain how things were run on other refugee (*olim*) ships; Oko, however, was unconvinced, and relations between him and the melavim were strained from the outset and remained so in the future.[45] Collectively, the testimonies of the melavim evince a strong disapproval of Oko and his methods of command. Significantly, however, Oko does not appear to have been critical of the melavim; he limits himself to the observation that there were aboard "young lads [...] called melavim. [They] are actually protectors of the passengers."[46] Final preparations on the ship were made the first week of

November. Several excellent photographs of the final stages of the process show supplies, materials, and luggage being loaded on the *Kefalos*.[47] They also portray a smiling Gladys on the bridge with the radio operator and some of the melavim, and in some of the photographs newly-stenciled markings "S.S. Kefalos — Panama" are clearly visible on lifesavers and a lifeboat. In one of the more striking photos, two men (perhaps melavim?) stand alone on an entirely empty and tidy deck, as if surveying with satisfaction the extensive work done on the ship — a vessel that in the following weeks would have thousands of refugees often squeezed shoulder-to-shoulder on the same deck [photograph 18].[48] On 6 November, Oko informed the port's inspector of customs that "bunkers, lube oil and diesel fuel" had been received aboard during the ship's stay in Naples.[49] And to tie up financial loose ends, as noted earlier, on the very next day, the captain made arrangements for all unpaid local bills to be paid by Rosenberg.[50] With all affairs seemingly in order, the *Kefalos* left Naples on 8 November at 4 p.m on its next mission.

While it is tempting to draw parallels between Tampico and Naples — among them, a prolonged involuntary stay at port, changes in personnel, unforeseen complications, and tussles with Israel's representatives — the differences far outweigh the similarities. Significantly, the *Kefalos* in Naples had not been immersed in contentious national political squabbles, as had occurred in Mexico. Likewise, in Naples there had been no hostile press publicity toward the ship or its crew. Also in Italy, Israel had a stronger presence and virtual free hand to operate as it wished, something that had been lacking in far-away Tampico. Finally, Naples port authorities did not interfere with the vessel's reconversion, and allowed the ship to leave unimpeded. Even so, sailing out of Naples and with the mission having radically changed, the vessel faced many imponderables and unknowns that it had not confronted when leaving Tampico. For one thing, Oko and the crew upon departing from Naples undoubtedly wondered whether transporting human cargo to Israel would prove more difficult or challenging than the recent smuggling of arms. The answer was far from easy — and not long in coming.

6

Rescues of Refugees

The Balkans and Their Aftermath

In two trips from Bakar to Haifa in late 1948, the *Kefalos* rescued 7,737 Jewish refugees stranded in the Balkans.[1] The first voyage took place between 14–23 November and the second one during 15–25 December. Neither of the two journeys was free of problems, complications, and hardships. Delays, bad weather and rough seas, ship malfunctions, limited and poor food supplies, overcrowding, tensions with local authorities, disagreements with the Israeli owners of the vessel, and dissent on board all combined to make the voyages of the rust bucket — particularly the second one — difficult and even perilous. Yet every individual who boarded at Bakar was evacuated safely to Israel.

Act I. First Rescue

When the *Kefalos* left Naples on 8 November its crew was slightly larger (42) than the one that had sailed from Tampico to Tel Aviv (38).[2] Also on board were several Israelis: five melavim and two members of the IDF (Israeli Defense Forces).[3] Traveling south through the Strait of Messina, around the "boot," and north through the Strait of Otranto, after picking up a pilot in Split on 12 November, the *Kefalos*, navigating quite slowly, arrived on 14 November in Bakar.[4] Putting into port was not easy because the harbor, as Oko observed, was in "a tight little cul-de-sac" that required delicate maneuvering; it was "so narrow that you have to put your bow on the beach to swing your stern."[5] Throngs of refugees met the ship upon its arrival. They had spent eight days on trains and had been waiting four days for the *Kefalos* to dock.[6] According to Oko, the refugees had run out of food and had been forced to do their laundry in salt-water. They had traveled to Bakar in boxcars similar to those that were used by the Nazis to take prisoners to concentration camps. A stunning photograph taken from the ship on the day of arrival shows large numbers of individuals in front of a large white building with a tall smokestack near the water, standing in front of a long line of boxcars, with no real port or dock to speak of. [Photograph 20] Although taken from a distance — a fact that makes it impossible to discern particular faces or expressions — the refugees are clearly looking intently toward the vessel that had come to evacuate them.[7] The captain recalled their miserable state, and yet the mass of refugees, in an extraordinarily moving scene, lined along the channel leading to the place of embarkment, while "both sides of the fjord echoed with the song 'Hatikvah' [...] and I can tell you frankly that there wasn't a dry eye aboard the ship."[8] It was an indelible memory that Oko would recall movingly:

> "I get a clutch from it, even now. Just thinking about those poor damned bastards standing there, spilling their hearts out at [the] sight of our frigging old Kefalos coming to get them. It kills me. I mean it. It does things to me that no man wants to admit. [...] These were people hounded by hate, herded into concentration camps, and subjected to every conceivable device destructive to human hope. Yet there they stood waiting on the shore, each finding somewhere in his or her tortured heart a voice of some kind to swell the chorus of unskilled hope to welcome us. [...] Bakar spelled out hope."[9]

The captain was not quite done, remarking incisively that these were "the remnants of the genocide, and these were all broken families, old men, young men, women, some children, various age groups and the like. The idea of departure into a dream and what it represented to them."[10] Two additional photographs of the refugees as they boarded the *Kefalos* eloquently illustrate their downtrodden state: ill-dressed and carrying their few possessions in bundles slung over their shoulders. Their demeanor is generally quite serious, although one senses a fleeting smile or ray of hope as they gradually filed deeper into the ship — in effect, as they realized that they were finally on board and headed for a new land.[11] [Photographs 21 and 22] A composite of the best testimonies suggests that the total number of refugees who boarded at Bakar on the first trip was between 4,000 and 4,500. Oko's estimate of 4,300 appears to be among the most reliable figure.[12] The vessel did not stay long in Bakar, leaving the very next morning for Split to pick up a local Yugoslavian pilot, a "fine [...] and a very sympathetic chap," according to Oko. The *Kefalos* left Split on 16 November, and then was on its own in the Aegean Sea and on its way to Israel. The seven-day voyage would prove rich in surprises and incidents, good and bad.

In a striking passage from his "1960 Account" that underscores the fleeting and improbable convergence of diasporas across centuries, geographies, and cultures, Captain Oko wrote, "The interesting thing was that my Spaniards were able to speak the antique Spanish of the days of the Inquisition of Cervantes to the women particularly aboard the ship. I was able to understand through a little knowledge of German, [and] enough Yiddish to be able to communicate with them."[13] In other words, the Spanish crew was able to communicate with Slavic Sephardic Jews, who doubtless knew or spoke some form of Ladino. Moreover, the captain, himself a Russian Jew, was able to share his thoughts with the refugees in another language some of them understood — Yiddish. The captain praised the Spanish contingent when matters got very rough during the first trip from the Balkans to Israel: "[Y]ou can't imagine the high morale that was sustained by the relationship of the people with my predominantly Spanish crew and to the ship and to each other."[14] Ratner, too, lauded the Spanish crew's steadfast loyalty to the humanitarian mission of the *Kefalos*: "the Spaniards proved trustworthy and even stayed with the ship [...] when we later carried refugees."[15] This was remarkable, as the captain put it, given the "stench and wretched condition of a vessel of 6,000 tons [dead weight] with 4,300 people aboard."[16] [Photographs of the crowded ship deck numbers 23, 24, 25; and of a more relaxed group of young passengers, numbers 26 and 27]

Oko emphasized the positive aspects of the refugees' conduct during this trip to Israel — social harmony and solidarity, music, marriages, and births — under exceedingly trying circumstances. In the captain's words, "the morale was tremendously high [and] there was an attitude of good cheer." Oko also pointedly noted that "there was no separation of feeling anywhere throughout the ship, but the greatest excitement for the arrival in Tel Aviv." Moreover, "we had a group of musicians aboard that gave of themselves continuously throughout the voyage."[17] The captain's notes relate that there was "music, singing and dancing on board the crowded ship during 8 days to Haifa."[18] [Photograph 29] Five marriages took place, some of which were captured in photographs. One of the most eloquent ones is of a happy wedding party of six, taken, as Gladys's caption explains, "just after the Captain had performed the ceremony, on the way to Haifa."[19] Several photographs of actual marriage ceremonies and the signing of a marriage contract exist as well.[20] Oko, who had for part of his life been brought up in a Reform household (although by his own admission he was not particularly religious), remarked that "we fortunately had a little rabbi who had a magnificent humor, and for the first time I saw the whole beautiful procedure of a truly Orthodox wedding."[21] Given how moved Oko was by this ceremony, it is hard to explain why he would try to minimize or deflect attention from his very direct participation in a wedding (perhaps the same one?). Chaya/Haya Kozlovsky, the vessel's radio operator, recalls in a stirring account how "three Bulgarian couples had decided that they wanted to enter Israel as married couples. The captain and a cantor conducted the marriage ceremony and we, the Israelis on the ship, were the 'givers away' of the brides; a choir sang songs, and there was a songfest. I stood there with tears in my eyes."[22] There were also three births during the voyage. According to the *Palestine Post*, "two boys and a girl born on the way, traveling in wicker baskets."[23] Mothers and newborns were given the best care possible under the circumstances; the ship's steward, Borrego, gave up his room to the new mothers and babies.[24]

However, another important participant of the first voyage episode remembered parts of the trip quite differently. While much of the photographic and anecdotal evidence appears to bear out the captain's decidedly rosy recollections, by contrast, Nathaniel Ratner's eloquent narrative details very negatively some of what occurred when the *Kefalos* left Bakar: "A storm kicked up. Captain Oko felt that as the ship was not very seaworthy, we should take shelter off the Italian coast until calmer sailing conditions prevailed. The Israelis felt that we should immediately proceed to Israel. The captain refused. The Israelis decided to take over the ship."[25] According to Ratner, Oko "was determined to resist, as he felt responsible for the safety of the passengers."[26] The crisis threatened to escalate into a full-blown mutiny, but Ratner, with the assistance of cooler heads, defused the situation by arguing that if a serious rebellion broke out, the mutineers would be tried in a Panamanian court. Moreover, he impressed upon them "that the ship was so rotted that there was a safety risk [involved] in the storm." As the malcontents acquiesced to the chief engineer's reasoning, in Ratner's words, "the comic opera" ended; it would not, however, be the only protest by refugees aboard the *Kefalos*.[27]

Ratner may be excused for making light of the episode; he clearly had much more serious and pressing concerns during those days. On 20 November, the chief engineer hastily scribbled a note for Oko with a host of mechanical problems on board. Ratner related that the steam cooking kettles would not withstand the ship's pressure, the electrical wiring for the ventilators in the passengers' quarters were defective, the diesel generator for the ventilators needed overhaul, the new piping was faulty, the passengers' toilets were not rigged for proper flushing, the boiler blower required balancing, and the vapor pressure regulating valve and two saltwater pumps needed overhaul.[28] This information was transmitted the same day to the Ha'Mossad Le'Aliya in Israel, which, in turn, asked if repairs were needed in Haifa, and, if so, which ones.[29] Demonstrating an unmistakable urgency, still on 20 November, Oko replied with a recommendation that the "complete overhaul [and] entire installation recently completed [in] Naples" should be reviewed "by a competent engineering authority on arrival."[30] It remains unknown whether the requested inspection was conducted; Oko's records are curiously silent on such an important matter.[31]

While Ratner worried about the *Kefalos*'s malfunctions, Oko, too, had other significant concerns to deal with. While the general health of the refugees appears to have been generally satisfactory, there were several cases of measles and whooping cough on board.[32] The numbers varied according to the day and appeared to be small (five measles, eight whooping cough). Nonetheless, the illnesses were highly contagious. Overseeing the care of the sick was Dr. Heinrich Keller, a surgeon and gynecologist who, according to Oko, had lost his wife, daughter, and son to the gas chambers. The doctor had been kept alive by the Nazis because they needed him to tend to storm troopers.[33] The captain was extremely grateful for Dr. Keller's medical services on this voyage. Oko was proud of the way Keller and Gladys had taken care "of the children and oldsters aboard that ship."[34] Oko noted as well that Gladys (a former superintendent of nurses at Green's Eye Hospital) had organized "the most beautiful hospital" on board.[35] On 22 November, Oko cabled the medical services in Haifa to have ambulance services ready for eight measles "isolation cases and eight hospitalization cases."[36] Upon entering port the next day, the *Kefalos* also had a quarantine flag raised.[37] [Photograph 30; unclear whether this was taken during the first or second voyage from Bakar]

A front-page article in the 24 November issue of the *Palestine Post,* headlined "4,000 Come in Ship Under Israeli Flag," heralded the ship's arrival in Haifa.[38] The wonderful piece began by evoking "a momentary illusion" of "a refugee vessel of pre-State days — for her deck was crowded black with people." A fantasy "broken by the sound of a shofar and then spirited singing came alongside the quay [sic]."[39] Most of the refugees, the article noted, were from Bulgaria. Some of the immigrants hoisted a portrait of Ben-Gurion above the ship's railings, taking turns holding it up until all had disembarked. According to the article, more than half of them belonged to the Workers Party (Mapai), "and even some of the youngsters wore party armbands." It took six hours for the refugees to be processed and receive documents from the Jewish Agency. The more fortunate ones had relatives to meet them. "The arrivals looked curiously at the Palmach inscriptions on the buses [...] which had taken part in the battle that made their coming possible, almost all with at least one bullet-hole." Other immigrants were taken by rail to a transit camp. The dozen men and women who registered them, the article underscored, "with the shrewd experience of having cared for tens of thousands [...], sized up the arrivals today as 'an excellent lot.'"[40] The captain and crew had accomplished successfully their task, safely delivering their human cargo under considerably less-than-optimal conditions. Oko, however, was still smarting for several weeks from the Neapolitan interlude and its concomitant problems, and he was eager to meet with Levi Skolnik to complain loudly about what had transpired there.

During the voyage from Naples to Haifa, the captain had cabled Skolnik three times (18, 21, and 22 November), requesting an interview with him upon arrival.[41] Oko's communications betrayed a pressing, almost desperate tone; he used such terms as "urgent" and "imperative." And the day before entering Haifa, Oko requested advice as to where Skolnik could be contacted upon arrival. The captain's troubled state of mind was abundantly evident in a note to Eric Forbes the very day the *Kefalos* entered Haifa. Oko informed his first mate that he would be away on business for several days, adding ominously that "should there be any change of plans such as my relinquishing command," Forbes would be advised to that effect "in person or in writing." Therefore, until the first mate heard from the captain, Forbes would assume "full command" of the vessel as soon as Oko left the ship for Haifa.[42] Could it be that Oko entertained notions of resigning? That would not be surprising given that, as noted in Chapter 5, he had thought of giving up command of the vessel on 31 October during the work on the conversion of the *Kefalos* in Naples. Still, if Oko could speak his mind fully in a meeting with Skolnik, perhaps they could reach a meeting of the minds on the numerous questions that troubled the captain. That is probably why Oko welcomed the news that Aryeh Mambush — the Haganah member who had traveled to Naples with Oko on the ship, who had spent more than two months with the vessel, and whom Oko liked — was attempting to arrange a meeting between the skipper and Skolnik.[43]

For reasons that are unknown, the encounter of Oko with Skolnik never took place, and this was doubtless a bitter blow to the captain. Skolnik might well have been busy with official matters, or perhaps he simply did not want to entertain Oko's complaints and bill of particulars. Recall that Skolnik and his wife, Elishiva, had visited Oko and Gladys on the ship shortly after the delivery of arms in September. The Okos had enjoyed their company, Oko had spoken admiringly of Skolnik ("a big Lincolnesque, open-shirted, direct fine person"), and Skolnik had sent a warm, personal, handwritten congratulatory note to the Okos ("to the true guides who had brought the boat safely ashore") along with a crate of gifts.[44] But with Skolnik's refusal to meet with Oko, the captain met instead with Tzvi Yechieli, a senior member of Ha'Mossad Le'Aliya Bet and head of the Marine Transportation Company. It would be Yechieli who gave Oko instructions for the second voyage to the Balkans.[45] Significantly, there was a marked change in Yechieli's *two* communications to Oko on 28 November, which had a more business-like and imperious tone than the comradely and amiable tone of earlier exchanges. Oko was now addressed as an employee and underling who took orders: "In accordance with our verbal discussion, you will sail your ship to Yugoslavia in order to embark people there for Israel."[46] The other note made it clear that whatever autonomy of action Oko may have had was about to end. Yechieli spoke as part of the "managers and agents for, and on behalf of, owners of the s/s Kefalos," and confirmed that the latter "were responsible for the payment of your crew's wages, other payments and bonuses, according to the articles signed on board." The communication added revealingly, "We are also responsible for the repatriation of your crew after being paid off, according to the agreement and order of your vessel."[47] If there was any doubt, the ship, already majority owned by Israel, was soon to be run entirely by a new administration, one in which neither the old crew nor its captain would play any part. Oko's days as master of the rust bucket were nearing their end. Even when faced with a bleak and uncertain future, on the evening of the same day he received Yechieli's two communications, Oko and the crew nevertheless sailed from Haifa to Bakar to carry out the next evacuation of refugees. The voyage would be part of the odyssey of the *Kefalos* under the command of Oko.

Act II. Second Rescue

The second trip to the Balkans and back to Israel would perhaps prove even more eventful than the first.[48] Arriving at Split on 6 December and then at Bakar on 8 December, the *Kefalos* would have to wait for several days before departing with the refugees. Although Oko offers no narrative on the stay at the port, his highly schematic notes, suggestively titled "Anxiety in Bakar," provide important glimpses of the heightened tensions the ship and crew encountered there.[49] Fortunately, the captain's fragmentary observations are supplemented with Ratner's accounts, Oko's primary document records, and some of the melavim's recollections. Numerous complications would quickly come into play at Bakar. First, the immigrants had not arrived. According to Ratner, "after about one week [...] the first freight train load of refugees arrived and were embarked."[50] In the meantime, another serious thorny problem ensued: a large cargo ship arrived at port "flying a 'baker' flag (dangerous cargo, probably munitions)."[51] Ratner adds that the *Kefalos* was "ordered to leave the dock to make room for this ship and its cargo. But if we left the dock, it would mean the 2nd trainload of refugees would be left in the boxcars, without sustenance. And who knew for how many days."[52] What to do then? Oko and Rather conjured up a number of delaying tactics, asserting necessary boiler repairs and invoking the perils to the passengers already on board if the *Kefalos* was moved. Compounding their troubles, strong winds made maneuvering the ship extremely difficult and dangerous.[53] Ratner relates that he notified Oko that he was repairing the boilers and could not move the ship. On 14 December, a flurry of communications ensued between Oko and Ratner on the one hand, and between Oko and the authorities on the other.[54] Ratner was "then called into the Yugoslav Commissar's office and told that we must move the ship." The chief engineer countered "through interpreters" that to do so "would endanger all the lives of those aboard, but that we could have the ship ready to sail by dawn the next morning."[55] As Oko and Ratner continued to stall for time, a sense of "anxiety permeated vessel" and "developed in crew almost defeatist attitude."[56] The sight of the *Kefalos* was not pleasant to some of those waiting on shore. Tommy Lapid, the noted Israeli personality and cabinet minister, recalls marching along with others "to the edge of the pier where a stubby, ugly little tub bounced up and down in the water."[57] The rust bucket may not have been pretty, but it represented the refugees' only means of getting to Israel safely.

The local authorities relented somewhat in their demands, but ordered that the ship should leave by dawn. Ratner, however, was adamant; as he later confessed, "I wasn't about to move that ship; I wasn't about to leave 2,000 people in boxcars."[58] To gain additional time under increasingly desperate circumstances, Ratner had the Spanish engineers, "to their confusion, remove some valves from the boiler" in case Yugoslavian officials came to inspect the progress of repairs. The ruse to delay worked in the nick of time: "[T]he train arrived [...] about midnight, and by 3 a.m. we had the 2nd load of refugees aboard and sailed at dawn as promised."[59] Well, not quite at dawn, actually. Oko's usually reliable log shows that the *Kefalos* left Bakar on 15 December at 11:45 a.m. He notes that "when we did get away, [we] ran the Israel flag up on the fore truck to give the refugees a lift. They started to sing the 'Hatikvah.' Tremendous relief — engine functioned [...] we were out of port. Out at the end of the cul-de-sac."[60] They were very happy to get out, but were also exhausted; neither Oko nor Forbes had slept for three days. Little wonder that Oko admitted they were "punchy coming from Split." Unlike the first voyage, the stop at Bakar during the second voyage had been far more than an adventure; it had proven an ordeal that had imperiled the crew, vessel, and passengers. The *Kefalos* had slipped away safely, but the ship was overloaded, conditions aboard were horrendous, and the weather soon became atrociously menacing.

Yehoshua Bar Lev, one of the Israeli officials (melavim) charged with escorting the passengers and looking after their well-being, graphically observed, "we shoved in men, women and children as if the 'Dromit' was the size of Australia [...] [H]ere we were with twice the number of olim [refugees] than had been expected."[61] Even if the *Kefalos* had left on time, "like an Italian train [...], the Adriatic Sea shot mountainous waves in our direction, [and] this torture continued for about three days in which we had made no headway."[62] According to Ratner, after leaving Bakar, the "refugees slept on wooden shelving, packed together like sardines [and] ate one meal a day."[63] Ratner asserts that the ship "almost sank in a storm with 4,000 refugees aboard," although he does not specify whether this was during the first of second voyage.[64] Bad weather and rough seas were prevalent during both journeys. The captain's log for 19–21 December vividly reflects the poor sailing conditions: "Hove to throughout night in Ely gale, rough to precipitous seas." Oko also noted reduced speeds of 4.3–4.7 knots.[65] By the 22nd, the ship had returned to a more respectable 7 knots, if still below its more usual 8–8.5 knots. Bar Lev relates that when the sea calmed, "life on deck went back to normal; normal but not good. The food was pretty bad and sleeping in the crowded holds on shelves was not pleasant. We were supposed to be en route for 8 days, but the storm added three more."[66] In effect, a voyage of eight days lasted nearly eleven.

Complaints, particularly about the food, began after the *Kefalos* had been at sea for six days. Bar Lev's account notes that the protests were justified, but that little could be done about it: "Legumes and stale bread was all we had [...] dry, stale biscuits, soup made of legumes, and tinned beef that we had collected from battlefields."[67] He remarked that "a rebellion was forming slowly but surely. A hunger strike was then declared." Bar Lev added, with a mixture of humor and sarcasm, that "this was the first and last time that I did not like people who had a healthy appetite."[68] During the uproar "three olim [refugees] approached the captain and complained," and, Oko, in a lie, "promised them access to the food supplies."[69] Bar Lev then asked the captain "if he had lost his mind." Oko justified this flagrant misrepresentation to Bar Lev by telling him "that sometimes a good lie can solve a bad problem."[70] Eventually, Bar Lev approached Ratner, who told him that he would intercede with the captain to make things right. It is not known what the chief engineer said or did, but here, again, Ratner apparently played a key role in quieting events. Bar Lev observed that they had arrived in Israel "weak and battered," but quickly added that "of course the olim were even weaker and more battered than we were" when the *Kefalos* put into Haifa on Christmas Day.[71] Upon reaching land, the immigrants "cheered," Ratner recalls, and "some of them kissed the ground."[72] According to Oko's figures, 3,800 olim arrived in Israel on the second voyage from the Balkans.[73] As opposed to the extensive front-page coverage after the arrival in Haifa during the first voyage, the second trip generated little publicity in the *Palestine Post*. A minuscule item in a regular column on 26 December noted that "4,200 immigrants have disembarked at Haifa port since Thursday."[74] In a masterful understatement, the captain succinctly summed up the second trip: "[I]t was like the earlier voyage, there were threats, [and] there was a bora blowing, which is a tremendously high wind in that area."[75]

During the two voyages the *Kefalos* and its crew had rescued a total of 7,737 refugees from their miserable state and had done so without a single loss of life.[76] But the two rescues had not been purely humanitarian. Oko was quick to point out "that on both voyages the bulk of the passengers were of military age, had been trained in the D.P. camps in guerrilla warfare, and immediately went in to man the arms in the Naga [sic] that we had brought from Tampico."[77] In sum, for all of these reasons the Okos proudly came to regard the rescues as their finest achievement, even more so than the smuggling of arms to Israel.[78]

However, immediately after the *Kefalos* returned to Haifa, the ship's owners were much less enamored of the accomplishments of the captain and crew. Undoubtedly, Oko had been a much less compliant employee than the Israelis would have wanted. He complained, protected turf, and insisted on doing things his way. A good example of this is what might be termed the Bari affair, an episode that had ruffled feathers on all sides. On the way from Haifa to Bakar during the second voyage, Oko had been instructed by Joseph Barpal, an Israeli official, to enter the port of Bari, but he had not been informed of the reasons for doing so.[79] Bar Lev, a melavim on the trip, relates that the ship had indeed received a telegram from Barpal inquiring whether there were "sufficient supplies and fuel to pick up some passengers."[80] The *Kefalos* indeed received a telegram from the Rome office that day with this text, "Proceed to Yugoslavia as in previous voyage. Give us requirements on fuel, water. Food and arrangements will be made for you to be supplied in Bari."[81] Perhaps the reason for suggesting Bari, as Yehuda Ben-Tzur speculates, was "most probably to check if [the vessel was] suitable to load tanks."[82] But there is no evidence that Oko was ever told of this possible reason, and, as Bar Lev asserts, the ship answered that it had enough food for 1,500 people for ten days or more. Moreover, Bar Lev was quick to note that "Barpal was a secretive person" and that he had not told the ship's crew that the vessel might have to take more than 1,500 refugees, but that he had *again* asked if the figures on board had been checked well. Barpal, according to Bar Lev, then suggested that the ship stop in Bari if more food or fuel were needed. However, the telegram that the ship received from Barpal on 6 December was anything but clear-cut; in fact, it was extremely ambiguous: "Because the immigration from Yugoslavia is delayed by three or four days, and because of this delay, please make another check on your fuel, water, food. If you require anything, please let us know, *and you may proceed to Bari*."[83] Barpal's telegram infuriated Oko: "Doesn't he think I know how to refuel my ship? If we have to go into Bari again, you'll have to walk to Haifa," the captain reputedly told Bar Lev.[84]

Barpal was told not to worry; the ship's figures were correct. In fact, Oko cabled Rome the same day with an adamant reply: "Repeat, No requirements providing no undue delays. Four days not considered undue delay. Arrival Split this evening."[85] Interestingly, not all communications went directly from Oko to Israeli personnel. Bar Lev, as a representative of the owners on board — in effect, the Mossad — engaged in candid back-channel communications with Israeli aides. In a telling statement, Bar Lev wrote the Mossad: "We have enough food for five days for 4,000 people. Remember that if you will direct us back to Bari, *the captain and the whole crew will be very much strongly against doing so.*"[86] According to Bar Lev, "Barpal did not make clear why they were to go to Bari," and he never found out what this official had in mind.[87] In conclusion, the *Kefalos* never entered Bari, and the mini-drama that was played out behind the scenes exacerbated the animosity that already existed for several weeks between the main protagonists: Oko and the crew on the one hand, and the ship's owners and Israeli maritime executives on the other.

Recall that already on 28 November, Tzvi Yechieli had raised the issue of payment for the crew's wages and their repatriation after settlement of their salaries.[88] Possibly wishing to stay one step ahead of the process, Oko, on the way back to Haifa on 18 December, took the unusual step to communicate directly with New York, something he had apparently not done in months. In a hastily written cable to "Jackson, Shipsage," as per the famous Instructions to Master, Oko pointedly wrote: "Due current conditions most crew and self with payoff Haifa or following European port. Who is Haifa agent. Stop. Reply urgent. Relay to ship thru Tarantoradio (counts as two words). Kay Master."[89] This might well have represented an attempt to bypass his employers in Israel and return to those he had dealt with initially in New York. If this was the skipper's intention, very soon he was about to be exceedingly disappointed. It is not known whether he received a reply from Jackson, Shipsage or Manuel Enterprises, assuming the latter still existed. But what is certain is that on 26 December, the very *next* day after disembarking the refugees, Oko received a jarring note from the ship's owners. The curt communication read in part: "Mr. [Yechieli] has requested me to ask you to prepare your ship's accounts for *tomorrow morning*, when he and Mr. Chovers will be on board to discuss matters with you."[90] It is difficult not to read this short note as anything other than payback for the problems that Oko had caused in recent weeks, including his failure to enter Bari. The captain's reaction to the letter is unknown, but the Okos were soon on the move to visit the camps that housed some of the refugees brought on the first trip.[91] Oko was quick to point out that travel to the camps had not been on government-escorted tours. In the camps the Okos were able to see for themselves what was happening to some of the immigrants they had transported earlier, and in the captain's words, "I can't say that we were anything but pleased, and their happiness was great."[92] It is good that the Okos were able to enjoy, even if briefly, the fruits of their labor; they were well aware that they were living in Israel, as it were, on borrowed time.

The hammer came down hard on 5 January 1949. On that day, Tzvi Jechieli addressed a short but unequivocally tough, brief note to Oko on behalf of the ship's owners (Shoham Ltd.), requesting that the skipper "hand over the ship 'Kefalos' (Pinzon) to Captain Golandski, who was appointed by our firm as Captain of the above ship."[93] To soften the blow somewhat, the communication thanked the captain for the services rendered and the hard work "to fulfill the job in the best possible way." They were polite words that hardly amounted to a ringing endorsement of what Oko and the crew had gone through in the previous six months. Although it is not known exactly when Oko and Gladys returned to the ship, by 7 January he was definitely on board to handle matters related to what came to be known as the Haifa payoff/payout. In effect, this was the liquidation of all outstanding wages owed to the crew and their official discharge from the vessel. The only two sets of documents of the payout that are known are those of Oko and Gladys.[94] Oko's wage voucher, dated 7 January, number 34, shows that he had served as captain of the *Kefalos* from 1 June 1948–31 December 1948 and during 7–9 January 1949. For his services he was owed US$4,989.50, from which was deducted US$3,000 for "allotments." Hence, the net amount due Oko, and presumably what was paid, was US$1,989.50.[95] Gladys's wage voucher, inexplicably dated two days later on 9 January, number 8, demonstrates that she served as purser during the same dates as her husband and was paid seven dollars. This document is the last of the captain's papers that carries the official seal of the *Kefalos* with Oko's signature on it.[96] It remains unknown when the Okos and the crew vacated the vessel, although it is almost certain that it was on 9 January or the next day. The Okos did not stay in Israel long; in late January or early February they returned to the United States. On 9 February, the captain, ever mindful of his crew, wrote brief recommendations for Borrego, Gutierrez, Larrauri, Rivera, and Sánchez.[97] Most of them appear to have had little luck finding employment in the Mediterranean, and in an intriguing twist of fate, at least three of the crewmen (Corino, Larrauri, and Sánchez) soon found themselves back in the San Francisco area aboard the *Adelanto*, the ship from which Oko had recruited them for the *Kefalos* six to seven months earlier.[98]

As the crew scattered in different directions in January and February 1949, the odyssey of the ship with three names had come to an end.[99] Yet important traces of it remained for years to come. Upon entering the Israeli merchant fleet, the vessel was officially renamed *Dromit*. And in yet another significant and perhaps improbable turn of events, its first full-time captain was Esteban Hernandorena, a Basque Republican refugee who had helped smuggle immigrants into Israel in 1947.[100] As for Oko, the inside cover of his large green log book, in which he meticulously recorded the voyages of the ships he captained, tellingly reads in bold handwriting, "A.S. Oko, Master, s/s Martin Alonzo [sic] Pinzon."[101] In conclusion, as noted before, in the six-month lifespan of the ship with three names, for a variety of historical and political reasons, both long- and short-term, there had been an unlikely intersection of diasporas across centuries, geographies, ethnicities, and cultures.

Conclusion

Roughly ten years after the *Kefalos* saga, Oko reflected on the success of the ship's operations. Although not particularly religious, Oko nonetheless mused about the possibility of divine intervention (and good fortune) in ensuring the missions' favorable outcome. In disconnected notes prepared for a chapter on Bakar that would remain unwritten, the skipper wrote, "[W]hen I think of the times that we could have missed all along the way. *Help from above.* Voyage a record of sheer luck (masel) — luck and determination to attain objective. And the unexplainable things (happening), aiding. Consistently violated every rule of seamanship and still came through. *Must be some force ruling.*"[1] In another passage, while discussing the unlikely arrival of the Exodus in Israel, Oko likened the Exodus's "miracle" to the *Kefalos*'s own voyage. To those who might question the rust bucket's equally improbable achievements, Oko had a ready answer: "[I]f you have any doubt, take a look at our log book. *There must have been some special providence taking care of sailors.*"[2] How else to explain that virtually nothing had gone according to plan during seven months, and that at numerous junctures the vessel had emerged unscathed and succeeded in its objectives? From the early fire right out of Portland, Maine, to the drawn-out crisis at Tampico that exposed and nearly sabotaged the mission, to the near mishap near Pantelleria, culminating in the arrival in Tel Aviv without radio contact and the alarming shortage of fuel and water — everything suggested favorable hidden forces at work. To a lesser extent the same was true of the rescues of refugees in the Balkans, most particularly that of the second voyage, which occurred under considerably dangerous conditions. Unquestionably, the *Kefalos* faced a panoply of seemingly insurmountable obstacles and pitfalls, any one of which could have scuttled its goals. Viewed in this light, it is understandable that Oko felt supernatural causes were wholly (or partly) responsible for the accomplishments of the *Kefalos*. However, a careful analysis of the totality of the vessel's operations convincingly demonstrates that a powerful combination of human actions and factors — political, economic, cultural, and maritime — preponderantly ensured the favorable outcome of all of the ship's missions. There was no hidden hand of fate or the divine; if anything, human hands and actions were the surest guides in nearly every important matter.

A significant ingredient in the successful smuggling of the arms cargo, as well as in the rescues of refugees, was the existence of a central Israeli organization that planned, directed, and coordinated the complex logistics involved in the operations. Using the fictitious Manuel Enterprises, Inc. as an imaginative, if not always efficient, front, the Israeli leadership was able to launch a daring and ambitious mission under the nose of U.S. authorities. There was a romantic conspiratorial aspect to the affair, complete with subterfuges, false papers and destinations, and misleading manifests of cargo, culminating with the change of appearance of the *Kefalos* and its change of name to *M.A. Pinzon*. And if the fanciful "Instructions to Master" were palpably laughable, at least they included communication channels through which the ship could stay in constant contact with New York for a time, and later with European and Israeli listening stations. Of course, as is now known, little went according to plan during the early stages of the arms-smuggling mission. The Tampico episode showed that much went wrong, and that events had come very close to unraveling plans completely. To be sure, the *Kefalos* enjoyed a great measure of good fortune at Tampico, but good fortune alone would not have sufficed had it not been for the effective assistance of key local participants of the Mexican Jewish community and considerable amounts of money handed out to Mexican government officials, which enabled the ship to leave port.

While it might be easy to minimize the monetary aspects of

the *Kefalos* enterprise, it would be a huge mistake to do so. This was not an operation done on the cheap; at every step money proved essential. The ship was bought, repaired, and supplied with food and fuel; the crew's wages were paid; and the bulk of the arms loaded in Tampico were bought from the Mexican government with generous bribes. Large sums were transferred from Europe (Geneva) to New York banks and from there to Mexico. FBI reports clearly illustrate an efficient money trail that financed a host of transactions at key junctures and locations. Ironically, there were continual — and at times long-lasting — mutual recriminations between Oko and Israeli representatives over wasteful or extravagant expenditures, notably in the United States, Mexico, and Italy. For instance, Oko was convinced that Elie Shalit and Rafael Recanati had paid too much to purchase the vessel, and Israeli officials insisted that Oko had over-spent at Naples in the conversion of the ship from a cargo to a passenger carrier. Regardless of what either party thought, money was the lubricant that facilitated crucial aspects of every operation.

It would be erroneous, too, to understate the significance of Oko's crew. A multi-national group, with a markedly Spanish and Latin American composition, the sailors with whom Oko surrounded himself had enormous maritime expertise. Many of them had sailed in a variety of seas, conditions, and circumstances. Not only did many of them know their positions on board well, they were also fiercely loyal to a captain whom they trusted and respected. This was particularly true of the *Kefalos*'s officers, many of whom had known the captain for some time. This tight-knit group remained loyal to the skipper, and to the ship during trying times, never wavering or rebelling. Numerous sailors, especially the Spanish ones, shared Oko's political sympathies on behalf of the Second Spanish Republic. This was perhaps even more true of the Basque contingent aboard. Losers of the Civil War, in which some had fought, they were exiled and became refugees, continuing to earn their livelihood as sailors in the late 1930s and 1940s under exceedingly difficult conditions. Many Basques demonstrated a remarkable affinity with the Israeli cause; as common victims of Fascism, they sympathized profoundly with the struggle and plight of Jews during and after World War II.[3] Some, such as Esteban Hernandorena, actively participated in operations to transport Jews from Europe to Israel in 1947–1948, and served the Israeli cause in other capacities.[4] A large number of Basque sailors, including Hernandorena, were interned in Cyprus in early 1948 after being caught by the British while helping Jews trying to enter Israel.[5] Although not Basque, Mariano Manresa, a native of Santander, was heavily identified with the Basque region. Manresa, as underscored in Chapter 1, played a central role in the *Kefalos* odyssey. Under circumstances that unfortunately remain unknown, Manresa and Oko had forged a close friendship in the mid-1940s.[6] Oko fervently admired Manresa's maritime savvy and the fact that as the de facto commander of the yacht *Vita*, he had been responsible for spiriting to Mexico a considerable fortune (the so-called Republican gold) to save it from falling into Francisco Franco's hands in 1939.[7] Also, during the Spanish Civil War, Manresa had commanded an armed transport, the *Tramontana*, a large former cod-shipping vessel that had belonged to PYSBE, and as such, had extensive sailing experience in the Mediterranean.[8] A seaman of Manresa's stature and sailing experience earned him the great respect and esteem of many others on the *Kefalos*, including Gladys; her wonderful smile in the photograph with Captain Manresa on the way to Tampico needs little interpretation. Regrettably, already very ill on the voyage to Mexico, Manresa could not continue the trip to Tel Aviv, a voyage he very much wished to make. As noted earlier, he would die in December 1948, and Oko was forced to scramble and find a replacement for his second mate. The captain chose Robert Keller, one of the five Jewish Americans sent by Haganah to serve aboard the *Kefalos* on the voyage to Israel.[9] [Photograph 7] Of the group, only Nathaniel Ratner stayed with the ship during its entire voyages. His accounts leave little doubt that he was well aware of the crew's Spanish Republican sympathies and that he admired the toughness and loyalty of the crew during all of its journeys. Although Ratner may not have been aware of it, in a small but particularly meaningful way his encounter with Spanish/Basque anti-fascists was a continuation of the ongoing rapprochement of different ethnocultural and political diasporas that had gradually converged for mutually beneficial considerations. Significantly, for a fleeting moment — if seven months can be characterized as such — the *Kefalos* had been the unlikely point for reuniting again peoples with a shared common past across many centuries, although they now lived in vastly separate and dispersed geographies.[10] Many Israelis acknowledged and long remembered the assistance rendered by Basque and Spanish sailors during their struggle for independence. The moving testimonies of *Palyamniks* in particular powerfully attest to Israeli gratitude for this help.[11]

There remains the important question as to which of the ship's different missions proved the more consequential: the first with arms or the second with refugees. In all likelihood there is no clear-cut answer; the first operation was important from a military and strategic perspective, while the second was significant from a humanitarian viewpoint. The smuggling of arms — even if not all that were brought to Israel were fully functional or state of the art — came at a crucial, perhaps even critical moment, especially with respect to the machine guns and airplane fuel. While it hardly tilted the military balance, the arms shipment was undeniably important politically and psychologically. Tellingly, Prime Minister Ben-Gurion paid close attention from the start to every aspect of the *Dromit* operation and received detailed reports on which armament had arrived on the vessel.[12] While Oko may have entertained less-than-satisfactory relationships with the leadership of Manuel Enterprises, Inc., and with Haganah's men in Mexico (especially with Greenspun, with whom he quarreled), overall the skipper did not experience acute difficulties with Israeli representatives during the arms smuggling voyage, despite glitches and communications problems. In fact, the Okos were extended a warm welcome in Tel Aviv. Recall, for instance, that Israeli officials visited the ship and brought gifts, all under an atmosphere of good will. Oko was then asked if he were willing to undertake a new and altogether different mission, which he gladly assented. Everything seemed to prophesy a fruitful collaboration. However, the spirit of cooperation and amity changed dramatically in Naples as Oko grew increasingly exasperated with delays, mismanagement, and incompetence, which he squarely laid at the doorsteps of Israeli aides in Italy. In turn, the Israelis blamed Oko for unnecessary and wasteful expenditures. Threatening to resign in a strongly-worded letter to Levi Skolnik, Oko's relationships with important Israeli officials rapidly deteriorated thereafter. Somewhat surprisingly, the transport of refugees from the Balkans to Israel proved far more conflictive and problematic than the smuggling of arms. Yet, the Okos came to regard the two rescues, both under trying and dangerous conditions, as their finest accomplishments.

In hindsight, the dramatic end of the saga of the ship with three names seems strangely odd and sad, although it was perhaps inevitable. Oko and the ship's management came from different cultures and traditions. Although Oko was undeniably and thoroughly Jewish, he never adapted to the Israeli mentality.[13] An accomplished sea captain whose life was formed in an entirely North American culture, Oko could never attempt, try as he might, to integrate himself into a tradition of struggle forged in clandestinity. In effect, Oko would not adapt to the culture of secrecy embodied by Haganah. The captain continually demanded accountability, competence, and seamanship, but his Israeli employers ultimately were less interested in the means than in the ends. Even if Oko and Gladys (who was quite probably more of an ardent Zionist than her husband) entertained the idea of settling permanently in Israel, this was at best a fanciful pipe dream that in all likelihood would never have worked. Admittedly, Oko was not easy to deal with. Equal parts pragmatist and idealist, he was high-strung, more than a touch neurotic, often outspoken, and quick to sense slights. On the other hand, Oko was extremely loyal to his crew and to the ship's owners even when he disagreed and clashed with them. He was also relentless in following through with tasks until the end. It is in this context that we should consider that even if he were ostensibly part owner of the *Kefalos* — at least on paper — Oko had tirelessly and unselfishly served Israel for seven months. In fact, in January 1949, at the time of the Haifa payoff/payout, neither he nor Gladys enjoyed any visible means of support; they had both heeded the urgent call of Israel, hurriedly packed, and left behind a recently completed home in the United States. The couple would return to the San Francisco area penniless and exhausted and would find little immediate recognition for their services.

Of course, not everyone who served on the ship's crew, or who assisted in the enterprise in one fashion or another, did so with the Okos' strong convictions. The motives of the crew members, and what might be labeled the entourage of the *Kefalos*, varied widely. They ranged from the need of employment and money to adventure, to friendship, to ties with other crew members, as well certainly to the desire to help the Israelis and their fellow Jews in the Balkans. Many of these individuals could have stayed home in safety, found less risky work, or simply looked the other way. In effect, there were numerous reasons for them to abstain from participation in the ship's missions. Whatever their motivations, they found themselves inextricably involved in a common operation to further the cause of the nascent state of Israel. The odyssey of the ship with three names may well have been a minor footnote in a much larger historical narrative with far-flung international dimensions, but for many of those who were directly affected, it was a singularly significant life-affirming and life-changing experience.

Back in Point Reyes in early 1949, exhausted by the travails of the past several months and devoid of resources, Gladys wrote a poignant letter that encapsulates the couple's approach to life:

> We are quite content to sink our roots in a small place (our bailiwick). The world may be large, but no man, after all, can occupy more than a fragment of it at one time. We happen to be convinced that Inverness is one of the happier fragments. A place is people. We like these people. And we like this way of life. You may be too young for a small town. It would destroy you if you could not find full expression for yourselves. But there is a prodigious legacy of work to be done here by us. We'll *always* be all right. Our best at least. Fortunately neither of us is ambitious for fame and fortune.[14]

No doubt, Inverness was mighty small in comparison with the vast expanses that the Okos had traveled during their voyages aboard the *Kefalos*. But despite their professed modesty and lack of ambition, as they settled into a new life, the Okos had abundantly demonstrated a remarkable ability to unselfishly assist their fellow human beings.

Epilogue
After the Kefalos

The Okos

Worn out and destitute, Oko and Gladys returned to Inverness in early 1949. Devoid of resources, in the aftermath of their return they sold prized possessions to make ends meet, obtained at least one short-term loan, and lived "on the hospitality of friends and acquaintances."[1] Oko never returned to the sea in an active capacity. Instead, he undertook the revitalization of the Inverness Yacht Club, almost single-handedly rehabilitating the institution. He also took a serious interest in Sir Francis Drake's journey to the area in 1579, and became a prominent student–researcher–explorer of the Golden Hind's exploits.[2] Some time in the mid-1950s Oko founded a real estate business, which was not very successful. He also opened an English-themed, pub-like restaurant that likewise did not meet with success. Perhaps more importantly, he took an active interest in civic and public affairs, coming to the defense of farmers and property owners whose interests were threatened by federal and state park services.[3] In characteristic fashion, Oko always seemed to side with the "little guys." In 1958, Oko went to England for a delicate operation to repair damage caused years earlier after being shot. Although seemingly fit much of his life, Oko's health deteriorated in the early 1960s, and he died of a heart attack in September 1963 at the age of fifty-eight.[4] Following his death, Oko received a stirring tribute from the California Legislature.[5] As for Gladys, she did not fare well after Oko's death. Without him, she seemed rudderless. Three years after Oko's death, Gladys liquidated the couple's estate, married a childhood friend, and moved to Massachusetts to take care of her sick husband. She, too, died of a heart attack in 1977 at the age of seventy-one.[6]

The Crew

Little is known about the majority of the *Kefalos*'s original crew following the ship's odyssey. However, some interesting details of their lives are known. Eric Forbes, Julio Larrauri ("Bermeo"), Carlos Sánchez, and Francisco Corino returned to the Bay Area (the latter two at least for some unspecified time), to continue to work as sailors and fishermen on the West Coast.[7] Félix Apaolaza, after traveling to Mexico, also worked in a factory in Central America and eventually as well in Peru. Harald Kalte ("Finland") sailed in the Caribbean in the 1950s. Casiano Totoricagüena and Lorenzo Aldalur, about whom little is known after their time aboard the *Kefalos*, settled in the New York region, where they worked in various capacities, but apparently not as sailors.[8] And Carlos Blanco Aguinaga returned to Mexico to continue his studies, earning an advanced degree. He became a literature professor and has had a long professional life in universities in the United States and Spain. Arye Kesselman and Jack Rothman, as noted earlier, died shortly after the ship's first arrival in Israel, on 21 November and 31 December 1948, respectively. Nathaniel Ratner returned to Chicago, married, raised a family, and worked as a plant engineer (1950–1954) and then as a plant and general manager of several companies (1954–1984). Robert Keller lived in a kibbutz for a while, then became director of supplies for Ta'as, then joined the American–Israel Paper Mills, and was associated with the Israel Productivity Institute. After returning to the United States, Keller worked in a number of businesses, notably the American Trade and Industrial Development with Israel, Inc., and export–import apparel and fashion enterprises.[9] And, finally, Al Ellis returned to the United States, traveling back and forth between the U.S. and Israel before settling down on the West Coast and later in Maryland. After completing a degree in aeronautical engineering at the University of California, Ellis worked in the aerospace industry. He eventually acquired a great deal of notoriety — and was involved in some controversy regarding credit — for his pioneering work on the development of pilotless drones.[10]

The Purchasers of the *Kefalos* and Other Important Figures

Raphael Recanati and Elie Schalit/Shalit, members of Haganah's Procurement delegation in New York, became important magnates in the shipping business as well as other enterprises. For instance, Recanati became the operations manager of the Israel–America Line, Ltd., and Schalit its traffic manager.[11] Both enjoyed long careers in commercial ventures. Teddy Kollek, the chief operative of Haganah in the United States at the time of the *Kefalos* missions, had an extraordinarily lengthy and successful political career, becoming mayor of Jerusalem for nearly three decades.[12] Eliyahu Sacharov, a Haganah Procurement officer who was active in the Mexican arms deal along with Hank Greenspun, developed and for a time headed the Israeli arms industry (Ta'as) after the War of Independence, retired as a Lieutenant Colonel from the IDF in 1952, and then worked in private business.[13] Finally, Levi Skolnik/Shkolnik, changed his name to Levi Eshkol, became a prominent politician, and served as the third Prime Minister of Israel (1963–1969).

Idalia Affair Protagonists

The two main figures, Hank Greenspun and Leland Robert Lewis, led distinctly different lives after 1948. Greenspun became an important and colorful newspaper editor (*Las Vegas Sun*), a vehement critic of Senator Joe McCarthy, a real estate developer, and an important long-time public figure in Las Vegas. He was indicted and tried twice for his involvement in the arms smuggling operation and illegal export of armament. Acquitted the first time, he was found guilty and fined after the second trial in 1950, although he served no time in prison. Lewis had his prized schooner/yacht confiscated by U.S. authorities, wrote books about the sea and the southern coasts of California and Mexico, and retired to Carmel, California.

Mexican Principals

Miguel Alemán served as President (1946–1952), and General Gilberto R. Limón Márquez was his Secretary of Defense (1946–1952). David Gritzewsky, an important participant in the arms operation in Tampico, worked as an industrial engineer in Monterrey. Elias Sourasky, a central figure in the purchase of the arms, afterward continued his significant involvement in industrial enterprises, banking, and insurance companies in Mexico. In addition, he became a renowned philanthropist, contributing important sums to educational, cultural, and scientific institutions and organizations in Mexico and Israel.

The Ship

The *Dromit* became the first cargo ship in the new company (from Ha'Mossad Le'Aliya Bet to Ha'Mossad Le'Aliya to Shoam to Zim). Its official number was 33. It served in the Israeli merchant marine until its official retirement on 6 March 1962, and was scrapped in 1963.[14] After some forty-five years at sea and seemingly endless sailings, the rust bucket had finally come to rest.

Appendix 1

Instructions to Master
Source: AJA 883.

New York
June 12, 1948

I. DESTINATION:

(1) Destination of vessel to be B.A. and first call at Tamp. is for bunkering purposes.
     From B.A. destination to be China.

(2) Crew should know such destination even after departure from Tamp.

(3) Master will be advised of any change in destination by new instructions.

(4) If for any reason entering Tamp. not desirable, Master to be instructed to cruise in Gulf
     Mex. until advised to proceed to Tamp. or to any other port.

II. PORTS OF CALL:

(1) Upon arrival in Tamp. papers will, in all probability not be examined. If examined,
     Master to explain change of name as caused by reluctance of crew to sail under K.

(2) In Tamp. Master to see the following:

                David Gritzewsky
                Productos Chemicos Estrella
                Tampico, Mexico.

     David to be asked to place person to person telephone call to NY at following:

                Hyman Padover
                EN dicott 2-2775.

     Afterwards, the Master will talk to H.P.

(3) In Tamp. Master to use his judgment to prevent harmful behavior from local persons.
     Nobody to be allowed to come aboard with the exception of the Agent or many other
     essential person which will not endanger the voyage by his presence on the vessel.
     NOTE CAREFULLY!

(4) Second port of call to be indicated to the Master while he is at first port.

(5) In Tamp. vessel to load bunkers up to full capacity of bunkers and as much as
     possible oil in barrels so as to permit reaching of final destination plus 2,000
     miles.

III. CABLES:

(1) Cables to be addressed to following:

                JACKSON
                SHIPSAGE
     and bearing signature KAY.

(2) Master to cable every 24 hours consumption and speed. Two days before
     reaching Tamp. Master to cable as follows:

                ETA 48.

(3) Cables from N.Y. to be signed JACKSON.

CABLES (Cont.)

(4) Cables from Mexico to be signed HYMAN PADOVER.

(5) If any normal trouble (machinery and the like) occur, Master to cable
     using words specifically.

-2-

III. AGENTS:

(1) In each port of call Master to use services of appointed agents for disbursements and any other problems concerning the vessel.

(2) Name of appointed Agent to be communicated to Master before arrival at port of call.

IV. CREW:

(1) Office to be advised of any changes in the crew at ports of call.

(2) In case of discharge before completion of voyage or at completion crew to be paid wages due to them plus air transportation to N.Y.

(3) Master to do utmost to develop teamwork with crew.

(4) If on the way South toomuch talk develops Master to cable as follows:

"CREW WORK UNSATISFACTORY" or "PARTIAL UNSATISFACTORY WORK" according to the extent of the talk. Master to send such cable only in case of disturbing talk and the to wait for instructions.

(5) At first port of call, crew to be kept on board working as much as possible.

V. FINANCES:

(1) Crew will be paid upon completion of voyage.

(2) Advances to be made at port of call according to Master's judgment, never in excess of wages due crew taking into account allotments.

(3) Advances in foreign port to be made in local currencies calculated at the offical rate of exchange.

(4) The Master is to cover all expenditures by vouchers.

(5) Accounts to be kept by the purser and to be mailed thru Agent in every port, after arrival, by Master.

(6) Even in case vessel trade in Europe after first voyage, financial matters to be centralized in N.Y., unless otherwise instructed.

VI. NAME OF VESSEL:

(1) Name to be changed on the way to Tamp. to Esperanza if and when advised by cable. (If no advise received name to be remains unchanged.) Master will be advised as follows:

HAPPY BIRTHDAY

(2) If Esperanza not suitable, name to be Adelanta. In such case, Master will be advised as follows:
HAPPY 42ND BIRTHDAY

(3) If both names referred to above not suitable the name to be Pinzon. Master to be advied as follows:
HAPPY 43RD BIRTHDAY

(4) Change of name will be approved by Pan Consulate in NY. Reason for change to be the reluctance of the crew to sale under K.

(5) Master to confirm change of name as follows
THANKS FOR WISHES

-3-

VII. SPECIAL SUPPLIES:

Master will be supplied with various protective instruments at first port of call.

VIII. GENERAL:

(1) Vessel to be conducted as a normal commercial venture. Vessel belongs to a commercial company and is managed xxx as any merchant vessel.

(2) Master has full responsibility of vessel and of all phases of the voyage and is in command of the voyage.

(3) Instructions while at sea or in ports to be received only from N.Y. unless otherwise instructed.

(4) Vessel may be escorted from Italy. Master will be advised to this effect.

(5) Master is holder of 50% of the company's shares. D.S. holds other 50% and is the representative of people in Switzerland.

(6) If any change of plan occurs execute carefully instructions.

(7) If vessel intercepted in mid-ocean Master to explain commercial nature of the vessel, and give destination as detailed in paragraph #I.

Appendix 2

Crew List of the Panamanian s/s *PINZON* ex *Kefalos*, Captain A.S. Oko, Jr.

Source: AJA 883.

CREW LIST.

of the Panamanian s/s "PINZON" ex "Kefalos" Captain A. S. Oko

No.	NAME.	Nationality.	Occupation.
1.	A. S. Oko Jr.	U.S.A.	Captain.
2.	Eric H. Forbes.	"	1st Mate.
3.	Carlos Sanchez.	Uruguayan.	3rd "
4.	Pedro Ilves	U.S.A.	Chief Eng.
5.	Fel. Apaolaza.	Costa Rican.	1st Asst Eng.
6.	August Karjus.	Estonian.	2nd " "
7.	Jose Bianco.	Spanish.	3rd " "
8.	Jack Rothman.	U.S.A.	Radio Oper.
9.	Gladys Z. Oko.	"	Purser.
10.	Peter Stojnic.	Yugoslavian.	Electrician.
11.	Julio Larrari.	Spanish.	Bosun.
12.	Francisco Corina.	"	Carpenter.
13.	William Wolders.	Dutch.	Sailor.
14.	Lorenzo Aldalur.	Spanish	"
15.	Joaquin Torrealday.	Spanish	"
16.	Florentino Ferreira.	Spanish.	"
17.	Harald Kalte.	Finnish.	"
18.	Honorio Fernandez.	Cuban.	"
19.	Perfecto Piñeiro.	Spanish.	"
20.	Hector Pineda.	Honduran.	"
21.	Jose Gacheiro.	Spanish.	Greaser.
22.	Everisto de Medisos.	Portuguese	"
23.	Joao de Almeidas.	"	"
24.	Miguel Urriolabeita.	Spanish.	Fireman.
25.	Calixto Diaz.	"	"
26.	Avaro Rufino Nuñez.	Portuguese.	"
27.	Emilio Suarez.	Spanish.	Wiper.
28.	Vicent Estrada.	"	"
29.	Jose Oliva Mateos.	"	"
30.	Ernest Borrego.	"	Steward.
31.	Daniel Dewitt.	U.S.A.	Cook.
32.	Jose Luiz.	Portuguese.	
33.	Jaime Rivera.	"	Sailor. (O.S.)
34.	Ricardo Gutiérrez.	Chilean.	Messman.
35.	Carlos Blanco.	Mexican.	"
36.	Cantana Totoricaguera.	Spanish.	"
37.	Philip Kellison.	U.S.A.	Officer.
38.	Jose Rivera.	Mexican.	Fireman.

Jose Rivero

Tampico Tam

A. S. Oko Jr.
Master.

Nathaniel Ratner   U.S.A.   1st Asst Eng.

No.	NAME.	Nationality.	Occupation.
1.	A. S. Oko Jr.	U.S.A.	Captain.
2.	Eric E. Forbes.		1st Mate.
3.	Carlos Sanchez.	Uruguayan.	3rd. "
4.	~~Pieter Dijvas~~	~~U.S.A.~~	~~Chief Eng.~~
5.	Félix Apaolaza.	Costa Rican.	1st Asst Eng.
6.	~~August Kariug.~~	~~Swedish.~~	~~2nd " "~~
7.	Jose Blanco.	Spanish.	3rd. " "
8.	Jack Rothman.	U.S.A.	Radio Oper.
9.	Gladys Z. Oko.	"	Purser.
10.	~~Peter Stojnic.~~	~~Yugoslavian.~~	~~Electrician.~~
11.	Julio Larrari.	Spanish.	Boswn.
12.	Francisco Coring.	"	Carpenter.
13.	William Wolders.	Dutch.	Sailor.
14.	Lorenzo Aldalur.	Spanish.	"
15.	Joaquin Torrealday.	Spanish.	"
16.	Florentino Ferreira.	Spanish.	"
17.	Harald Kalte.	Finnish.	"
18.	Honorio Fernandez.	Cuban.	"
19.	Perfecto Piñeiro.	Spanish.	"
20.	Hector Pineda.	Honduran.	"
21.	Jose Cacheiro.	Spanish.	Greaser.
22.	Everisto de Medisos.	Portuguese	"
23.	Joao de Almeidas.	"	"
24.	Miguel Urriolabeita.	Spanish.	Fireman.
25.	Calixto Diaz.	"	"
26.	Avaro Rufino Nuñez.	Portuguese.	"
27.	Emilio Suarez.	Spanish.	Wiper.
28.	Vicent Estrada.	"	"
29.	Jose Oliva Mateos.	"	"
30.	Ernest Borrego.	"	Steward.
31.	Daniel Dewitt.	U.S.A.	Cook.
32.	Jose Luiz.	Portuguese.	"
33.	Jaime Rivera.		Sailor. (O.S)
34.	Ricardo Gutiérrez.	Chilean.	Messman.
35.	Carlos Blanco.	Mexican.	"
36.	Casiano Totoricaguera.	Spanish.	"
37.	~~Philip Kellison.~~	~~U.S.A.~~	~~Officer.~~
38.	Jose Rivera.	Mexican.	Fireman.

Jose Ruis

Tampico Tam.

A. Oko Jr.

A. S. Oko Jr,
Master.

Nathaniel Ratner   USA.   1st Asst Engr.
Robert Keller   USA.   2nd mate
Arye Kanelman   Palestinian   2nd Radio Op.
Abraham Elyacoff   USA   Supercargo

Ruth Tartakoff

Tartakoo

Appendix 3

Crew Members' Ages and Length of Service at Sea
August-September, 1948 Voyage

Sources: AJA 883, Ancestry.com, and other primary and secondary sources

No.	Name	Age	Length of Service at Sea [years]
1.	A. S. Oko Jr.	43	ca. 10 [1922-26, 1942-48]
2.	Eric E. Forbes	35	15-18,*
3.	Carlos Sánchez	30	unknown,*
5.	Félix Apaolaza	34	unknown,*
7.	José Blanco	35	no information,*
8.	Jack Rothman	37	USMM, WWII
9.	Gladys Z. Oko	42	none
11.	Julio Larrauri	30	fisherman in Spain,*
12.	Francisco Corino	35	12,*
13.	William Wolders	39	22
14.	Lorenzo Aldalur	25	4
15.	Joaquín Torrealday	33	11
16.	Florentino Ferreira	49 [?]	unknown
17.	Harald Kalte	32	11
18.	Honorio Fernández	32 or 33	6 or 8 [a]
19.	Perfecto Piñeiro	34	16
20.	Hector Pineda	25	4 or 8 [b]
21.	José Cacheiro	46	3-10 [c]
22.	Everisto de Medisos	39	3
23.	Joao de Almeida	51	31
24.	Miguel Urriolabeitia	35	20
25.	Calixto Díaz	54	26
26.	Álvaro Rufino Núñez	31	unknown [d]
27.	Emilio Suárez	45	21
28.	Vicent Estrada [e]	51	20
29.	José Oliva Mateos	32 or 33	5 months
30.	Ernesto Borrego	46 or 47	30
31.	Daniel Dewitt	41 or 42	unknown

32. José Luiz	31 or 32	unknown [f]
33. Jaime Rivera	20 or 21	2
34. Ricardo Gutiérrez	no information	no information
35. Carlos Blanco	21	none
36. Casiano Totoricagüena	no information	no information
38. José Rivera	no information	no information
Nathaniel Ratner	26	served at sea in WWII [g]
Robert Keller	24	Merchant Marine, officer in WWII[h]
Arye Kesselman	23	none
Abraham Elazaroff [Al Ellis]	22	about 1 [i]

Notes

* Denotes crew member who had served previously on *Aries/Adelanto*. Ilves and Manresa had also served on that vessel but did not make the trip from Mexico to Tel Aviv.

a. This individual's full name was Honorio Román Cortinas Fernández. However, he is routinely referred in nearly all documents simply as Honorio Fernández.

b. Discrepancies in documentation. 3 years service in 1947 according to one document; 9 years service in 1949 according to another.

c. Discrepancies in service due to descriptions of various positions held at different times: as oiler (3-10 years in 1947-1949), fireman (25-26 years in 1952) and trimmer (25 years in 1949).

d. Only one individual with this precise name, but document has no information on experience at sea. There is another person with a similar name but different spellings, but he does not appear to be the same individual.

e. Crew member's exact name was Vicente Valebona Estada. A 1953 ship manifest lists his length of service as 30 years, which is probably exaggerated.

f. Appears on many lists as a cook, 2nd cook, and assistant cook. However, on a February, 1948 manifest, an individual with an identical name is listed as a "porter." The latter person may or may not be the same individual since this is a common name.

g. Served in U.S. Navy four years. Full Lieutenant. Listed his military specialty during the War as "Naval Engineering and Line Officer."

h. Served on two Victory ships, October 1945-April, 1946.

i. Served on two merchant ships, October, 1947-May, 1948.

Appendix 4

Crew Salaries
Source: AJA 883 and other primary
and secondary sources

	Name	Occupation	Salary
1.	A. S. Oko Jr.*	Captain	4,702.50 U.S. $[1, 2]
2.	Eric E. Forbes*	1st Mate	4,363.85
3.	Carlos Sánchez *	3rd Mate	2,894.02
4.	Félix Apaolaza*	1st Asst. Eng.	2,434.75
5.	Jose Blanco*	3rd Asst. Eng.	1,787.25
6.	Jack Rothman*	Radio Oper.	1,022.97
7.	Gladys Z. Oko *	Purser	7.00
8.	Julio Larrauri *	Boswn	2,486.33
9.	Francisco Corino*	Carpenter	2,265.00
10.	William Wolders*	Sailor	1,719.33
11.	Lorenzo Aldalur *	Sailor	1,702.55
12.	Joaquin Torrealday*	Sailor	1,410.22
13.	Florentino Ferreira*	Sailor	790.67
14.	Harald Kalte*	Sailor	1,917.17
15.	Honorio Fernández*	Sailor	1,003.02
16.	Perfecto Piñeiro*	Sailor	1,484.47
17.	Hector Peneda*	Sailor	927.77
18.	José Cacheiro*	Greaser	3,111.32
19.	Everisto de Medisos*	Greaser	1,360.38
20.	Joao de Almeidas*	Greaser	749.13
21.	Miguel Urriolabeitia*	Fireman	1,464.22
22.	Calixto Díaz*	Fireman	755.54
23.	Álvaro Rufino Núñez *	Fireman	748.60
24.	Emilio Suárez*	Wiper	1,271.17
25.	Vicent Estrada*	Wiper	808.69
26.	José Oliva Mateos*	Wiper	808.67
27.	Ernest Borrego*	Steward	2,567.97
28.	Daniel Dewitt*	Cook	1,148.76
29.	José Luiz *	Cook	1,986.50
30.	Jaime Rivera*	Sailor (O.S.)	1,462.72

31. Ricardo Gutiérrez*	Messman	1,282.57
32. Carlos Blanco*	Messman	735.91
33. Casieno Totoricabuena*	Messman	1,244.02
34. José Rivera *	Fireman	1,210.08
35. Nathaniel Ratner *	1st Asst. Engr.	3,538.33
36. Robert Keller *	2nd Mate	687.50
37. Arye Kesselman*	2nd Radio Op.	352.30
38. Abraham Elazaroff *	Supercargo	352.38
39. Miguel López**	unknown	881.25 [3]
40. Mariano Manresa+	2nd Mate	507.50 [4]
41. Bernard Marks ++	unknown	228.75 [5]
42. Francisco Morales**	Messman	445.67
43. [Manuel] Ramón Ruiz **	unknown	500.67
44. Joaquín Martínez**	unknown	906.25
45. [Eleuterio] Herrero Poza**	Wiper	594.20
46. Salvador Mirralles [sic]**	unknown	489.42
47. Leslie Solomon ++	unknown	400.00
48. Gonzalo Salazar**	unknown	546.63
49. Juan Alonso/Alonzo **	2nd Cook/Baker	813.50
50. Alfonso Álverez [sic?]**	Fireman	596.45
51. Manuel Díaz **	unknown	1,015.52
52. Benito Echeverría**	3rd Cook	634.25
53. Samuel Habuba**	unknown	368.33
54. Peeter Ilves +	Chief Eng.	1,056.25
55. Donald Jackson ++	unknown	122.90
56. Castaldi Vincenzo [sic]**	unknown	482.00
57. August Karjus +	2nd Asst Eng.	1,019.00

Total $ 72,174.12

Source: Information is from an undated handwritten list compiled by Oko. Source: AJA, Microfilm 883. Spelling and names have been preserved as they exist on the list. First names have been added when missing. In "And It Was So," Notes 3, this notation: "57 men went through the ship – 37 to 43 in crew."
1. On margin after Oko's name: "(shore allowance to be completed)"
2. * Traveled on ship from Tampico to Tel Aviv (nos. 1-38), N=38.
3. ** Crew members who served on the ship after Naples (nos. 39, 42-46, 48-53, and 56), N=13.
4. + Traveled only from NYC to Tampico (nos. 40, 54 and 55), N=3.
5. ++ Did not travel with the ship or their fate is unknown (nos. 41, 47 and 55), N=3.
6. Not included in list is Peter Stojnic, electrician, who traveled from NYC to Tampico and was discharged there from vessel.

Appendix 5

Captain Oko's Complete Ship Log
Source: AJA 883

<u>S/S KEFALOS</u>   PASAGE TO TAMPICO FROM NEW YORK

JUNE	NOON POSITION	RUN	SPEED	CRSE	TOT.DIST.	
14	Ambrose Light	dept. 8:30 p.m.DST				draft fwd 9' aft 12'7"
15	35 15N 72 38W	210	8.5			
16	32 44N 75 50W	200	8	216d T		
17	30 48N 77 30W	148	6.2	210		
18	28 N 79 46w	207	8.6	215	850	
19zx25z52Nzx82zl5Wzx zx181 z2x2z zxz 1021						
19	25 42N 79 56w	138	5.8	185	988	
20	23 52N 82 15w	181	7,5	var	1169	
21	23 15n 85 51w	203	8.1	260	1372	
22	23 n 90 16w	245	10.0	267	1617	
23	22 47n 94 24w	228	9.5	267	1845	9:25pm reduced to 30 revs
24	22 29n 97 29,5w	186	var	var	2031	arrived Tampico 3:10p.m.

TAMPICO TO TEL AVIV

AUG	NOON POSITION	RUN	SPEED	CRSE	TOT.DIST.	
3	Tampico, Mexico	dept. 12:30p.m.				draft fwd 13'8" aft18'10" M 16'3"
4	22 17n 94 24w	187	7.95	90	2218	
5	22 47n 90 53w	198	8.25	81t	2416	
6	22 41n8 87 31w	190	7.91	92	2606	
7	22 20n 84 20w	180	7.5	77	2786	
8	24 16n 80 40w	211	9.1	74	2997	
9	28 32n 79 42w	271	11.29	var	3268	
10	31 21.5 77 54w	202	8.41	var	3470	
11	33 34.5 75	200	18.55	48	3670	
12	35 37 72 10	187	7.79	47	3857	advanced clocks 1 hour
13	36 36 69 03	163	7.08	69	4020	
14	37 49 65 29	185	7.7	67	4205	
15	39 21 61 39	202	8.41	63	4407	
16	40 15 57 56	179	7.45	72	4586	advanced clocks 1 hour
17	41 16 54	189	7.87	72	4775	
18	41 12 49 51	187	8.13	91	4962	
19	48 28 45 20	201	8.37	86	5163	
20	41 23 40 57	198	8.25	92	5361	advanced clocks 1 hour
21	41 20 36 41	192	8.34	91	5553	
22	40 58 33 04	166	6.91	98	5719	
23	41 00 28 43	197	8.2	90	5916	dead reconingn no sun
24	40 25 13	172	7.16	111	6088	advanced clocks 1hr
25	39 12 21 23w	185	8	105	6273	
26	38 08 17 35	189	7.87	109	6462	
27	36 35 13 52	200	8.33	118	6662	
28	36 11 9 35	209	8.7	97	6871	clocks advanced to GCT
29	36 5 12	216	9.4	var	7087	/Gibralter 10:50p 8.5 mi
30	36 34 35w	226	9.41	81	7313	
31	37 23n 3 05E	183	7.62	75	7496	
SEPT						
1	37 30 6 47e	176	7.33	88	7672	
2	37 16 11 02E	206	8.95	var	7878	12:40 cape bon 10 mi
3						conning lites thru Sicily S

S/S KEFALOS   TAMPICO TO TEL AVIV   1948   2

	NOON POSITION	RUN	SPEED	CRSE	TOT.DIST.	COMMENTS
SEPT						
3	35 12N 14 34E	213	8.87	var	8091	to go 1026m (5da)
4	34 47 18 41E	205	8.54	97	8296	to go 821m
5	34 28 22 31	192	8.34	95	8488	clocks advanced 1hr
6	34 22 26 36	203	8.5	92	8691	to go 436mi
7	34 03 31 09	226	9.41	95	8917	to go 210 mi
8	Tel Aviv	210	9.4		9127	from Tampico 7096mi 35d

TO NAPLES

12	Dept Tel Aviv 6:15 a.m. standing off, various courses and speeds					
13	32 46N 34 42E	100	standing off, var cses and spds Revs. 60			
	Departure Haifa 10 p.m.					
14	32 58 32 21	119	8.5	276	119	
15	33 18 28 43	185	7.4	277	304	clocks retarded 1 hr
16	33 58 25 36	165	6.8	285	467	
17	35 16 21 50	205	8.5	293	671	
18	36 44 18 03	204	8.5	286	875	
19	38 23 15 38.5	180	7.2	var	1055	Cape Spartevento 4pts 0450h
	0645 entered Messina Straits cleared 1054					

SPLIT-BAKAR-HAIFA

NOV						
8	4p.m. depart Naples					
9		130	6.5	var	130	noon Stromboli Isl 3m beam
10	38 30N 17 13E				302	NEgales watersouts th and ltr
11			6.5	var		
12	10:45pm arrive Split		5.5			headwinds
13	7:25am depart Split					
14	11:50am arrive Bakar					
15	8:20 a.m. depart Bakar					
16	11:43am arrive Split Depart 11:49am					
17	40 56N 18 03E	186.5	7.7	var	186.5	3:30p Pt San Cataldo 8mi
18	38 19 19	191	7.9	varE	377.0	
19	35 47.5 22 34	187	7.8	133	564.0	clocks advanced 1 hr
20	34 22 24 51	147	6.4	101t	711	
21	33 35 28 40	197	8.17	101	908	
22	33 05 31 45	171	7.13	98	1079	
23	7:53 a.m. arrive Haifa					

SPLIT-BAKAR-HAIFA

28	8:40 p.m. depart Haifa					
29	33 05 33 05	95	6.3	277	95	
30	33 48 29 50	179	7.4	284	274	
DEC						
1	34 10 27 25	123	5.1	280	397	
2	34 16 25 07	114	4.7	274	511	
3	35 37 21 58	176	7.3	298	687	
4	37 56 19 41	177	7.3	322T	864	
5	40 47 18 09	186	7.8	var	1040	Noon Brindisi 12mi off Master Conning W Coast Italy
6	8:05pm arrive Split 3h 55m detention at sea, no water passng to boiler					
	42 42 16 00	155	6.4	var	1195	(1295 Haifa to Split)

S/S KEFALOS   .3

DEC	NOON POSITION	RUN	SPEED	CRSE	TOT.DIST.

7   11 a.m. depart Split   Capt. Bozo Koracic conning minefields to Bakar
8   4:50 p.m. arrive Bakar

15 11:45am depart Bakar
16 10:45pm arrive Split 10:46pm depart Split
17 42 09,5 16 42.5 93.9 7.1 var 1353.4
18 39 50N 18 45E   179   7.4 var 1532.4   1215p C.Sta.Maria Di Lenca
19 38 35   18 40   72   S   1604.4   dead reconing
    Hove to throughout night in Ely gale, rough to precipitous seas,
      currently at Half Ahead for steerage way on 150deg true
20 36 59   19 58   113   4.7 149 1717
21 35 20   20 39   103   4.3 161 1820
22 34 30   23 51   168   7   101 1988
23 33 53   27 01   163   6.6 104 2152
24 33 17   30 14   167   7   167 2319   Christmas eve and no
                                              proper GROG aboard
25 32 58   33 47   185   7.7 95   2499.4 Merry Christmas
                                              Arrival Hiafa
                                              To Go: 60 mi.

[1] *The* Larranga *with armament during World War II, 16 November 1942. Source: NARA, Record Group 26 (Records of the U.S. Coast Guard) Entry A1 180 (Merchant Vessel Information Files, 1939-1952).*

[2] *The* Kefalos *in early 1948 in the vicinity of Montevideo. The photograph, credited to Raul Maya, is from the William Schell Collection. It was made available to me by Mr. Schell.*

[3] *Oko captured the ship's disastrous condition at Portland, Maine. Source: Courtesy of the Jacob Rader Marcus Center of the American Jewish Archives, Cincinnati, Ohio; AJA, 883. All photographs with this call number are from the same source.*

[4] *Manresa and Gladys in route from New York City to Tampico, June, 1948. AJA, 883.*

[5] *Photograph of ship in the middle of the River Pánuco in Tampico, June–August, 1948. AJA, 883.*

[6] *Barrels and cases of water or fuel loaded in Tampico. AJA, 883.*

[7] *Jewish volunteers in Tampico recruited by Haganah to serve on the ship.*
Courtesy of the Ratner Family.

[8] *Panamanian sailing papers issued to First Mate Eric Forbes by the consul of that republic for the voyage, New York, 2 June 1948.*
Courtesy of the Forbes Family.

ESTADOS UNIDOS MEXICANOS

FORMA 12

SERVICIO DE MIGRACION

VALOR $ 5.00

181979

TARJETA DE IDENTIFICACIÓN PARA TRIPULANTES

NACIONALIDAD / NATIONALITY __U.S.A__

ESTADO CIVIL / SINGLE OR MARRIED __SINGLE__

COMPLEXION / BUILD __FAIR-__

ESTATURA / HEIGHT __5' 8"__

RAZA / RACE __

COLOR / COLOR __WHITE__

SEÑAS PARTICULARES / IDENTIFICATION MARKS __

LUGAR DE CONTRATACION / PLACE WHERE CONTRACTED __N.Y. CITY N.Y.__

NOMBRE DEL VAPOR / NAME OF STEAMER __S/S KEFALOS__

VENCE EL CONTRATO EN / CONTRACT EXPIRES __

AGENTES CONSIGNATARIOS / AGENTS __

OTROS DATOS / OTHER INFORMATION __CHIEF OFFICER__

NOMBRE DEL TRIPULANTE / NAME OF SEAMAN __ERIC FORBES__

LUGAR Y FECHA / PLACE AND DATE __

FECHA DE NACIMIENTO / DATE OF BIRTH __

FIRMA DEL TRIPULANTE / SIGNATURE OF SEAMAN __

LUGAR DE NACIMIENTO / PLACE OF BIRTH __CANADA__

FIRMA DEL CAPITAN / SIGNATURE OF MASTER __

SAN FRANCISCA-CALIF

[9] *Ship document issued to First Mate Eric Forbes by the Mexican Government for the voyage, unknown where issued, undated. Courtesy of the Forbes Family.*

[10] *First Mate Eric Forbes, overboard, changing the ship's name. AJA, 883.*

[11] *The ship's bridge before carpenter Francisco Corino's changes. AJA, 883.*

[12] *The ship's bridge after carpenter Francisco Corino's changes. AJA, 883.*

[13] *M.V. Pinzon*
Source:www.photoship.co.uk/JAlbum%20Ships/
Old%20Ships%20P/slides/Pinzon-02.html

[14] *Gladys hanging laundry, most probably on the way to Tel Aviv. AJA, 883.*

[15] *After entering the Mediterranean, on captain's orders, some Jewish volunteers mounted machine guns on deck to defend the ship in the event of attacks from hostile forces. AJA, 883.*

[16] *Seven crewmen on board in Tel Aviv alongside a life-saver stenciled "S.S. M.A. PINZON. PANAMA" Source: Ben-Tzur, "An Arms Ship to Israel in the War of Independence S/S Kefalos > 'Dromit,'" p. 14.*

[17] *Photograph that captures the satisfaction of Oko and Gladys on way from Tel Aviv to Naples. Name Pinzon still visible on lifeboat. Source: Marin Independent Journal, 22 April 1961.*

[18] *Empty ship at Naples. Source: Palmach Museum.*

[19] *Melavim, radio operator and Israeli officials at Naples. Palmach Museum.*

[20] *Photograph taken from the ship on the day of arrival at Bakar, November, 1948, shows large numbers of refugees in front of a large building near the water's edge. Note railroad cars behind the olim. AJA, 883.*

[21] *This and the next photograph eloquently illustrate the refugees'*
downtrodden state as they boarded the ship at Bakar. AJA, 883.

[22] *Refugees boarding ship at Bakar. AJA, 883.*

[23] *The vessel swarming with people. Palmach Museum.*

[24] *Passengers apparently requesting, or fetching water. Undated.*
Courtesy of the Forbes Family.

[25] *An extremely crowded ship. Note laundry hanging in lower center of photograph. Undated. Courtesy of the Forbes Family.*

[26] *This and the next photograph of relaxed groups of immigrants during the second voyage are titled "Young people on the deck of the illegal immigrant ship 'Kefalos', 1948." This is factually incorrect since it was no longer illegal in late 1948 to migrate to Israel. Date on back of item call number 3883/4168 shows that the photograph is from second voyage from Bakar: 26/12/1948. Source: Yad Vashem Photo Archive.*

[27] *Explanation for this photograph in previous caption.*

[28] Musician with accordion. Source: AJA 883.

[29] A happy wedding party on board. AJA, 883.

[30] *Ship steaming toward Haifa with passengers, November-December, 1948,*
photograph taken by Baruch Geller, chief engineer of the Israeli vessel INS Maoz,
K 24. Source: www.palyam.org/English/ArmsShips/hy_Dromit.

[31] *Front left to right, Apaolaza, Gladys and Larrauri. Lifeboat still sports the name S.S. M.A. PINZON. AJA, 883.*

[32] *Gladys and four crew members. The only ones who can be identified with certainty are Larrauri (far right) and Apaolaza (squatting). AJA, 883.*

[33] *Corino at work with an unidentified companion who may have been Totoricagüena or Forbes. AJA, 883.*

[34] *Captain Oko was a strong proponent of safety drills at sea. Blanco Aguinaga is at the far left wearing a life vest. Courtesy of Carlos Blanco Aguinaga.*

Endnotes

Chapter 1. *The Rust Bucket*

1. The first epigraph is from Oko's "THE KEFALOS" (henceforth "THE KE-FALOS"). A copy of this document with Oko's extensive handwritten revisions is in the American Jewish Archives, microfilm no. 883, (henceforth AJA, 883). The second epigraph is from Oko's 1960 account (henceforth "1960 Account"). See Unpublished Sources in the Bibliography for complete references for these documents.

2. See www.shipbuildinghistory.com/history/shipyards/1major/inactive/bethsanfrancisco.htm. See also Daniel Strohmier, "A History of the Bethlehem Steel Company Shipbuilding and Ship Repairing Activities," *Naval Engineers Journal*, 77:2, 1963. There are several general brief overviews and histories of the ship, some of which can be found online. See the following: [1] www.sjohistorie.no/skip/d/Dicto%201917; [2] www.warsailors.com/freefleet/norfleetd.html (title "Other ships by the name *Dicto*"); [3] www.shipscribe.com/usnaux/AK/AK59.html;_[4] (a) www.palyam.org/English/ArmsShips/hy_Dromit (by Hillel Yarkoni, from his book *75 Years of Hebrew Shipping in Eretz, Israel*), and (b) www.hma.org.il/Museum/Templates/showpage.asp?DBID'1&LNGID'1&T-MID'84&FID'1753&PID'5055 (also from the same source); and [5] www.de.wikipedia.org/wiki/Dvora. See also Norske Veritas (Organization). *Register of Norwegian, Swedish, Danish, Finnish, and Icelandic ships and of Other Ships Classed with Det Norske Veritas*. Oslo: Det Norske Veritas, 1900s; and Tony Starke; William A. Schell, *Register of Merchant Ships Completed in 1917*. Peer-reviewed Kent, World Ship Society, 1998, 19. For the last days of the vessel, see *Marine News*, vol. XVI, No. 7, July 1962, 179; and Web page 4(b) to this note.

3. Bjørkelund, Leif M., and E. H. Kongshavn. *Våre gamle skip: skipshistorisk billedbok for Haugesund, Kopervik og Skudeneshavn*. [Aksdal]: Lokalhistorisk stiftelse, 1996, 355. I base the amount in U.S. dollars for 1917 on Øyvind

Eitrheim, Jan Tore Klovland, and Jan F. Qvigstad. "Historical Monetary Statistics for Norway 1819–2003," Norges Bank Occasional Papers No. 35, Oslo 2004. See Table A-2. Exchange rates monthly 1914–1940, 313.

4.   The Hoover Institution, *Register of the Commission for Relief in Belgium Records, 1914–1930.* Box 332, Folder 4, *Dicto*, 1918–1919. One of the earliest photographs of the *Dicto* shows the vessel with its owner's insignia on the chimney and a large banner on its side that reads "BELGIAN RELIEF"; in Bjørkelund, Leif M., and E. H. Kongshavn. *Våre gamle skip: skipshistorisk billedbok for Haugesund, Kopervik og Skudeneshavn.* [Aksdal]: Lokalhistorisk stiftelse, 1996, 355.

5.   Bjørkelund, Leif M., and E. H. Kongshavn. *Våre gamle skip: skipshistorisk billedbok for Haugesund, Kopervik og Skudeneshavn.* [Aksdal]: Lokalhistorisk stiftelse, 1996, 355. The amount in U.S. dollars for 1928 is based on Øyvind Eitrheim, Jan Tore Klovland, and Jan F. Qvigstad. See Table A-2. Exchange rates monthly 1914–1940, 313. A photograph of the *Dicto* under E. B. Aaby ownership ca. 1928–1933 online at www.shipscribe.com/usnaux/AK/AK59.html.

6.   E-mail from Mr. Torsten Hagneus of Vastra Frolunda, Sweden, March 4, 2009. The information is from Norske Veritas (Organization). Det Norske Veritas. *Register over norske, svenske, danske, finske og islandske skip.* Oslo, 1925–1968, 1931, No. 66; see also Steamers & Motorvessels, no. 77.

7.   It is not known how much the ship was sold for in 1933. On entering U.S. ownership, the vessel was assigned no. 232352 (its official number) by the U.S. Department of Commerce. Its radio call letters were WNEA.

8.   As *American Cardinal*, see *The Log*, vols. 22–24, 1933, 147; *Marine Engineering & Shipping Age*, vol. 38, 1933, 314; *Pacific Marine Review*, vol. 32, 1935, 282; *Marine News*, October, 1936, 84; *Marine News*, December, 1936, 119 (name changed to *Mallard*); *Annual Report of the Department of Health of the State of New Jersey*, 1936, 74; United States. *Bureau of Marine Inspection and Navigation Bulletin*, vols. 1–2, 1936, 23 Washington, DC: U.S. Government Printing Office; *The Baltimore Sun*, March 12, 1937, 29; Pacific Steam Navigation. *Sea Breezes: The Ship Lover's Digest,* vols. 19–20, 1955, 108. Liverpool [etc.]: Charles Birchall & Sons.

9.   Baughman, J. P. *The Mallorys of Mystic.* Middletown, CT: Wesleyan University Press, 1972, pp. 324–25 [n. 35, 388]; and *Marine News*, December 1936, 119 (name changed on 10 September 1936).

10. Baughman, *The Mallorys of Mystic*, 324–25.

11. National Archives and Records Administration (NARA) Record Group 41, U.S. Bureau of Marine Inspection and Navigation, entry 126, Official Number Files, 1876–1958, file for vessel no. 232352 (its official number), the *Larranga*. Information received courtesy of Ms. Kim Y. McKeithan, archives specialist at NARA, sent on 17 October 2008.

12. In the yearbooks titled *Merchant Vessels of the United States.* Washington, D.C.: U.S. Government Printing Office, for the years 1942–1949, the ship is listed as *Larranga* (595) and as *Larrañaga* (758) in 1942; as *Larranga* from 1943–1945; as *Larrañaga* during 1946–47; and as *Larranga* in 1948. The

permanent certificate of registry of the ship issued by the Department of Commerce when the ship was eventually surrendered to its new owner at Newport News, Virginia, on 30 September 1947 calls the vessel *Larrañaga*; see previous note for full reference. A large part of the confusion concerning *Larranga*/*Larrañaga* stems from the fact that the change from *Mallard* to its new name was done by telephone on 5 December 1941; see the certificate of registry referenced earlier in this note.

13. See www.shipscribe.com/usnaux/AK/AK59.html, title "Class Notes," compiled by Stephen S. Roberts. The author notes correctly that *Larranga* was often spelled *Larrañaga*.

14. A good photograph of the ship with armament can be found on the website cited in note 13 and is dated 16 November 1942. I have obtained a similar photograph, dated 26 October 1942, courtesy of Ms. Kim Y. McKeithan, archives specialist at NARA, sent on 28 May 2008. The latter photograph has a lower definition than the first one, but the vessel is clearly recognizable.

15. www.convoyweb.org.uk/hague/index.html. In this website, see page related to the *Larranga* titled "Ship Movements," with detailed dates of departures and arrivals, as well as destinations.

16. www.ibiblio.org/hyperwar/USN/Admin-Hist/173-ArmedGuards/173-AG-2.html, p. 19 (my emphasis). According to this site, "The principal source of information on Armed Guard Combat is the confidential Voyage Report which was prepared by the Armed Guard officer and sent to the Chief of Naval Operations." This report can be found in numerous subsequent works. For an erroneous report, probably intentionally misleading, that the ship had been sunk by an Italian submarine in the Atlantic in late December 1941, see *The Baltimore Sun*, 28 December 1941, article titled "Ship 'Larrinaga' Sunk, Says Rome," p. 6. Curiously, both accounts, unreliable and mistaken, may have been unwillingly related.

17. See www.shipscribe.com/usnaux/AK/AK59.html, title "Class Notes," compiled by Stephen S. Roberts. More on this matter in Property Management & Archive Record System (PMARS), basic ship data for the vessel *Larrañaga*, https://pmars.marad.dot.gov/detail.asp?Ship'2954. In particular, see Custody Card, back, which asserts that the ship was "time chartered to Iceland in 1944 & 1945" (https://pmars.marad.dot.gov/New-Cards/2954_5495AB.jpg).

18. www.convoyweb.org.uk/hague/index.html, title "Ship Search" *Larranga*; see also page titled "Ship Movements," www.convoyweb.org.uk/ports/index.html?search.php?vessel'LARRANGA~armain.

19. PMARS, Custody Card, front (https://pmars.marad.dot.gov/New-Cards/2954_5495AF.jpg).

20. "TROOP TRANSPORTS OFFERED FOR SALE: Maritime Commission Invites Bids on George Washington and the City of Norfolk." *New York Times* (1923–current file), 28 December 1946, retrieved from www.proquest.com.proxy.cc.uic.edu/ (accessed 27 May 2011). The article notes "The *Larrañaga* [was] once chartered by the Government of Iceland."

21. PMARS, Disposal Card. See https://pmars.marad.dot.gov/DisposalCard/All/2954_AF.jpg.

22. Ibid. All bids offered under Invitation for Bids PDX-279 were turned down. The bidding was renewed under Invitation for Bids PDX-330.

23. NARA, Record Group 178, Records of the U.S. Maritime Commission, Minutes of the Maritime Administration, 1946–1950. Information courtesy of Mr. Richard Peuser, assistant chief, Reference Section at NARA, 22 May 2009. See also PMARS, Custody Card, front (https://pmars.marad.dot.gov/DisposalCard/All/2954_AF.jpg). Additional information on how the purchase was made in Report of Earl L. Fuoss, title, Adolph Sigmund Oko, Jr., Washington, D.C., 21 October 1948, Federal Bureau of Investigation, file 100-19508. The FBI mistakenly asserts that "on June 24 1947, BONICOS took delivery of the ship SS Larrañaga." He would not take possession of the vessel until August–September, 1947.

24. PMARS, Custody Card, front (https://pmars.marad.dot.gov/NewCards/2954_5495AF.jpg).

25. NARA, Record Group 41, U.S. Bureau of Marine Inspection and Navigation, entry 126, Official Number Files, 1876–1958, file for vessel no. 232352 (its official number), *Larranga*. Information received courtesy of Ms. Kim Y. McKeithan, archives specialist at NARA, sent on 17 October 2008. In the section of the permanent certificate of registry titled "Why Surrendered," the document reads, "Vessel sold alien to Panamanian registry and flag. U.S. Maritime Commission Transfer Order No. C-5669, dated August 7, 1947." See *Merchant Vessels of the United States, 1948*, section "Vessels Sold or Transferred to Aliens," p. 867.

26. See *Merchant Vessels of the United States, 1948*, section "Vessels Sold or Transferred to Aliens," p. 867. For the transfer of the ship to Panamanian registry, see *Gaceta Oficial. Órgano de Estado* (Panama), issue no. 10465, 4 December 1947. Additional information on subsequent transfers and related administrative procedures in nos. 10501, 10628, 10655, and 10680. It is unclear how the new name was arrived at. There are two locations in Greece named Kefalos. However, a more plausible explanation for the ship's new name is that *kefalos* in Greek alludes to different fish (e.g., a mullet, chub, common grey mullet, dace, or flat-head grey mullet). Or perhaps, as Oko asserts, *kefalos* simply meant "big head," a term in keeping with fish with large heads. See "And It Was So," chapter 1, p. 3. See also an explanation regarding this document in Unpublished Sources in the Bibliography for this book.

27. Ancestry.com, New York Passenger Lists, 1920–1957, crew record of the *Alicante*, 21 March 1917; and Ellis Island crew record of the *S.S. West Gambo*, 1 March 1919.

28. Ancestry.com, World War I Draft Registration Cards, 1917–1918. I could not find a date on the card.

29. NARA, Mid-Atlantic Region, Record Group No. 85, E181, File 96. Aliens' Applications for Permission to Depart from the United States, 1918–1919, ARC entry: 567234. Information received courtesy of Ms. Gail Farr, head, Reference Services at NARA Mid-Atlantic, sent on 17 November 2008.

30. Ancestry.com, New York Passenger Lists, 1820–1957, arrival in New York on board the *Lake Yelverton*, 22 January 1920; Ancestry.com, New York County Supreme Court Naturalization Petition Index, 1907–1924, petition dated 18 March 1921, vol. 491, p. 131; and Ancestry.com, Index to Declaration of Intent for Naturalization, New York County, 1907–1924, petition 382.

31. Ancestry.com, 1930 United States Census. Bonicos arrived as a passenger in New York on the *Aquitania* on 6 February 1930; see also Ancestry.com, New York Passenger Lists, 1820–1957.

32. Ancestry.com, U.S. World War II Draft Registration Cards, 1942.

33. Oko, "1960 Account," p. 5. Gerassimos Bonicos, born between 1890 and 1893, had been a captain in the Atlantic and the Pacific for a long time. See Ancestry.com, New York Passenger Lists, 1820–1957, and Seattle Passenger and Crew Lists, 1882–1957; and *Portland Press Herald*, 2 April 1948. In an unconfirmed report, Captain Gerassimos was lost at sea with his ship in October 1950. See *Facts on File: Weekly World News Digest with Cumulative Index*. New York: Facts on File News Services [etc.], 1950, p. 344. According to this account, the Greek freighter *North Voyageur* sank off Newfoundland on 22 October and 11–12 crewmen were missing, including the captain. See "Search for 11 'Lost' on Sunken Ship Ends," *New York Times* (1923–current file), 26 October 1950, p. 63. Retrieved 25 May 2011, from ProQuest Historical Newspapers, *New York Times* (1851–2007). (Document ID: 88411917). Also "Vessel Feared Lost in Atlantic with 24 Men," *Los Angeles Times*, 23 October 1950.

34. "And It Was So," chapter 1, p. 1.

35. Ibid., p. 3; Oko recounts the same story in "1960 Account," p. 5.

36. "And It Was So," p. 28. Oko asserts that the ship was in such poor shape that "at Buenos Aires, one trip, all the men in that Greek crew reported to their consul that they were venereally diseased — to get off the ship." In this same passage, Oko remarks that the *Kefalos* had experienced "two degrading years" under Bonicos; this is, however, inaccurate. Michael Bonicos (and perhaps also his brother Gerassimos) had only owned the vessel since September 1947. Hence, the new owners had held the ship for at most less than one year. Perhaps Oko was calculating the ship's tenure under the Bonicos in *calendar* years (1947–1948)? See also "THE KEFALOS," p. 2, in which Oko writes that under the ownership of the Bonicos the vessel had made eight voyages. It is worth underscoring that the Buenos Aires episode was apparently not the first time Captain Bonicos had experienced problems with sailors. See *The Meriden Daily Journal* (Connecticut, USA), 27 December 1933, "Eight Greeks Desert Ship." They had abandoned the steamship *Kalypso Vergotti*, commanded by Bonicos.

37. "And It Was So," chapter 1, p. 3.

38. Ibid., chapter 1, pp. 3–4. More on the shipment of China clay and the ensuing complications in *Portland Press Herald*, 2 April 1948 and following days. See also note 71 below.

39. "And It Was So," chapter 1, pp. 2–3.

40. Ibid., pp. 14–5.
41. Ibid., p. 29.
42. Ibid, p. 30. "Platte" is surely an allusion to the Rio de la Plata or its vicinity. Two excellent photographs of the ship in early 1948 were taken in this area. The photographs, credited to Raul Maya, are from the William Schell Collection. Both were kindly made available to me by Mr. Schell.
43. Ibid., p. 31. Oko's emphasis.
44. Ibid.
45. Ibid.
46. Ibid., pp. 31–32.
47. This exact letterhead appears in numerous documents in AJA, 883. In Spanish, the "S.A." stands for *Sociedad Anónima*; however, nearly all English-language references to this company, including those in FBI documents, carry "Inc.," after the business's main name.
48. "And It Was So," chapter 1, p. 7. Oko's "1960 Account" tells essentially the same story, but makes the point that he was asked "to come immediately [...] to New York, and to accept an assignment on a vessel that Israel had purchased in which they wished to carry arms from Tampico, Mexico into Tel Aviv" (p. 2). However, whether Oko already knew, while inspecting the *Kefalos*, that it had already been bought is doubtful.
49. Ibid., p. 8.
50. Ibid.
51. Ibid. Oko makes the same points in "THE KEFALOS," pp. 1–2. More on the purchase price of the ship in note 72.
52. Special Agent in Charge [SAC], New York Office to FBI Director, 1 June 1950, (word redacted) was. et al. Neutrality Act, Conspiracy, Bureau File 2-1004. See also letter from the FBI Director to the CIA Director, 9 June 1950, (word redacted) with aliases, et al. Neutrality Act, Conspiracy, Bureau File 2-1004-231. Shipowners Agency was located at 39 Broadway, New York, 6. Its cable address was Shipsage, and its telephone number was Whitehall 3-7843. More on the close relationship between Manuel Enterprises, Inc., and Shipowners Agency in note 57.
53. Report from San Francisco Office, by Douglas G. Allen, 7 April 1949, Bureau File 100-28664, 2. Extensive information on the purchase of the vessel by the Israelis in memorandum from SAC, New York Office, to FBI Director, 27 September 1948, subject Manuel Enterprises, Inc., Neutrality Act, Bureau File 64-32444-8. This extensive document details the complex transactions and monetary transfers involved in the acquisition of the *Kefalos* by Shipowners Agency and Manuel Enterprises, Inc. The files concerning Manuel Enterprises, Inc., include both 64-HQ-32444 and NY 2-420; letter of the FBI to this author, 17 May 2011, FOIPA No. 1159782-000. Additional information on Manuel Enterprises, Inc. and Shipowners Agency in the voluminous FBI files on Lloyd I. Rosenblum, et al., sent by the bureau to this author, 23 June 2010, FOIPA No. 1132423-001. See SAC, Los Angeles Office to FBI Director, 19 May 1950, (subject title redacted) was., et al., Neutrality Act, Conspiracy, Bureau File 2-1004-222;

report from Los Angeles Office, 19 May 1950, Neutrality Act, Conspiracy, Bureau File 2-1004-223, Los Angeles File 2-105, p. 8; Bureau teletype, 22 May 1950, Bureau File 2-1004-230; memorandum from FBI Director to CIA Director, 9 June 1950, (subject title redacted) with aliases, et al., Neutrality Act, Conspiracy, Bureau File 2-1004-231; memorandum from SAC, New York Office, to FBI Director, 1 June 1950, (subject title redacted) was., et al. Neutrality Act, Conspiracy, Bureau File 2-1004-231 (no explanation for repetition of file number); and report from New York Office, 19 June 1950, (subject title redacted) was. et al., Neutrality Act, Conspiracy, Bureau File 2-1004-261, pp. 11–13 (these pages are heavily redacted). Additional details on the purchase of the *Kefalos* in Eliyahu Sacharov, *Out of the Limelight,* pp. 178–87.

54. Letter from George M. McConnaughghey, chairman of the Federal Communications Commission to the U.S. Attorney General, 10 September 1956, Bureau File 2-1004-317.

55. Telegram from Acheson, Department of State to U.S. Embassy, Geneva, Switzerland, 3 July 1950, Bureau File 2-1004-288. Of the amounts that are known, Dr. Hayman paid $300,000 for the purchase and repair of the *Kefalos,* $500,000 to Western Ordnance Corporation, and $1.3 million to Hank Greenspun. The latter two payments were made in Mexico. The exact relationship between Dr. Hayman and the chief cashier of Haganah in Geneva at the time, Pinchas "Pini" Ginzberg, is unknown to this author.

56. "Instructions to Master," section VIII, item 3.

57. Oko writes of Schweitzer, "We [Gladys and himself] came to regard her as the heart of Manuel Enterprises and the mainspring of Ship Owners Agency, another dummy set-up that fronted for the ship," in "And It Was So," chapter 4, p. 41. In a letter to Oko, dated 15 October 1948, about maritime matters and the *Kefalos,* George C. Stern, of Shipowners Agency, wrote the captain, "I have conveyed your regards to everyone and have in person delivered the hug from yourself and your good wife to Diane. By the way, Diane is getting married very shortly." (AJA, 883)

58. This and much of what follows is from "And It Was So," chapter 4, pp. 4–6 passim. See also Oko, "1960 Account," p. 2.

59. Oko's "1960 Account" explicitly asserts that the vessel in question was the future Exodus (see p. 1).

60. "And It Was So," chapter 4, p. 6. More on Oko's Jewishness and his political trajectory in Chapter 2.

61. Ibid.

62. For the 10 May visit of Shalit to the West Coast, see report from San Francisco Office, by Douglas G. Allen, 9 September 1948, Bureau File 100-356037-9, p. 2. This is the only reference to this meeting that I could find; not even Oko mentions it. The important document is lengthy and detailed. Significantly, the same information can be found in a separate, shorter memorandum from SAC, San Francisco Office, to the FBI Director, 9 September 1948, Bureau File 100-356037-9. No reason is given as to why both documents carry the same bureau file number. The first doc-

ument asserts that Oko left San Francisco for New York on 21 May; the second gives 23 May as the date of departure. Both documents provide significant information on Oko's preparations to head east with his crew.

63. Report from San Francisco Office, by Douglas G. Allen, 9 September 1948, Bureau File 100-356037-9, p. 1. The *S.S. Adelanto*, formerly the *S.S. Aries*, was a vessel that Oko and several business associates purchased in the spring of 1947. In February 1948, "the name of the ship was changed to SS Adalento [sic], and the Adalento [sic] [Steamship] Company was formed under California law" (p. 2). March 1948 is probably a more correct date (see Chapter 2, note 90). The objective was to refurbish it and resell it for a profit. This did not happen, and the *Adelanto* gave Oko nothing but headaches during the time he owned shares in it. Mrs. Okamoto worked for Oko from February to June 1948, presumably at the Adelanto Company. Given her position, she was well situated to know a great deal about the captain's business affairs and other personal matters.

64. "And It Was So," prospectus for chapter 2, p. 1. Pointed remarks on Oko's anti-Fascist, anti-Francoist views in Blanco Aguinaga, Carlos. *Por el mundo: infancia, guerra y principio de un exilio afortunado*. Irún: Alberdania, 2007, p. 235.

65. Ibid., chapter 4, p. 8.

66. Ibid., p. 8; see also pp. 6 and 9. That Sunday was Memorial Day, and Monday was Memorial Day holiday. A telegram of 27 May 1948 from Michael Bonicos to Chase, Leavitt & Co., Portland, advises the ship's local agent to "give letter to Captain Oko now enroute Portland by plane [and] allow him inspect Kefalos [...] give every assistance" (Maine Maritime Museum, MS-49: Chase, Leavitt & Co.). The telegram does not identify the letter in question.

67. The names of some of those who flew east with Oko and Gladys are in the 9 September 1948 FBI documents cited in note 62. Though Corino's name does not appear in these two lists, Oko's "1960 Account" asserts that he, too, was flown from the West Coast with the others. Quite possibly the eighth individual was Carlos Sánchez, whom Oko mentions in his 1960 recollection, pointedly, next to Apaolaza. We would be on surer footing if we possessed crew lists of the *Aries* and its successors, the *John J. O'Hagan* and *Adelanto*, which, unfortunately, we do not.

68. FBI documents cited in note 62.

69. Oko, "1960 Account," p. 7. This document is quite informative on how Oko recruited crewmen from the *Aries/Adelanto* and transported them to the East Coast (pp. 7–8).

70. Ibid., chapter 2, p. 10.

71. AJA, 883, letter from Shipowners Agency to Consulate General of Argentina, 15 June 1948. More on the vessel's poor condition upon its last arrival in Portland, after a 20-day Atlantic crossing, in *Portland Press Herald*, 2 April 1948, "Storm-Battered Freighter Arrives in Port Under Jury Steering Rig." The ship had arrived from Fowey, England, with a large cargo of china clay.

72. "And It Was So," chapter 2, p. 15.

73. *Portland Press Herald*, 9 April 1948, "Ship Stoppage Settlement Hinted." According to this article, thirty-one crewmen had called a strike, and when ninety longshoremen reported for work, they had found a sign on the gangplank that read "Strop [sic] — Strike." Additional details of the episode and its ramifications are found in the same newspaper in the following weeks. The work action by the sailors on the *Kefalos* and their legal claims against the ship owners would have direct impact on the purchase price. According to the *Portland Press Herald,* 2 June 1948, "Claims Against Ship to Be Settled Today," $99,500 in claims were included in the sale price of $190,000. In effect, the ship itself had cost only $90,500, or slightly less than what Bonicos had paid for it the prior year. While this issue of the Portland newspaper asserted that the buyers of the vessel were "two New York men, believed to be engaged in the ship chandlery business," an earlier telegram from perhaps Michael Bonicos to G. Michalitsianos, 18 May 1948, cryptically asserted that "Chinese Greek buyers seem interested" (Maine Maritime Museum, MS-49: Chase, Leavitt & Co.) The local agent for the vessel was Chase, Leavitt & Co. No additional information in the dossier casts light on the mysterious would-be purchasers. More details of the work stoppage episode, and the settlement of claims, in Maine Maritime Museum, same file.
74. "And It Was So," chapter 2, p. 15. According to Oko, Pluskewicz said, "He signed on to spite the ex-owners as much for money [...] He hated the former owners' guts and felt sympathy for the ship as something as mistreated as he had been. He said he had barely escaped being murdered in England [...] and insisted that what looked like a willful attempt to kill him must have been instigated as a try to avoid giving him some $3,000 back pay." (p. 14)
75. Ibid. For the 3 June 1948 departure from Portland, see Maine Maritime Museum, MS 49: Chase, Leavitt & Co. One document is titled "Coasting Manifest," the other "Statement of Master of Vessel Regarding Changes in Crew Prior to Departure." The latter has Oko's signature. Unfortunately, the list of "Seamen Signed on at This Port" is missing. The file contains at end "a list of crew discharged at Portland, Maine." It is composed of thirty-three individuals, twenty-one of them Greek.
76. Ibid., chapter 3, p. 17.
77. Ibid., p. 18. Important accounts of the fire and the crew's role in putting it out in *Portland Press Herald*, "Damaged Vessel to Alter Course" (p. 5), and 8 June 1948, "South Portland Pilot Tells How He Saved Ship, Crew." Curiously, the Mexican daily *Excelsior* carried a brief Associated Press wire story in its 5 June 1948 edition. Headlined "Incendióse un Barco Panameño en Boston," the item noted that the merchant vessel was named Kefalos, and that the fire had been quickly put out (section 1, p. 11). While the story may appear insignificant, it was probably of interest to Haganah associates in Mexico, who *may* have had some inkling of the ship's mission.
78. Oko, "1960 Account," p. 9; Bancroft, Mss 68/39c, carton 2, small snapshot of the Israeli flag flying atop the ship; and photograph in *Marin Independent Journal,* 22 April 1961, p. 13.

79. "And It Was So," p. 23. Apparently, all radio communications and records between the *Kefalos*, the U.S. Coast Guard, and shore have been preserved (see AJA, 883).
80. Ibid.
81. Ibid., p. 22.
82. Ibid.
83. *Portland Press Herald*, 8 June 1948.
84. Report New York Office, by Lawrence W. Spillane, 1 December 1948, Manuel Enterprises, Inc., Neutrality Act, New York File 2-420. This document is also filed as New York Office, Bureau File 64-32444-13. Although identical in content, curiously, the latter version is unsigned. Also, the latter document contains more redactions. Much of what follows is taken from this report.
85. I owe this suggestion to Mr. Yehuda Ben-Tzur.
86. In a message to Manuel Enterprises, Inc., shortly after the fire on board, Oko instructed, "hold complation [sic] purchase for my report." See AJA, 883, undated handwritten communication by Pluskewicz, the radio operator.
87. AJA, 883, work orders and bills for repairs at Todd Shipyards Corporation, Brooklyn division, for job number 7228. Perhaps the order had been pre-dated? This would account for the mistakes and discrepancies in the document.
88. See note 81.
89. Ibid.
90. AJA, 883, eleven-page itemized bill from Todd and the one-page settlement agreement, both dated 12 June 1948. A slight discrepancy in the total cost can be found in the 1 December 1948 documents cited in note 81. According to these, the bill for repairs came to $50,892. The detailed bill reveals exactly everything that was done to the ship at Todd Shipyards in the surprisingly short period of four days. Regrettably, it is not known as of this writing how the bill was paid.
91. US$240,000 in 1948 would equal US$2,214,000 in 2010.
92. "And It Was So," chapter 5, p. 43.
93. Oko, "THE KEFALOS," p. 2. This quote also appears in "And It Was So," chapter 5, p. 36.
94. Oko, "1960 Account," p. 9. See also "And It Was So," chapter 5, p. 38.
95. Unless stated otherwise, the quotes and information that follow are from "And It Was So," chapter 5.
96. Ibid, p. 37.
97. Unfortunately, I was unable to obtain any information on this important matter from the Panamanian consulate or that nation's government, despite repeated requests. The notes for "And It Was So," prepared by Aline Merritt, the ghostwriter, assert that the crew and officers signed articles before the Panamanian Consul between 9–11 June 1948. However, the only two original Panamanian certificates that I consulted, those of Eric Forbes and Gladys Oko, are dated 2 June 1948. Were they backdated? It is impos-

sible to know.

98. "And It Was So," chapter 5, p. 39.

99. Ibid., p. 36. Over time, Rothman would also become a kind of father figure to the four American Jewish volunteers who boarded at Tampico.

100. Ibid., p. 39.

101. Ibid.

102. Ibid., p. 43, emphasis added.

103. Ibid., p. 34.

104. Ibid., p. 38.

105. AJA, 883, Shipowners Agency to Consulate General of Argentina, 15 June 1948. A vessel is usually considered arriving or departing "in ballast" if no cargo is loaded when leaving a port or no cargo is unloaded when arriving at a port.

106. "Shipping — Mails: All Hours Given in Daylight Saving Time." *New York Times* (1923–current file), 15 June 1948. Retrieved from www.proquest. com.proxy.cc.uic.edu/ (accessed 27 May 2011).

107. "And It Was So," p. 45; AJA, 883, contains a copy of the "*INSTRUCTIONS TO MASTER*" given to Oko, which in all likelihood was his personal copy. This document's title is in capitals and is underlined.

108. According to Amitzur Ilan, "from mid-May 1948, Kollek headed the [Haganah] mission" in New York. See *The Origin of the Arab–Israeli Arms Race: Arms, Embargo, Military Power and Decision in the 1948 Palestine War*. (New York: New York University Press, 1996), p. 90. More on Kollek's activities on p. 65 and p. 90 ff. This work casts a considerable light on Israeli efforts and projects to secure arms and materials in the United States and in Latin America (see 63–104 passim). For a good summary of these actions, see Table 4, p. 94. Amitzur's book is an excellent complement to Leonard Slater's trailblazing account, *The Pledge* (New York: Simon and Schuster, 1970).

109. "And It Was So," chapter 6, pp. 45–46.

110. The clause "If examined" is unclear and confusing. For one thing, it assumes that the vessel's name had already been changed from Kefalos, a fact that is not in evidence. From everything that is known, the ship entered Tampico as *Kefalos*. Could the ship possibly have carried into port a double set of papers? This appears unlikely. More on this question in Chapter 3 (see note 23).

111. This matter would come into play at various junctures, particularly at Tampico, where Oko suddenly found himself acting in the triple capacity of captain, ship agent, and owner. See "And It Was So," chapter 8, pp. 66–67.

Chapter 2. *Oko and Gladys*

1. State of New York, Certificate and Record of Birth, number 56693, 14 December 1904. The father's residence is listed as 605 E. 11th Street. Weisinger is listed as having the same address. He was twenty-two years old, and she was eighteen. Weisinger is sometimes also spelled Weissinger.

2. Much is known about Oko Jr.'s father, given his important career and notoriety. See the following: a good introduction to the life of the elder

Oko in Andrew B. Wertheimer, "Oko, Adolph S.," in *American National Biography*, John A. Garraty and Mark C. Carnes (eds). New York: Oxford University Press, 1999, 16, pp. 661–662. Available online at www.anb.org.proxy.cc.uic.edu/articles/09/09-01118.html?a'1&n'adolph%20s.%20oko&d'10&ss'0&q'1; the biographical sketch to the Inventory to the Adolph S. Oko Papers at the AJA, available at www.americanjewisharchives.org/aja/FindingAids/oko.htm; his obituary "Dr. Adolph S. Oko, Spinoza Scholar: Ex-Librarian of Hebrew Union College, Cincinnati, Dies. Edited Jewish Bimonthly." *New York Times* (1923–current file), 4 October 1944, retrieved from http://www.proquest.com.proxy.cc.uic.edu/ (accessed 31 May 2011); Carroll R. Bowman, "The Spinozism of Adolph S. Oko," *Southern Journal of Philosophy*, 6(3) (1968: Fall), p. 172; and "Adolph S. Oko," in *Encyclopaedia Judaica, Second Edition*, Michael Berenbaum and Fred Skolnik (eds). Detroit: Macmillan Reference, USA, 2007 (part of Gale Biography in Context biographical research collection). There are also numerous articles about Adolph S. Oko's activities and accomplishments in national and local newspapers.

3. 1900 United States Census, Manhattan, New York, NY, Roll T-623 1086; Page 12B. On Etta Oko, see Ancestry.com, Ohio Deaths, 1908–1932, 1938–1944, and 1958–2002, vol. 4524, certificate 44757, date of death 7 August 1924. According to her death certificate, State of Ohio, Department of Health, Division of Vital Statistics, file no. 44757, she was born in Austria on 12 May 1884 to Bernhard Weisinger and Kate Scharp, both Austrians. The information was provided by her surviving husband, Adolph S. Oko. A brief death notice appeared in the *Cincinnati Post*, 8 August 1924, p. 15.

4. Although Pearl's date of birth is known from several sources, notably travel records and passenger lists, no birth certificate for her has been found despite requests to New York state authorities. In effect, Pearl was twenty-three days older than her brother Adolph.

5. Regrettably, little is known about when Rose traveled to California and where and when she married Peter Isaak.

6. 1910 United States Census. San Francisco Assembly District 32, San Francisco, CA, Roll T624_96; Page 7B; Enumeration District 37; Image 943. Peter Isaak's trade is listed as "iron worker" engaged in "display fixtures." Oko Jr. is listed as a "step-son." At this time Peter was twenty-eight years old and Rose was twenty-four.

7. *Marin Independent Journal*, 22 April 1961.

8. Ibid.

9. Ibid. Oko claims in this article that "he won an art scholarship which might have taken him to Israel for study under Abel Penn." This assertion cannot be confirmed. See also AJA, 883, letter from Oko to Penn, 12 November 1953.

10. 1920 United States Census. Hamilton, Cincinnati, Ohio; Series T625; Roll 1395; Page 87.

11. See www.americanjewisharchives.org/aja/FindingAids/oko.htm

12. See obituary cited in note 2.
13. *Marin Independent Journal*, 22 April 1961.
14. RG 178, Records of the USMC. National Archives and Records Administration (NARA). War Shipping Administration, Division of Operations, Service Record, 22 January 1943. Definitions of these terms can be found at http://freepages.genealogy.rootsweb.ancestry.com/~nzbound/nautical_terms.htm. OS, or ordinary seaman, is a seaman of the lowest grade in the merchant marine. AB, or able seaman or able-bodied seaman, is an experienced seaman certified to perform all routine duties at sea.
15. *Marin Independent Journal*, 22 April 1961 (my emphasis). This was Oko's unmistakable way of underscoring his dual loyalty to the United Sates and to his Jewish identity.
16. Ibid.
17. City and County of San Francisco marriage license no. 3439. Oko was employed at Gump's Arts Goods Store for a year or so.
18. Ancestry.com, California Birth Index, 1905–1995 (the entry incorrectly lists him as Adolph Sigmund Oke); and Social Security Death Index. Aaron's newspaper obituary mistakenly asserts that he was born in 1922 in Jalapa, Mexico; *The World Newspaper* (Oregon), 21 May 2002. His name is listed as Aaron S. "Turk" Oko. His death certificate repeats the erroneous place of birth, provides an incorrect date of birth, and affirms that his mother was Gladys. He was seventy-four when he died. More on Aaron in San Francisco Office report by Douglas G. Allen, 13 May 1948, Bureau File 100-356037-1 (San Francisco file 100-28664), title "Adolph Sigmund Oko, Jr. — was A.S. Oko, A.S. Okovich, 'Igor,'" Internal Security –R, pp. 5 and 7. (Hereafter the title of the file and the character of the case will be omitted.)
19. Same sources as in note 18. In particular, see San Francisco Office report by Douglas G. Allen, 13 May 1948, Bureau File 100-356037-1 (San Francisco file 100-28664), p. 5: "Gladys Z. Oko appeared before the [U.S. Shipping] Commission, February 1944 and affirmed that Adolph Sigmund Oko and Aaron Steffins Oko are one and the same person."
20. Bancroft Mss 68/39c., carton 3. In August 1928, Oko is listed as the editor of this publication's apparent first issue. Another one is dated September 1928. Also among these papers is another publication titled *Pacific Skipper*, which lists Oko as publisher. One issue is dated January 1937. Another issue is dated February 1937, in which Oko appears as president (p. 5); in the same magazine issue he is also listed as publisher (p. 28). I have been unable to determine how many issues of each of these two publications saw the light of day.
21. San Francisco Office report by Douglas G. Allen, 13 May 1948, Bureau File 100-356037-1 (San Francisco file 100-28664), p. 10. The 19 October incident was reported in the *San Francisco Examiner*, 20 October 1928; the article noted that Oko was the editor of a yachting magazine.
22. 1930 United States Census. San Francisco, California; Roll 203; Page 13B; Enumeration District 225; Image 92.0. According to the Crocker-Langley San Francisco 1929 city directory, p. 1154, Oko and Madge resided at 1715

Broadway.

23. San Francisco Office report by Douglas G. Allen, 13 May 1948, Bureau File 100-356037-1 (San Francisco file 100-28664), p. 9.

24. In the Superior Court of the State of California, in and for the City and County of San Francisco, Decree of 1 March 1933, No. 238230. Madge Oko, Plaintiff vs. Adolph Oko, Defendant. Madge was awarded custody of their son and received the sum of $40 per month for the maintenance of the infant as well as the right to resume her maiden name. However, the case dragged on until 27 August 1934, and, in the interval, there were several orders modifying the interlocutory decree of divorce. Some of the modifications appear to have favored Oko, who earned joint custody of their son in a complex arrangement.

25. San Francisco Office report by Douglas G. Allen, 13 May 1948, Bureau File 100-356037-1 (San Francisco file 100-28664), pp. 6–7; see also p. 3.

26. Ibid. Not that Oko had been enamored of work at the newspaper. Years later, Lawton Kennedy, a printer, recounted that he had met Oko on the street and asked him what he was doing. "Oh, not much of anything right now [...], [H]e said he was pimping for the Call-Bulletin." Asked by Kennedy what he meant by that, Oko replied, "I am soliciting want ads." See *Lawton Kennedy: A Life in Printing*, an oral history transcript and related material, 1966–1967: http://ia600308.us.archive.org/14/items/lifeinprintinglawt-00kennrich/lifeinprintinglawt00kennrich.pdf, pp. 75–76.

27. *Marin Independent Journal*, 22 April 1961: "It was during the advertising phase that he met his wife Gladys." Unfortunately, despite strenuous efforts, I have been unable to find the exact date of the marriage. Even the FBI is uncertain on this matter, providing two different years for the matrimony. See San Francisco Office report by Douglas G. Allen, 13 May 1948, Bureau File 100-356037-1 (San Francisco file 100-28664), pp. 2–3. The FBI gives two dates without explanation: 18 August 1933 (at Salinas) and 1934 (without additional details).

28. Standard Certificate of Death, County of Alameda, Oakland, California, number 2335. The document lists her as a teacher of dancing and art, a fact confirmed, with additional significant details about her life and work, in the *Berkeley Daily Gazette* obituary of 20 August 1936.

29. See note 20.

30. San Francisco Office report by Douglas G. Allen, 13 May 1948, Bureau File 100-356037-1 (San Francisco file 100-28664), p. 3. According to this report, on 23 July 1937, Oko had debts totaling $51,000 and assets of $100.

31. *Marin Independent Journal*, 22 April 1961.

32. Ancestry.com, California Voter Registrations, 1900–1968, 1939, lists him as a "publicity man" and a registered Democrat; the 1939 Polk's Crocker-Langley San Francisco city directory lists his office at 681 Market, room 424; the 1940 Polk's Crocker-Langley San Francisco city directory repeats this information and has two specific mentions of Oko Public Relations, one for his home and another for his office. Oko's papers at the Bancroft Library contain an envelope with miscellaneous items, among them several

business cards. One of them is for Oko Public Relations at the Monadnock Building; see Bancroft Mss 68/39c, carton 3. An article in the 27 August 1940 issue of the *Oakland Tribune* reports that Oko, as president of Oko Public Relations Co., has been angling for the Albany track account; retrieved from www.newspaperarchive.com/SearchResultsV3.aspx#refine.

33. Bancroft Mss 68/39c, C-B 920 Oversize. This very large album — a kind of scrapbook — also contains two photographs of Oko from 1938, one an excellent original and the other from a newspaper.
34. Several bulging oversize albums compiled by Oko are among his papers at the Bancroft Library. Some of the articles go back as far as 1934 when he worked for the *San Francisco Call-Bulletin*.
35. Bancroft Mss 68/39c, C-B 920 Oversize. Good publicity poster of Gene Krupa at the Shalimar Bowl. This album contains numerous clippings, articles, and publicity materials, for the most part dated January 1939, from the *San Francisco Chronicle*, the *Los Angeles Examiner*, and many other newspapers.
36. San Francisco Office report by Douglas G. Allen, 13 May 1948, Bureau File 100-356037-1 (San Francisco file 100-28664), pp. 3–4, testimony of W. F. Bradley, credit manager of Gump's Arts Goods Store. Whether Rose Isaak's role was that significant is unknown. According to Jack James and Earle Vonard Weller (authors of *Treasure Island, "The Magic City," 1939–1940; The Story of the Golden Gate International Exposition*. San Francisco, CA: Pisani Printing and Publishing Co., 1941), she's listed only as having a 1940 concession of Russian arts and crafts (Appendix, p. xxxiv). However, given her prominence as a Soviet sympathizer, the FBI kept a close watch on Rose Isaak, and her name is continually brought up in Oko's bureau files.
37. San Francisco Office report by Douglas G. Allen, 13 May 1948, Bureau File 100-356037-1 (San Francisco file 100-28664), pp. 3–4. Oko was a close associate of Philip Soljak in public relations and also worked with him in presenting lectures and motion pictures. According to the 1940 Polk's Crocker-Langley San Francisco city directory, they shared the same business address.
38. *Marin Independent Journal*, 22 April 1961.
39. U.S. Department of Homeland Security, U.S. Coast Guard, Department of Commerce, Bureau of Marine Inspection and Navigation, Shipping Section, 6 April 1942, San Francisco. This file also includes some documents from service at sea in the 1920s, as well as subsequent service in World War II. His identification number was Z-192633. Additional materials on Oko's sea service record in SAC, San Francisco report to FBI Director, 2 June 1948, Bureau File 100-386037-3; and, as noted earlier, in RG 178, Records of the USMC. NARA. War Shipping Administration, Division of Operations, Service Record, 22 January 1943.
40. SAC, San Francisco report to FBI Director, 2 June 1948, Bureau File 100-386037-3, p. 2. See also *Full and Down* — U.S. Maritime Service Officers' Training Station, Government Island, Alameda, California. Class of summer 1942.

41. SAC, San Francisco report to FBI Director, 2 June 1948, Bureau File 100-386037-3, titled "Sea Service Record for Adolph Sigmund Oko, Jr."

42. Bancroft Mss 68/39c, carton 3. The Okos kept not only the paper documents, but also the actual metal bars. In carton 1, among the correspondence, there are two photographs of Oko apparently from his merchant marine service. He is in uniform and wearing shorts.

43. Bancroft Mss 68/39c, carton 1, 4 November 1942.

44. Bancroft Mss 68/39c, carton 3. *National Organization Masters, Mates & Pilots of America Membership Book.* The certificate of membership is number 2988, dated 1 January 1947, in San Francisco. It is followed on the next page by a personal description with basic facts about birth, hair color, eye color, weight, height, and so on. It also states that he joined on 3 February 1943, and that his Social Security number was 568-09-2043. Then there is information on dues paid for February–May 1947, although they seem to be for the entire year. An unidentified source stated in 1948 that Oko "had resigned from the union recently." See San Francisco Office report by Douglas G. Allen, 13 May 1948, Bureau File 100-356037-1 (San Francisco file 100-28664), p. 5.

45. Much of what follows is from a statement of the ship captain, B. W. Dutton, that is in the vessel's official log and that was transcribed for FBI purposes. See Boston Office report by Clement A. O'Brien, 3 August 1948, titled Adolph Sigmund Oko, Jr. – was A.S. Oko, A.S. Okovich, "Igor," Internal Security –R (San Francisco [?] file 100-21739), Bureau File 100-356037-8. There are other accounts of the incident: see *San Francisco Chronicle,* 5 November 1945; *Chicago Daily Tribune,* 7 November 1945; "More Marines at Chinwangtao," *New York Times* (1923–current file), 8 November 1945, retrieved from www.proquest.com.proxy.cc.uic.edu/ (accessed 3 June 2011); *Stars and Stripes* (China Edition), 9 November 1945; and *Marin Independent Journal,* 22 April 1961. In Oko's papers at the Bancroft Library (Mss 68/39c, carton 1), in a large folder labeled "Oko in China," there is a large stack of extremely small photographs that show Oko being foisted on a makeshift stretcher that is being carried by four villagers. In the pictures Oko is heavily bandaged and seems very uncomfortable and unable to move freely. I did not find an explanation of the history of these photographs or how Oko came to possess them.

46. Ancestry.com, California Passenger and Crew Lists, 1893–1957. Oko arrived by U.S. Air Force plane and was transferred to Marine Hospital in the same city.

47. San Francisco Office report by Douglas G. Allen, 13 May 1948, Bureau File 100-356037-1 (San Francisco file 100-28664), p. 6, testimony of Allan K. Hulme, vice president of the General Steamship Co., Ltd. He "advised that his company had sold the SS Amur, now the Far Eastern Carrier, to the subject, who was acting as agent of China Hellenic, Ltd., [...] Shanghai, China." See also *Marin Independent Journal,* 22 April 1961.

48. Ibid. These accusations are at the start of the latter document.

49. See Boston Office report of Clement A. O'Brien, 3 August 1948, note 45.

50. *Marin Independent Journal*, 22 April 1961; and Bancroft Mss 68/39c, carton 3. Oko meticulously recorded his voyages by hand in a large green log book. For the *Kefalos* journeys, Oko transcribed the data into a neatly typewritten three-page document that is divided into the following sections: (a) "S/S KEFALOS PASSAGE TO TAMPICO FROM NEW YORK; (b) TAMPICO TO TEL AVIV; (c) TO NAPLES; (d) SPLIT-BAKAR-HAIFA; and (e) SPLIT-BAKAR-HAIFA. A copy of the document in AJA, 883. See Appendix 5, this volume.

51. *Marin Independent Journal*, 22 April 1961. See also "And It Was So," chapter 1, p. 3.

52. "And It Was So," chapter 1, p. 3. Of course, Oko's dates here are confusing; he and Gladys could not have been married for twenty years in 1946. He had married his first wife, Madge, in 1926, and his matrimony to Gladys had only taken place in 1933 or 1934.

53. Ancestry.com, California Passenger and Crew Lists, 1893–1957. What remains unclear is whether Oko had stayed in China after sailing the *Far Eastern Carrier* there in April–May (and possible also June) 1946, or whether he had returned to the United States shortly thereafter and then returned to China again in July of that year. On board this vessel was Manuel Galdos, a former ship captain in the Basque region and associate of Mariano Manresa. A further complicating factor in the timeline is another unexplained earlier trip by Oko, this time from Leyte (Philippines) to the United States on board the *S.S. George R. Holmes*, the same vessel he had sailed on when he was shot in November 1945. The *Holmes* arrived in Seattle on 3 June 1946; see Ancestry.com, Seattle Passenger and Crew Lists, 1882–1957. On this voyage, had Oko simply "hitched" a ride back to the United States after the voyage aboard the *Far Eastern Carrier*? It is impossible to know at this point.

54. *Marin Independent Journal*, 22 April 1961. See also "And It Was So," chapter 1, p. 3.

55. California State Board of Health, Bureau of Vital Statistics Certificate of Birth, County of Alameda, City of Oakland, State Index No. 116, Local Registered No. 153. Certified copy, Office of the Recorder, County of Alameda, Oakland, 3 November 2008. Otto Zemple had been born in September 1878 and Belva Anderson in 1878 or 1879; hence, they were both twenty-seven or twenty-eight years old when Gladys was born. For Otto (last name also spelled Zimpel in places), see Ancestry.com, 1880 United States Census, Dayton, Richland, Wisconsin; Roll T9_1445; Family History Film 1255445; Page 45-4000; Enumeration District 232; 1900 United States Census, Butternut, Ashland, Wisconsin; Roll T623 1777; Page 1A; and Ancestry.com, U.S. General Land Office Records, 1796–1907. Otto G. Zemple of Douglas County, Wisconsin, had purchased land in Minnesota in 1904. For Belva Zemple (nee Anderson), see Ancestry.com, 1910 United States Census; Oakland Ward 2, Alameda, California; Roll T624_70; Page 12A; Enumeration District 94; Image 267. According to the 1910 census, Belva's father was born in Norway, and her mother in Wisconsin. As recently as June 1905, Belva had resided in Waupaca, Wisconsin; see Ances-

try.com, Wisconsin state censuses, 1895 and 1905.

56. Oko, "1960 Account," p. 3: "It is interesting to note that my wife is not a Jewess [...]; [she is] of Norwegian Lutheran background."

57. Ancestry.com, California Voter Registrations, 1900–1968, Alameda County, 1908, City of Oakland, Third Ward, 11th Precinct.

58. Ancestry.com, 1910 United States Census. Oakland Ward 2, Alameda, California; Roll T624_70; Page 132; Enumeration District: 94; Image 267. Belva's entry in the 1910 census lists her as widowed. This would also explain the absence in this census of Otto Zemple, Belva's husband and Gladys's father.

59. Ancestry.com, 1920 United States Census. San Francisco Assembly District 30, San Francisco, California; Roll T625_139; Page 1A; Enumeration District 229; Image 206. The census entry lists Belva as divorced, which I believe is mistaken.

60. Ancestry.com, California Voter Registrations, 1900–1968. Oakland, precinct number 222.

61. Ancestry.com, 1930 United States Census. Alameda, Alameda, California; Roll 100; Page 10B; Enumeration District 229; Image 876.0. Efforts to locate Gladys in the 1930 census have been unsuccessful.

62. Polk's Crocker-Langley San Francisco city directory, p. 1269. She lived at "r 770 Calif[ornia]." According to the abbreviation section, 'r' stands for "roomer or resides." No information of where she was employed. Interestingly, Oko is not listed that year.

63. Polk's Crocker-Langley San Francisco city directory. Belva resided at 278 Dolores, while Oko lived at 228 Dolores (p. 1268). Belva is listed as a householder; Oko as a resident or roomer (p. 878). He is listed as an advertising salesman. Vernon, Gladys's younger brother, although listed alongside his mother, lived as a resident or roomer at 669 Ellis and is listed as a clerk. Gladys's absence from this directory is puzzling.

64. Polk's Crocker-Langley San Francisco city directory, p. 881.

65. What follows is from the *Marin Independent Journal*, 22 April 1961. See note 27 for the possible time of their first meeting.

66. Bancroft Mss 68/39c, carton 1.

67. Throughout Oko's Bureau Files, 100-356037, and related dossiers, Rose Isaak repeatedly appears as a prominent Communist sympathizer, as the executive head or secretary of the American Russian Institute in San Francisco and member of its board of directors, as a frequent visitor to the Russian Consulate in that city, and as an associate of Gregori Kheifets, Vice-Consul at the consulate. San Francisco Office report by Douglas G. Allen, 24 June 1949, (San Francisco file 100-28664), Bureau File 100-356037-17, asserts that Kheifets was "a known Russian espionage Agent" (pp. 7–8). Kheifets was an associate of Erick (also Eric and Erich in some documents) F. Stuewe, who was married to Mildred Stuewe, Oko's half-sister born to Rose and Peter Isaak. According to this report, Mildred was a member of the Los Angeles Communist Party and held 1944 Communist Party Membership Book No. 49430, p. 8. I have not ascertained when Mildred and Erick mar-

ried, but according to the 1930 United States Census, the couple was living with Rose in Sausalito, California; Census place Sausalito, Marin, California; Roll 177; Page 1A; Enumeration District 35; Image 232-0. Mildred was twenty-two years old, Erick was thirty-nine, and Rose was forty-three.

68. Complete reference to this report in note 18.

69. *Marin Independent Journal*, 22 April 1961.

70. Ibid.

71. Ibid.

72. "And It Was So," chapter 1, p. 4. At some point Oko and Gladys had a mezuzah in their house at Inverness. Made of wood and copper, it was created by the noted artist Victor Ries. It is now owned by Oko's granddaughter, Angi Dega.

73. An indication of Rose's political orientation in the 1910s see Ancestry.com, California Voter Registrations, 1900–1968, Marin County, 1900–1918, Index to Registration Affidavits, 5 November 1918, p. 11. Rose registered as a Socialist. Her views must have crystallized in the previous five years because in the 1913 San Francisco County Voter Roll she is identified as "Dec.," or a "Declined-to-State" party voter.

74. For Yiddish, see "1960 Account," p. 21; for Jewish proverbs, see letter from Oko to Gershon Agron, 1 November 1949 ("To cheat a gentile is worse than cheating a Jew," etc.), AJA, 883; for "schlemiels," see "And It Was So," chapter 1, p. 4 (my emphasis); for a quote from the Old Testament, see AJA, 883, letter from Oko to Marvin and Sylvia Lowenthal, 15 March 1949; for "chosen people," see "1960 Account," p. 1. During World War II, Oko was issued a pocket-size volume titled *Readings from the Holy Scriptures Prepared for Use by Jewish Personnel of the Army of the United States*. Washington, DC: U.S. Government Printing Office, 1942. The volume shows Oko as the owner and lists Gladys as nearest of kin, both in Oko's handwriting. Like the mezuzah cited in note 70, this book is owned by Oko's granddaughter, Angi Dega. Finally, it should not be forgotten that Oko chose a biblical reference for the title of his proposed *And It Was So*.

75. For anti-Semitism among the board of the Adelanto Steamship Company, see AJA, 883, letter from Oko to Marvin and Sylvia Lowenthal, 15 March 1949; for the anti-Semitic tracts that Oko received in November 1957, see Bancroft Mss 68/39c, carton 1. He reported it to the FBI (all materials in the 1956–1959 correspondence).

76. "And It Was So," chapter 1, p. 6 (my emphasis).

77. Ibid., chapter 1, p. 4.

78. Ibid.

79. Ibid., p. 6.

80. Ibid., p. 7. D.P. Camp is short for displaced persons camp, a site where refugees of various conditions and nationalities congregated after the war.

81. Unless otherwise noted, all of the correspondence is from AJA, 883.

82. My emphasis.

83. Details on the purchase of the *Aries/Adelanto* can be found at https://pmars.marad.dot.gov/detail.asp?Ship'308. The documents are mistakenly

filed under the ship *Andalien.*

84. "And It Was So," chapter 1, p. 7.

85. "1960 Account," pp. 1–2.

86. More on the history and actions of the *Aries/Adelanto* can be found at:
    www.history.navy.mil/photos/sh-usn/usnsh-a/ak51.htm
    www.shipscribe.com/usnaux/AK/AK51.html
    https://pmars.marad.dot.gov/detail.asp?Ship'510
    www.navsource.org/archives/09/49/49037.htm
    http://en.wikipedia.org/wiki/USS_Aries_%28AK-51%29
    www.convoyweb.org.uk/ports/index.html?search.php?vessel'ARIES~ar-
    main.
    See also Department of Investment, Division of Corporations of the State
    of California, Permit, File no. 628383 F, 14 May 1948. This permit au-
    thorized the company to sell and issue its securities. Finally, see RG 178,
    Records of the U.S. Maritime Commission, Minutes of the Commission,
    1936–1950, 1 November 1949. NARA. Information courtesy of Mr. Rich-
    ard Peuser, assistant chief, Reference Section, at NARA, 4 November 2010.

87. San Francisco Office report by Douglas G. Allen, 13 May 1948, Bureau File
    100-356037-1 (San Francisco file 100-28664), p. 2. The investigation's first
    interviews were conducted in January of that year and lasted through the
    end of April. Purportedly, the ship had been purchased for $180,000. The
    FBI's information on the price, even though it appears to have come from
    Gladys, is mistaken. According to PMARS, the vessel had been bought by
    Oko under bid PDX-296 for $106,310 (see https://pmars.marad.dot.gov/
    DisposalCard/All/308_AF.jpg). More on the sale in note 92.

88. Ibid., p. 4. Other parts of the report also contain information on the *Aries/
    Adelanto.*

89. Ibid., pp. 7–8.

90. Ibid.

91. Ibid. According to this report, Oko had been a subscriber to the *Daily Peo-
    ple's World* in San Francisco as late as 13 May 1947. Whether he still was at
    the time of the FBI investigation is unknown.

92. SAC, San Francisco Office report to FBI Director, 9 September 1948. Sub-
    ject: Adolph Sigmund Oko, Jr. — was. Neutrality Act, Bureau File 100-
    356037-9, p. 2. According to PMARS, the ship had been sold "for operations
    March 21, 1947." However, *delivery* was to be made "on or before 4/24/47"
    (see https://pmars.marad.dot.gov/DisposalCard/All/308_581AF.jpg).

93. "And It Was So," chapter 1, p. 7. The consortium that owned the vessel,
    the Adelanto Steamship Co., was incorporated on Wednesday, 3 March
    1948, in the state of California. State reference ID 00225319. Source:
    Public record data, Department of State, Division of Corporations. See
    http://www.corporationwiki.com/Unknown/Unknown/adelanto-steam-
    ship-co/42066257.aspx. More information in note 83.

94. AJA, 883, night letter, from Philip S. Ehrlich to David R. Wahl, 20 May
    1948.

95. AJA, 883, letter from Ehrlich to Oko, 22 May 1948.

96. Memorandum from SAC, San Francisco to FBI Director, by Douglas G. Allen, 9 September 1948. Subject: Adolph Sigmund Oko, Jr. — was. Neutrality Act, Bureau File 100-356037-9, p. 2. These accusations lingered, and Oko was confronted with ugly rumors regarding the misuse of funds when he returned home in early 1949 following the *Kefalos* saga.

97. See note 83. The U.S. Maritime Commission *approved* the sale on 1 November 1949, transfer order number C-6528 (see https://pmars.marad. dot.gov/DisposalCard/All/308_CF.jpg). It remains unknown when the sale was finalized.

98. "And It Was So," chapter 1: "I wired Gladys and hopped the next plane to San Francisco. She packed while I attended to details and picked up my crew." (p. 8) And "[We] spent three days under our own roof by our fireside." (p. 7)

99. They would remain together until his death of a heart attack on 25 September 1963. According to Bonnie Shrewsbury Arthur, fittingly, Oko died in Gladys's arms at a Marin County Historical Society banquet in San Rafael, where he had been invited to read a scholarly paper (*The Inverness Tales*, p. 57). See County of Marin, San Rafael, California, Certificate of Death No. 2100–719. Lengthy obituaries in the *Marin Independent Journal*, 26 September 1963 (followed by an editorial two days later titled "Oko of West Marin Fought for All He Deemed Right"), and the *Pacific Sun*, 3 October 1963. Gladys never fully recovered from the loss. As Jack Mason related, "three years after Oko's death, she sold everything they owned on Point Reyes, went East and married a childhood friend, Charles [S.] Helmholtz of Reeding [sic], Masschusetts. Her passing was remarkably like Oko's. She fell dead at the breakfast table on a spring morning in 1977." (*Point Reyes West*, p. 186). See The Commonwealth of Massachusetts, Standard Certificate of Death, Place of Death: Middlesex County; Winchester, no. 29291, Registered No. 122, Date of Death, 11 May 1977. The certificate lists the immediate cause of death as acute myocardial infarction.

Chapter 3. *Tampico and Arms*

1. "And It Was So," chapter 7, p. 52.

2. Ibid., chapter 8, p. 56.

3. A "Reliable Confidential Informant" cited by the Legal Attaché of the U.S. Embassy in Mexico thought the figure was considerably lower ("$1,200 USC a day"); see letter of John N. Speakes, Legal Attaché, Embassy of the United States, Mexico City, to FBI director, 26 July 1948. Subject: Manuel Enterprises, Inc., No. 2 Broadway, New York City, Panamanian Ship, "Kefalos," Foreign Miscellaneous, Neutrality Act, Bureau File 64-32444-1. More on this document in note 15.

4. Ibid., chapter 6, p. 49.

5. Oko was critical of this question as laid out by the personnel of Manuel Enterprises, noting "such evidence of ignorance of ordinary port practice as was indicated by the first 'instruction,'" "And It Was So," chapter 6, p. 47.

6. Ibid., chapter 6, p. 46.

7. Ibid., chapter 7, p. 51.

8. Ibid., chapter 7, p. 47. The messages were sent from the ship to Shipowners Agency and not to Manuel Enterprises, Inc.; see AJA, 883, cables dated 22 and 23 June 1948.

9. AJA, 883, Oko to Manuel Enterprises, Inc., and Shipowners Agency, 19 June 1948.

10. "And It Was So," chapter 6, pp. 6–7.

11. AJA, 883, certificate of the health authorities of the Port of Tampico, 24 June 1948, after inspection of the vessel. The document stipulates the forced arrival of the *Kefalos* due to fuel problems ("arribada forzosa por combustible"). The certificate notes that there were no passengers aboard and that the ship had a crew of thirty-seven, carried no cargo, and would berth at the main depot.

12. "And It Was So," chapter 7, pp. 52–53.

13. Ibid.

14. AJA, 883, permit of the consul at Tampico, 25 June 1948.

15. AJA, 883, letter is undated but from the text it is clear that it was written on 25 June. It is written in Spanish, and quite possibly was the work of the López Hermanos Agency. Oko had asked them to draw up a *cause majeure* "in their language and manner of presenting things." This letter asserts that the ship was bought on 1 June 1948. See also "And It Was So," chapter 7, p. 54. Important information on the ship, its arrival in Tampico and subsequent developments, including repairs, in letter of John N. Speakes, Legal Attaché, Embassy of the United States, Mexico City, to FBI Director, 26 July 1948. Subject: Manuel Enterprises, Inc., No. 2 Broadway, New York City, Panamanian Ship, "Kefalos," Foreign Miscellaneous, Neutrality Act, Bureau File 64-32444-1. The Legal Attaché relayed to headquarters the information gathered by a "Reliable Confidential Informant" who was sent to Tampico by Mexican authorities to investigate the facts surrounding the vessel. The informant apparently turned in his report to Colonel Santiago P. Pina Soria, Chief of the Military Aides to President Alemán, who told the informant that "he must forget the entire matter," and that he had "seen nothing and heard nothing." The Legal Attaché, however, gained access to the report and communicated its main points to the FBI. According to the informant's report, Oko alleged problems with the ship's speed, an excessive consumption of oil, contamination in the water tanks, and bits of concrete in the boilers; that repairs were necessary to the engine; that it was necessary to install fans in the engine room to reduce the temperature; and that "extensive boiler and radio repairs" were needed (p. 3). Some crew members knew better. One of them told the informant "that it was not correct that the ship had entered port in an emergency condition, but that it had come to Tampico especially to carry a cargo of arms that the Government of Mexico was selling to another Government," a statement explicitly supported by none other than Mariano Manresa. This report and other documents from Bureau File 64-32444 on Manuel Enterprises, Inc., contain important information on the ship's layover in Tampico.

16. "And It Was So," chapter 7, p. 54.
17. AJA, 883, Shipowners Agency to Oko, 25 June. The telephone number Oko was to call in New York, Whitehall 37785, was not that of the agency or Shalit. Oko reproduced the telegram, adding sarcastically, "the message as received looked as though a nervous breakdown in New York had been transmitted" (see "And It Was So," chapter 7, p. 54).
18. Oko related these missteps with relish (see "And It Was So," chapter 7, pp. 54–55; and "1960 Account," pp. 10–11.
19. Oko, "1960 Account," p. 11.
20. "And It Was So," chapter 8, p. 58; see also AJA, 883, letter from Jackson (perhaps actually Kollek or Shalit; I have been unable to ascertain who hid behind the pseudonym) to Oko, 17 July 1948, apparently hand delivered by Louis Markovitz, a prospective sailor on the *Kefalos*. The communication deals with financial matters; however, the exact nature of the complex transactions remains rather unclear.
21. "And It Was So," note 2 of the eleven single-spaced observations drafted by Aline Merritt to serve as reminders of key events and individuals during the vessel's voyages.
22. AJA, 883, Schweitzer to Oko, 23 June 1948.
23. Ibid., "PATENT PROVISICIONAL [sic] DEL NAVEGACION [sic]," and so forth. In addition, unfortunately without elaboration, Oko asserts that he had been "shoved out in front with two sets of phony ship's papers" (see "And It Was So," chapter 7, p. 51).
24. "And It Was So," chapter 8, p. 62.
25. My father, who had recently been signed on as a mess man, suggests that Ilves left suddenly and without explanation; in effect, "jumped ship." See Blanco Aguinaga, Carlos, "A crew member's story of the SS Kefalos in the summer and early fall of 1948," p. 9. Additional information, if sketchy, in *Excelsior*, 6 August 1948: "Después de haber zarpado el barco Kefalos se supo que desertó un marinero." Oko's interpretation is far more benevolent (see "And It Was So," chapter 8, pp. 62–63).
26. "And It Was So," chapter 8, p. 63. My father is certain that Manresa misrepresented the situation to Oko, most likely in an attempt to convince the captain to take my father on board. More on the circumstances on my father's "recruitment" by Manresa and his time in Tampico in Blanco Aguinaga, *Por el mundo*, pp. 230–249 passim, and in "A crew member's story of the SS Kefalos in the summer and early fall of 1948," p. 6ff.
27. "And It Was So," chapter 8, p. 63.
28. Ibid.
29. AJA, 883, letter from Manresa to Oko, 16 July 1948.
30. Copies of official Mexican and Spanish documents kindly provided to me by Manresa's daughter, Esperanza, in January 2012.
31. "And It Was So," chapter 8, p. 64.
32. AJA, 883, telegram of David Gritzewsky to his brother Luis, 13 July, sent apparently from New York to Tampico with instructions to transmit the information about Marks to Oko; see also telegram of Jackson to Oko, July

14. More on Marks and the *Exodus* in various sources at the U.S. Holocaust Memorial Museum (e.g., http://resources.ushmm.org/inquery/uia_doc.php/photos/21085?hr'null; http://resources.ushmm.org/inquery/uia_doc.php/photos/18121?hr'null). Oko claims that he was "bombarded with orders to release Marks." All of the communications that Oko kept are in AJA, 883. The New York offices sent cables under different names and signatures (e.g., Manuel Enterprises, Inc., Marshall, or Jackson). (I have been unable to ascertain who hid behind the pseudonyms.) These were probably by no means the only ones the captain received; there may well have been other cables, letters, and telegrams, judging from collateral documentation alluded to elsewhere.

33. Oko's assessment of Markovitz was harsh: "The man they sent in [Marks's] place, I could not use. He was an unstable type, scared silly, a man I dared not take on board," "And It Was So," chapter 8, p. 64.

34. AJA, 883, telegram from Manuel Enterprises, Inc., to Oko.

35. See Apaoloza's account in www.elcorreo.com/vizcaya/prensa/20070531/sociedad/buque-canones-obuses-para_20070531.html. This is also a noteworthy article because it contains the only photograph unearthed to date that shows the *Kefalos* at Tampico with arms ready to be loaded. It has been impossible to obtain a copy of the original. See also *El Correo Espanol–El Pueblo Vasco*, 5–6 October 1985. According to SAC, New York Office to FBI Director, 7 September 1948, Bureau File 64-32444-5: "three photographs reflecting the loading of the cargo aboard the S.S. Kefalos" were forwarded to the bureau. Unfortunately, they cannot be located (very poor copies of the photographs were eventually released to me after the manuscript was completed). Blanco Aguinaga's undated clipping from an unidentified Tampico newspaper, referred to in the Introduction to this volume, includes the caption "El Barco 'Kafalos' Cargando El Armamento" and captures the hoisting of a box of weapons on board; however, it does not show the stacks of weapons at dockside, as Apaolaza's photograph does.

36. AJA, 883, letter from Oko to the port captain: "He preferido fondear mi buque frente a Cd. Madero a fin de evitar entorpecimientos en las operaciones portuarias de otros buques, y por convenir asi a la naturaleza de las reparaciones que se estan efectuando a bordo del mismo."

37. AJA, 883, letter from Captain Jorge Aguirre Ortiz to Oko; "ASUNTO:-Que se comisiona a un empleado de esta capitanía para tomar nota de las reparaciones del vapor 'KEFALOS.'"

38. "And It Was So," chapter 8, p. 62.

39. Ibid., p. 64: "I was advised that López Hermanos were washing their hands of us."

40. AJA, 883, letter from Captain Jorge Aguirre Ortiz to Oko, 17 July 1948.

41. AJA, 883, document titled "Basic Requirements before Vessel Is Ready for Sea," 17 July. It was signed by Ilves and approved by Oko. According to this list, the main areas of concern were the engine room, fuel, and water. Even after being at port for twenty-two days, no repairs of any kind had been made on the vessel. More on these matters in note 15.

42. AJA, 883; although the original is undated, Oko dated it 17 July. See "And It Was So," chapter 8, pp. 64–65, where it is reproduced in its entirety. Gritzewsky especially warned Oko about an unidentified "bald-headed" individual.
43. "And It Was So," chapter 8, p. 65.
44. Ibid., p. 66ff.
45. AJA, 883, hand-delivered letter (by Louis Markovitz) from Jackson to Oko, 17 July 1948 and night letter from Jackson to Oko, 18 July 1948.
46. "And It Was So," chapter 8, p. 67.
47. Ibid.
48. Ibid., p. 68.
49. Ibid. I have been unable to determine exactly which MSTs Oko was alluding to.
50. Ibid.
51. AJA, 883, letter of Oko to Dr. Juan Gómez Sariol, 19 July 1948. Of course, Shanghai was also part of the elaborate fiction.
52. Ibid. Significantly, the endorsement of Oko's request by the head of the customs office, on the same sheet of paper, is unsigned.
53. AJA, 883, "Vino a Tampico un Barco Sospechoso para Llevar un Cargamento de Armas." I have been unable to find a copy of the original; therefore, I am relying on Oko's copy. All of the information that follows in this discussion of the catalyst for the subsequent events is from this issue. The captain kept a large collection of the Tampico dailies that wrote of these events.
54. *Excelsior*, 19 July 1948.
55. Ibid., 20 July 1948. Also on the daily's front page. Oko asserts that another prominent Mexico City daily, *Novedades*, "carried two front page stories" on the affair (see "And It Was So," chapter 8, p. 73). The *New York Times* on 20 July 1948 carried a brief item under the byline "Arms at Tampico Investigated" (p. 7). *New York Times* (1923–current file), 20 July 1948, retrieved from www.proquest.com.proxy.cc.uic.edu/ (accessed 27 July 2011). The piece noted that it had been "reported without confirmation that a Jewish group was shipping the weapons from the United States to Palestine via Mexico."
56. Well before these events, questions surrounding Israel and the Middle East had been the object of considerable attention in the Mexican press. See Gloria A. Carreño and Ethel Gerbilsky de Glusman, *El Estado de Israel en la Opinión de la Prensa Mexicana: Abril, Mayo, Junio de 1948*. México: Centro de Documentación e Investigación de la Comunidad Ashkenazí de México, 1995.
57. AJA, 883, letter of Captain Jorge Aguirre Ortiz to Oko: "*Que el vapor Panameño 'Kefalos' debe fondearse a medio rio.*" See also telegram from Harold B. Quarton, U.S. consul at Tampico, to U.S. Department of State, 21 July 1948. The consul wrote that "after loading one day, collector customs suspended operations." National Archives and Records Administration (NARA), 711.00111 Armament Control/7-2148, Telegram 4. The no-

tation "XR 001.BB Palestine" appears in pencil on the left-hand margin. Quarton pointedly wrote in the communication that the "destination of cargo still unknown, but believed to be Palestine."

58. "And It Was So," chapter 8, p. 71.
59. *El Mundo*, 22 July 1948, and *Excelsior*, 20 July 1948. General Sánchez Acevedo's quote is in *Excelsior*.
60. *El Mundo*, 22 July 1948.
61. *El Mundo*, 23 July 1948. Piece signed by Porfirio M. Ramos.
62. AJA, 883. It is almost impossible to read the date on the copy in Oko's papers, but judging from other information on the page, it appears almost certain that it was the 20 July issue.
63. In addition to Quarton's telegram cited in note 58 above, see 4 August 1948 telegram of Raymon H. Geist, Counselor of the U.S. Embassy in Mexico to the U.S. Secretary of State, NARA, RG 59, 1945–1949, Central Decimal Files. See also letter of John N. Speakes, Legal Attaché, Embassy of the United States, Mexico City, to FBI Director, 26 July 1948. Subject: Manuel Enterprises, Inc., No. 2 Broadway, New York City, Panamanian Ship, "Kefalos," Foreign Miscellaneous, Neutrality Act, Bureau File 64-32444-1, cited in notes 3 and 15.
64. "And It Was So," chapter 8, p. 72. The captain's self-serving remarks, of course, were not exactly true.
65. AJA, 883, *El Universal*, 20 July 1948; and "And It Was So," chapter 8, p. 73.
66. The information that follows is from Carlos Blanco Aguinaga, *Por el Mundo*, pp. 239–243. See also Blanco Aguinaga, "A crew member's story of the SS Kefalos in the summer and early fall of 1948," pp. 8–9.
67. See Appendix 4, this volume. There is only one list of the crew's salaries. Compiled by Oko, it contains no information on whether the salaries were monthly or for the duration of the voyages.
68. *El Mundo*, 21 July 1948, and AJA, 883, letter of Oko to the Minister of the Aduana. Because the communication is in English, it is impossible to know for certain to which individual or department the letter was addressed. Since previous letters had gone to the head of the customs office, Dr. Gomez Sariol, I tend to believe that this communication was also meant for him.
69. AJA, 883, letter of Oko to the Minister of the Aduana, 23 July 1948.
70. "And It Was So," chapter 8, p. 75.
71. Ibid., chapter 8, pp. 75–76.
72. *Excelsior*, 22 July 1948. In the telegram from Harold B. Quarton, U.S. consul at Tampico, to U.S. Department of State, 21 July 1948, the consul wrote that the loading of the arms had ceased "pending investigation by President Alemán's agents as military explanations deemed unsatisfactory" (see note 58). There are other clear indications of the intervention by the office of the Mexican president (e.g., see note 74).
73. *Excelsior*, 24 July 1948. In "And It Was So," Oko wrote that on Monday, 26 July [1948], the daily "*Novedades* in Mexico City announced the return to the capital of various government agents who declared that the arms and

munitions inspected and released for shipment were to be taken to Europe for training purposes, and that the Kefalos would sail soon" (chapter 8, p. 82).

74. *El Mundo,* 23 July 1948. The same article asserted that the *Kefalos* would leave port shortly.

75. The article in question is among Oko's papers in AJA, 883, but it is not clearly identified. However, judging from the type and tone, it certainly appears to be from *La Tribuna.*

76. AJA, 883, document titled "Informe general de los trabajos verificados por el vapor panameño 'Kefalos' entrado a este Puerto en junio 24 de 1948. Operación verificada en el Muelle del Golfo." Signed "E. Forbes," 29 July 1948. The typewritten document is two pages long.

77. Ibid. The report specifies in which of the four cargo holds the materials were placed. It is clear that the sugar was placed on top of the arms to disguise the shipment in the event they were intercepted at sea. As for the water, the document details 382 water drums, 128 cases water tins, and 37 water barrels on cargo hold number 3, as well as 62 water drums on cargo hold number 4. The difference between drums, water tins, and barrels is not given. See also "And It Was So," chapter 8, p. 80, where Oko summarizes the totals of the shipment.

78. AJA, 883, receipt signed by Oko, 26 July 1948. Apparently, the transaction took place aboard the ship. Note the discrepancy between the number of cars given by Oko and those reported in the newspapers (see comments earlier in text). Additional important information on the arms is included in the 26 July 1948 letter of the U.S. Legal Attaché (cited in note 3 and elsewhere in this chapter). The communication provides specific information about the Mexican military officials involved in the arms transfers as well as precise details of the shipping orders.

79. AJA, 883, manifest for this cargo, Tampico, 27 July 1948.

80. AJA, 883, manifest for this product, Tampico, 27 July 1948. Curiously, the document only stipulates the shipment of 10,000 sacks of sugar, or 500 tons. Forbes's countersigned report gives twice the amount, or 20,000 sacks.

81. "And It Was So," chapter 8, p. 80.

82. Ibid., p. 81.

83. *Excelsior,* 3 August 1948: "Hace seis días que los tripulantes se hallan a bordo, esperando la orden para zarpar."

84. AJA, 883, letter of Jorge Aguirre Ortiz to Oko, 2 August 1948. The order carried an implicit threat. Failure to do so, according to the port captain, would result in the removal of the *Kefalos* from the dock by tugs because the berth was needed for other ships.

85. AJA, 883, discharge papers dated 2 and 3 August 1948, respectively. There is good reason to believe that both Estonians had reservations about making the voyage. Also, on 27 July, Oko had informed Manuel Enterprises, Inc., that Peter Stojnic, an electrician on board, was leaving the ship because he had the opportunity to obtain Canadian citizenship. Stojnic, a dis-

placed person and possibly a Yugoslavian citizen, carried a passport issued by the International Red Cross. Oko asked the New York office to assist Stojnic, who appears to have left the ship in good standing because the captain wrote that his services to the vessel had been "very satisfactory."

86. AJA, 883. It is impossible to know which port person or authority sent the letter to Oko; the document carries no identification and the signature is extremely difficult to make out.

87. AJA, 883. It was signed by Port Captain Jorge Aguirre Ortiz.

88. *Excelsior*, 4 August 1948. The brief article cited sources of the customs office in Tampico. The daily correctly noted that the documentation from the customs administration, while mentioning the sugar, made no mention of the arms. However, the article had several important mistakes. *El Universal* the same day carried a similar story, indicating that the *Kefalos* had left port loaded with arms and sugar, although its destination remained a secret.

89. Oko, "THE KEFALOS," p. 4.

90. Greenspun, Hank, and Alex Pelle, *Where I Stand; The Record of a Reckless Man*. New York: D. McKay Co, 1966 (hereafter *Where I Stand*), pp. 73, 75–92 passim; Slater, *The Pledge*, pp. 198–200; and Ben-Tzur, http://palyam.org/English/ArmsShips/kefalostranslationlatest1by. However, none of these authors consulted the extensive FBI files on the episode.

91. According to Greenspun's account — one that should be taken with an enormous grain of salt given his tendency to embellish facts with self-serving statements and his propensity to make glaring factual errors — he left his home in Las Vegas on the night of the grand opening of KRAM, a local radio station, in late December 1947. He had been persuaded to make the trip to Hawaii by Adolph Schwimmer and by Hank's cousin, Reynold Selk (*Where I Stand*, pp. 82–85).

92. As noted below, there is considerable discrepancy in the number of crates, according to FBI records.

93. Greenspun arrived in Los Angeles on flight number 80625 of Pan American Airways, and Sosnow arrived in San Francisco on flight number 588 of United Airlines (Ancestry.com, Hawaii Passenger Lists, 1942–1948). From the time difference between their arrivals, one might deduce that Sosnow had stayed behind in Hawaii an extra month to make the shipping arrangements.

94. Extensive information on the Hawaii episode is included in FBI files. See, in particular, Los Angeles Report, 19 April 1950, Bureau File No. 2–105, pp. 5–14; and arrival of guns in Los Angeles, p. 14ff. See also Salt Lake City Report, 10 January 1958, Bureau File 92-3244-2, Herman Milton Greenspun wa., "Hank," Anti-Racketeering, p. 16. Finally, see Greenspun indictments and trials, U.S. v. Herman Greenspun et al., No. 21266, U.S. District Court, Los Angeles, and U.S. v. Herman Greenspun et al., No. 20927, U.S. District Court, Los Angeles. I consulted these trials in 2009–2010 at NARA, Pacific Region, Laguna Niguel, California. The records are now at NARA's new facility at Riverside. Some of the principals involved in the Hawaiian epi-

sode testified at the trial of Greenspun and the other defendants in 1950. One of the witnesses was Perry G. Edmonson, the former superintendent of the Universal Airplane Salvage Corporation (*Los Angeles Times*, 7 July 1950, p. B7). Shaul Avigor wrote in February 1948 that "a group in Hawaii is giving us [arms] for free" (Shaul's Copybook, unpublished; originals are kept at Israel Defense Forces (IDF); I received translations of these documents from Yehuda Ben-Tzur). Oko casually observed that the *Kefalos* carried "some highjacked aviation armament that later won the interest of the F.B.I," ("1960 Account," p. 11); and Nathaniel Ratner remarked that he had later discovered that "Hank had illegally acquired [arms] in Hawaii," in "Nathaniel (Nat) Ratner — American Veteran of Israel, 1946–1949," p. 2.

95. Los Angeles Report, 19 April 1950, Bureau File No. 2-105, p. 5. At one of Greenspun's later trials in 1949–1950, the indictment charged that he had given Liff $4,200 for labor and shipping. See U.S. v. Schwimmer, et al., No. 20636 Cr., p. 4 of the indictment. It is worth noting that Greenspun collected some funds in Hawaii from a group of Jewish businessmen assembled by Liff to assist with the shipment charges (*Where I Stand*, pp. 90–92).

96. Ibid. In Los Angeles Report, 19 April 1950, Bureau File No. 2-105, see pp. 5, 14–15; and in trial No. 20636, p. 4 of the indictment.

97. Los Angeles Report, 19 April 1950, Bureau File No. 2-105, p. 7.

98. While the $2 million figure may seem slightly exaggerated, it was repeatedly cited by the prosecutors in the trials of Greenspun and his associates, possibly in an effort to magnify the culpability of the defendants. The *Los Angeles Times* and other dailies continually used the $2 million figure in their reports.

99. Los Angeles Report, 19 April 1950, Bureau File No. 2-105, p. 15.

100. Los Angeles Report, 19 April 1950, Bureau File No. 2-105, pp. 15–21. See also Greenspun, *Where I Stand*, pp. 93–96.

101. Los Angeles Report, 19 April 1950, Bureau File No. 2-105, p. 15ff. Despite a wealth of facts and details from testimonies given to the FBI, it is not altogether clear why the bureau's agents and other authorities failed to locate these sixteen crates. This is all the more strange in that the entire ninety-five boxes, by the FBI's own admission, arrived safely at Maxwell Associates and were stored in a yard. However, it appears that after the boxes arrived, some were taken away to other locations in small pickup trucks.

102. *Where I Stand*, p. 95.

103. For the basic general accounts of the *Idalia*, see *Where I Stand*, pp. 96–116; and Slater, *The Pledge*, pp. 201–204. The primary sources, notably FBI files, are detailed below in this note. Descriptions of the arms taken in Hawaii and shipped on the *Idalia* can be consulted in Greenspun's 1950 trial, key parts of which are laid out later in the chapter. See U.S. v. Greenspun, et al., No. 20927 Cr., Bill of Particulars; U.S. v. Herman Greenspun, et al., Defendants, No. 21266 Cr., Motion for Bill of Particulars, Points and Authorities; U.S. v. Herman Greenspun, et al., Bill of Particulars; and U.S. v. Herman Greenspun, et al., Defendants, No. 21266 Cr., Amended Bill of Particulars. See also Yehuda Ben-Tzur's treatment of the episode at, www.

palyam.org/English/ArmsShips/The_Idalia_caper. This valuable account utilizes hitherto unknown Israeli sources.

104. Christen, Arden G., and Peter M. Pronych, *Painless Parker: A Dental Renegade's Fight to Make Advertising "Ethical."* Baltimore, MD: Distributed for the American Academy of History of Dentistry by Samuel D. Harris, National Museum of Dentistry, 1995, chapter 10, in particular pp. 355–359. See also John R. Adams, "Picture Ship," *Sea, The Pacific Yachting Magazine,* May 1949, 8, pp. 43–44. In Report of Legal Attaché, John N. Speakes, U.S. Embassy in Mexico, to FBI Director, 11 August 1948, Bureau File 2-1004-7, p. 3. Lewis is quoted as saying that he had served in the Merchant Marine from 1940 through 1946, and "had done work for Naval Intelligence." Lewis also declared that at the time he held "valid Radio licenses 1st Telegraph and a 1st Telephone issued at Los Angeles, California," p. 4.

105. *San Diego Journal,* 14 April 1948; Greenspun, *Where I Stand,* p. 96.

106. Important information on the *Idalia* arms in Los Angeles Report, 19 April 1950, Bureau File No. 2-105, sections titled "'Idalia' Used to Transport Guns to Mexico," and "Defendants in Los Angeles Area During Pertinent Period," pp. 29–68; and "Interviews with Defendants," pp. 68–87. See also Bureau File No. 2-1004, Reports of the Office of the Legal Attaché, John N. Speakes, U.S. Embassy in Mexico, to FBI Director, dated 8 July, 24 August, and 11 August 1948. See also "Nathaniel (Nat) Ratner — American Veteran of Israel, 1946–1949," pp. 1–2; and letter of Ratner to Greenspun, 11 April 1967, paragraph 2 (document provided to the author by the Ratner Family).

107. Los Angeles Report, 19 April 1950, Bureau File No. 2-105, p. 33.

108. Additional information on damage to the *Idalia* in Report of the Legal Attaché, John N. Speakes, of the U.S. Embassy in Mexico, to FBI Director, 24 August 1948, Bureau File 2-1004-5, p. 4; and Los Angeles Office, 9 September 1948, Bureau File 2-1004-16, p. 13.

109. Taped interview of Ratner by his daughter, Nancy, 5 January 2000, provided to the author by the Ratner Family.

110. *Where I Stand,* pp. 105–106; see also pp. 107 and 112. Slater asserts that Greenspun "was pugnacious from the beginning" (p. 112).

111. "Nathaniel (Nat) Ratner — American Veteran of Israel, 1946–1949," pp. 1–2.

112. *Where I Stand,* p. 110.

113. Report of the Legal Attaché, John N. Speakes, U.S. Embassy in Mexico, to FBI Director, 24 August 1948, Bureau File 2-1004-5, p. 5: "[Lewis] indicated that since he is an 'idealist' and this arms venture was being done with an idealistic motive, he was at least partially in sympathy with it."

114. *Where I Stand,* pp. 105, 110–112; see Slater, *The Pledge,* pp. 201, 204.

115. One of his most thorough testimonies is in Los Angeles Report, 19 April 1950, Bureau File No. 2-105, pp. 31–41, given in Honolulu, on 27 June 1949. (This lengthy report also carries the bureau notation 2-1004-198; the document runs ninety-one pages. It will be cited here by its point of origin and original bureau file number.) The bureau called it "probably

the most accurate and incorporates the pertinent information set out in his other statements." See also "Statement of [name redacted], taken on Friday, August 6, 1948, 2:30 P.M. at 548 South Spring Street, Suite 510, Los Angeles, California," Bureau File 2-1004-16. This document is ninety-two pages long, and was taken before a notary public, even though the copy I consulted is not signed. Lewis later sued Greenspun for damages in a civil case, which dragged on until 1958 and was decided against Lewis because he had waited too long to file it. See Leland Robert Lewis, Appellant, v. Herman Greenspun, Respondent, Civ. No. 22570, Court of Appeals of California, Second Appellate District, Division Three, 160 Cal. App. 2d 711; 325 P.2nd 551; 1958 Cal. App. LEXIS 2175. 22 May 1958. As of this writing (November 2012), Lewis resides in California. I first made contact with him in April 2009, and periodic correspondence between the two of us followed. Lewis was helpful in providing me with some facts about of the *Idalia* episode. It is worth nothing that although he is an author of several books, Lewis has never written about the affair, largely, he asserts, because all of the particulars are deceased, and therefore, have no way of defending themselves against what he may have written. While his position is understandable, it is unfortunate that he chose not to provide readers with his views of the episode.

116. A summary of the laws broken by Greenspun et al. in Los Angeles Report, 19 April 1950, Bureau File No. 2-105, pp. 3–4, sections titled "Statute of Limitations" and "Prosecutive Action Taken." It is worth noting that the trials that resulted from these and related actions have not been the object of a single study, despite a wealth of primary sources.

117. Report of Legal Attaché, John N. Speakes, U.S. Embassy in Mexico, to FBI Director, 8 July 1948, Bureau File 2 1004-5, p. 3.

118. Report of Legal Attaché, John N. Speakes, U.S. Embassy in Mexico, to FBI Director, 24 August 1948, Bureau File 2-1004-5, p. 6. See also Lewis testimony, 27 June 1949, cited in note 105, p. 39 ("took us fourteen more days to sail to Acapulco"), and p. 43 ("left Wilmington approximately June 1").

119. Lewis testimony, 27 June 1949, cited in note 105, p. 40; see also, p. 43 ("the Mexican officer in charge [...] at the Navy docks was apparently a three-star Mexican General [...] [Lewis] was of the impression that the Mexican government was completely involved in the gun-running transactions." See also report of Legal Attaché, John N. Speakes, U.S. Embassy in Mexico, to FBI Director, 24 August 1948, Bureau File 2-1004-5, p. 6; and report of Legal Attaché, John N. Speakes, U.S. Embassy in Mexico, to FBI Director, 11 August 1948, Bureau File 2-1004-7, p. 2. In the latter report, Speakes cites a confidential informant who had been present in Acapulco when the *Idalia* arrived. According to this source, the "arms had been removed by military or naval personnel at the navy yard." (It is unclear why the last two reports are out of sequence.) The yacht's correct name was *Sotavento*. Additional important reports from the Legal Attaché to the FBI Director concerning these matters dated 26 July 1948, Bureau File 64-32444-1; 8 September 1948, Bureau File 64-32444-6; and 27 September 1948, Bureau

File 64-32444-8. See also the letter of the FBI Director to the Legal Attaché, 13 August 1948, Bureau File 64-32444-3. The last four documents concern the FBI's investigation of Manuel Enterprises, Inc., the "Panamanian Ship 'Kefalos,' Foreign Miscellaneous; and the Neutrality Act.

120. "Nathaniel (Nat) Ratner — American Veteran of Israel, 1946–1949," p. 2. See Amitzur, *The Origin*, p. 100, n. 66, for more information on these arms and correspondence between the Israelis involved in the matter.

121. Los Angeles Report, 19 April 1950, Bureau File No. 2-105; Fuchs was interviewed by two FBI special agents on 19 October 1949, pp. 75–84.

122. Ignacio Klich. "Latin America, the United States and the Birth of Israel: The Case of Somoza's Nicaragua," *Journal of Latin American Studies*, vol. 20, no. 2 (November 1988), in particular pp. 398 and 428; Slater, *The Pledge*, p. 134 (also pp. 228 and 238). See Amitzur Ilan, *The Origin*, p. 96ff. According to this author, "The Latin American project, code-named 'Dromi,' was to become an alternative focus of Israeli arms-purchase activities in America in the post-Arazi period" (p. 96). For the *Dromit* and its code name, see www.hma.org.il/Museum/Templates/showpage.asp?DBID'1&LN-GID'1&TMID'84&FID'1753&PID'5055. In addition, when Al Schwimmer and a large number of confederates were indicted by a grand jury in June 1948, the charges indicated that at least some of the acts they were accused of had taken place as early as September 1947 in a number of places, among them Mexico City (Case 21299, District Court of the United States for the Southern District of Florida, Miami Division). I consulted this transcript at NARA, Laguna Niguel, California. However, some of the "overt acts" that were specifically singled out occurred in May–June 1948. For additional evidence of Latin American assistance to the Israeli cause, see David Jay Bercuson, *The Secret Army*. New York: Stein and Day, 1984, c1983 (Panama, pp. 40–41, 83, 86–87, 89, 95-8, 112, 120, 139–140, 171, 182, 191, 229; Mexico, 88, 132, 182 [*Kefalos*], 229; Nicaragua, 133, 229). Panamanian consuls, for example, facilitated by providing sailing papers for sailors and ships. Paul Kaminetzky, a U.S. volunteer, received a "Certificado de Idoneidad" (No. 668, 17 May 1948) from the Panamanian consul in New York, enabling him to sail as a third-assistant engineer aboard a ship of the Panamanian Merchant Marine. The document in question, which is identical to those of Eric Forbes and Gladys Oko (and which was expedited in connection with the *Kefalos*), is in the possession of Paul (Kaminetzky) Kaye, its owner. For the original, see http://israelvets.com/picts/rescue_fleet_launched/full_size_images/KayeSeamanPapers.jpg.

123. See report of Legal Attaché, John N. Speakes, U.S. Embassy in Mexico, to FBI Director, 3 November 1948, Bureau File 2-1004-34, p. 6, in particular section titled "Haganah Activities in Mexico as Reported by [name redacted]," pp. 2–3ff. This lengthy report (twelve pages) contains a wealth of important details on Israeli/Haganah activities in Mexico. A key passage reads, "it must be recalled that the simplest method of operations for Haganah is to have the Mexican Government purchase arms and planes from the United States obtaining a legitimate export permit by virtue of the official

nature of the purchase. However, the Mexican government merely serves as a conduit to Haganah, the usual arrangement as worked out by Ives and [Rosenblum] being a fixed fee plus ten percent of the war goods or arms purchased, these to remain with the Mexican Government" (p. 6). At the start of this report, the Legal Attaché references a number of prior communications he had made to the FBI, some of which dealt with Manuel Enterprises, Inc. (Bureau File 64-32444), and with another one captioned "SALE OF C-46 CARGO AIRPLANES TO THE STATE OF ISRAEL. NA." The Legal Attaché explained that "reference is being made to all of the foregoing since they all have to do with Haganah activities carried on by the same group of individuals" (p. 1).

124. Shaul's Copybook, p. 19. See note 95.
125. See NARA, RG 319, Records of the Army Staff, Army Intelligence Document Files, Entry 85, File 470505.
126. See NARA, RG 59, 1945–1949, Central Record File, confidential letter of Raymond H. Geist, Counselor of U.S. Embassy in Mexico, to U.S. Secretary of State, no. 1277, 4 August 1948. The letter is captioned "Departure SS PINZON ex-KEFALOS from Tampico Loaded with Arms and Ammunition for Shanghai." The communication also deals with other arms-related matters.
127. Slater, *The Pledge*, pp. 134, 235, and 238.
128. Abundant information on the role of these officers can be found in FBI files. See reports of the Legal Attaché, John N. Speakes, U.S. Embassy in Mexico, to FBI Director, 10 September 1948, Bureau File 2-1004-15; report of 12 January 1949, Bureau File 2-1004-45; and report of 27 October 1949, Bureau File 2-1004-137. Paredes, about whom little is known, is merely referred to by Greenspun as an engineer (*Where I Stand*, p. 120). Perhaps significantly, General Limón had been awarded the Legion of Merit by the U.S. government just after the arms were loaded on the *Kefalos* and prior to the sailing of the vessel (see photograph in *Excelsior*, 22 July 1948, in which the U.S. Ambassador to Mexico, Walter Thurston, confers the honor on the general). There were other important politicians and government officials implicated in the arms operations, among them the former president, Lázaro Cárdenas (see report of Legal Attaché, John N. Speakes, to FBI Director, 23 September 1948, Bureau File 2-1004-25); and the Beteta brothers, one of whom, Ramón, was the Secretary of the Treasury, and the other, General Ignacio Beteta (report of Legal Attaché, John N. Speakes, to FBI Director, 3 November 1948, Bureau File 2-1004-34). See also the informative and revealing declaration of Lawrence C. Ives to FBI agents, on 15 April 1949, which explicitly implicates important Mexican military aides, including President Alemán, in arms deals (Los Angeles Report, 19 April 1950, Bureau File No. 2-105, pp. 70–74).
129. Report of Legal Attaché, John N. Speakes, U.S. Embassy in Mexico, to FBI Director, 3 November 1948, Bureau File 2-1004-34, pp. 11–12. However, the Legal Attaché was quick to point out that Serrano's reputation was not good, and that the Greenspun group was none too happy "because too

many have 'gotten into the picture,' and it is expensive to pay them off."
Still, it is worthy of note that as of this late date, Greenspun and his associates were intent on procuring planes and tanks in Mexico.

130. Report of Legal Attaché, John N. Speakes, U.S. Embassy in Mexico, to
FBI Director, Bureau File 2-1004-7, p. 5. Although undoubtedly correct in
the conclusion that the Mexican president was involved, the Legal Attaché
probably erred in believing that the purchasers of the arms were Mexican
nationals. Significantly, two weeks earlier, the Legal Attaché wrote the FBI
Director that "several months ago, an unconfirmed report was received
that President MIGUEL ALEMAN had received the sum of one million
dollars [...] in order that he would give his consent for the overall project
of utilizing Mexico for such a supply place" to "Israelite Haganah forces"
in Mexico (Report of Legal Attaché, John N. Speakes, U.S. Embassy in
Mexico, to FBI Director, 26 July 1948, Bureau File 64-32444-1, p. 1). The
report provides important details regarding the *Kefalos* in Tampico. Much
of the information conveyed by the Legal Attaché came by way of a "Reliable Confidential Informant." British intelligence sources, too, accused
the president of Mexico of taking a $1 million bribe from the Haganah for
similar arms-buying and transport considerations. And Panama's president
received a $100,000 payment for the establishment of Lineas Aéreas de
Panamá Sociedad Anónima (LAPSA), officially Panama's national airline.
(See Amitzur Ilan, *The Origin of the Arab–Israeli Arms Race: Arms, Embargo,
Military Power and Decision in the 1948 Palestine War*. New York: New York
University Press, 1996, p. 101.)

131. Report of Legal Attaché, John N. Speakes, U.S. Embassy in Mexico, to FBI
Director, Bureau File 2-1004-137, pp. 1–2. In a separate report from Mexico City, also dated 27 October 1949, Bureau File 2-1004-140, mention is
made of those in "the Mexican Department of Defense which participated
in graft," (p. 1a); and "that during 1949 some of these same officials have
been active in other arms transactions connected with Central American
and Caribbean politicians," (p. 7). According to the Central Intelligence
Agency, "There have been recent indications of increasing dissatisfaction
with the Alemán Government and of increasing legal and illegal arms traffic into Mexico although the ultimate destination of the arms in question
may be Palestine or some other trouble spot, the conjunction of these two
developments may be ominous," (*Review of the World Situation as It Relates to
the Security of the United States*, CIA 5-48, 12 May 1948), p. 10.

132. Report of SAC, Los Angeles Office to FBI Director, 28 October 1949, Bureau File 2-1004-143.

133. Several examples abundantly underscore this point, including, ironically,
Greenspun's own words (see *Where I Stand*, pp. 121–122 on the subject of
bribes [*mordidas*]). In a 7 June 1948 report on "Haganah Activities in Mexico," the U.S. Air Attaché in the capital reported that President Alemán had
received $1.5 million for his cooperation (see NARA, RG 319, Records of
the Army Staff, Army Intelligence Document Files, Entry 85, File 470505).
Slater writes that Al Schwimmer, another key protagonist of pro-Israel ac-

tivities in the United States at the time, traveled to Mexico — presumably in the summer of 1948 — "to deliver 260,000 in cash to his government friends for the long-postponed purchase of Mexican arms" (p. 308); see also pp. 134 and 153. As noted earlier, Captain Oko learned that $36,000 had been paid out in Tampico to port authorities to allow the ship to leave (see also note 84). Perhaps it was these "pay-offs to port officials in Tampico" and to General Ignacio Beteta that were alluded to in the extensive report of Legal Attaché, John N. Speakes, U.S. Embassy in Mexico, to FBI Director, 3 November 1948, Bureau File 2-1004-34, p. 5. See also letter of Assistant Attorney General James M. McInerney, Criminal Division, to FBI Director, 29 June 1950, which discusses "payoffs to various Mexican government officials which were necessary and customary in Mexico," Bureau File 2-1004-271 or 272. (It is impossible to read the notation at the bottom of this letter; however, the communication immediately follows another one from the same party to the Director dated 22 June 1950, and that appears to be Bureau File 2-1004-271.)

134. *Where I Stand*, pp. 121–122.
135. Sacharov, *Out of the Limelight*, p. 187; on Arieh Dulzin, see pp. 182–83. Lewis declared that "the Jews with whom he came in contact with in Mexico were all very concerned as to the time of his departure from Mexico, and that he was suspicious that these individuals had close contact with the Haganah organization" (Los Angeles Report, 19 April 1950, Bureau File No. 2-105, p. 42).
136. Report of Legal Attaché, John N. Speakes, U.S. Embassy in Mexico, to FBI Director, 23 September 1948, Bureau File 2-1004-25, p. 5. According to this report, the bureau's files contained information on Phillips's smuggling activities. The FBI believed that Phillips "had an important position in the Haganah organization in Mexico." The bureau noted that Phillips had handled the shipping expenses of the bodies of Glenn King and Bill Gerson, two U.S. pilots who were killed on 21 April 1948, when their heavily overloaded C-46 crashed on take-off at Mexico City Airport. Additional important information on Phillips can be found in the report of the Legal Attaché to the FBI Director, 3 November 1948, Bureau File 2-1004-34, p. 6; and New York Report, 19 June 1950, [New York] File 2-434 (also Bureau File 2-1004-261), pp. 20–21.
137. Report of Legal Attaché, John N. Speakes, U.S. Embassy in Mexico, to FBI Director, 23 September 1948, Bureau File 2-1004-25, pp. 6–9, section titled "Investigation at Tampico, Mexico." Though his name is not explicitly mentioned, it is clear that this section refers to Gritzewsky's actions in that port. It is worth noting that his brother, Luis, had a minor role as well in the *Kefalos* affair.
138. George C. McConnaughey to the Attorney General. This letter was declassified by the FBI on 30 June 2010, in response to a request of mine based on the Freedom of Information Act. It is Bureau File 2-1004-317. The correct spelling is Hayman. Important details on these transactions in report from SAC, New York, to FBI Director, 1 June 1950, Bureau File 2-1004-

231; and in confidential letter by special messenger from FBI Director Hoover to Director of the Central Intelligence Agency, 9 June 1950, Bureau File 2-1004-231 (although different, both documents have the same Bureau File number). See also telegram of Secretary of State Acheson to the U.S. Embassy in Geneva, 3 July 1950, requesting information on the identity and relationship of Dr. Erwin Hayman to "Israeli Arms transactions." The communication wishes to confirm upon whose orders Chase National Bank, New York, and Banco del Ahorro Nacional, Mexico City, "paid large sums" to Herman Greenspun and defendants in the ongoing criminal trial in Los Angeles. This document is Bureau File 2-1004-288. See also Los Angeles Report, 18 August 1950, Neutrality Act, Conspiracy, Los Angeles File No. 2-105, Bureau File No. 2-1004-292, pp. 1–4; and Salt Lake City Report, 10 January 1958, titled "Herman Milton Greenspun, wa., "Hank" Greenspun" (last name handwritten the second time), "ANTI-RACKETEERING," Bureau File 92-3244-2, p. 19.

139. *Where I Stand*, p. 122. Clearly the amount paid was lower than the total money Greenspun had reportedly received. Perhaps this is why George C. McConnaughey's letter, cited in note 138, hinted at improprieties on Greenspun's part. His letter reported that "a source of unknown reliability asserted that Greenspun and an associate involved in the arms operation received a 10% 'kick back' of the gross amount involved in an unidentified arms deal." Was the difference between the amount received and the amount paid to the Mexican government, in effect, Greenspun's kickback?

140. Report of SAC, Los Angeles Office to FBI Director, 19 May 1950. Subject: [redacted] was., et al., Neutrality Act, Conspiracy (underneath this notation: "Your File 2-105"), Bureau File 2-1004-222. See also Los Angeles Report, 19 May 1950, Los Angeles File No. 2-105, Bureau File 2-1004-223, in particular pp. 5–9. Finally, see Los Angeles Report, 18 August 1950, Los Angeles File No. 2-105, Bureau File 2-1004-292.

141. See note 117.

142. *U.S., Plaintiff, v. Herman Greenspun, Defendant*, No. 21266, pp. 339–340. Greenspun reiterated these points in a later exchange with the judge: "The activities were mostly in Mexico, your Honor. They were perfectly legal down there. We purchased it right from the Mexican government and they consented to it" (p. 348).

143. Ibid., p. 341. At least one of Greenspun's acquaintances thought that he had profited from the arms transactions. Henry Bellows, according to an unidentified source, volunteered that Greenspun "was motivated in the Israeli arms shipments, including the Idalia, by money alone"; Los Angeles Report, 19 May 1950, Los Angeles File No. 2-105, Bureau File, 2-1004-223, p. 9. Bellows, however, was a reputedly shady character and probably not the most reliable source.

144. More on this trial and the circumstances of Greenspun's sentencing in *Where I Stand*, pp. 188–192. Agreeing to plead guilty to a misdemeanor and not to a felony spared Greenspun jail time. It should be noted that some of Greenspun's comments in these passages do not square with the official

trial transcript. Whether this was his fault or that of his ghostwriter is open to debate.

145. See, in particular, reports of the Legal Attaché, (John N. Speakes), U.S. Embassy in Mexico, to the FBI Director, dated 3 September 1948 (Bureau File 2-1004-21); 10 September 1948 (Bureau File 2-1004-15); and 23 September 1948 (Bureau File 2-1004-25). Additional information on Greenspun and his group can be found in subsequent reports of the Legal Attaché from 1948–1949. These reports are in the series Bureau Files, 2-1004, as well as in the FBI's investigation of Manuel Enterprises, Inc., Bureau Files 64-32444.

146. Report of the Legal Attaché to the FBI Director, 3 September 1948, Bureau File 2-1004-21; see previous note.

147. *Where I Stand*, pp. 121–122.

148. *Out of the Limelight*, pp. 183 and 187. His account is significant because it casts considerable light on the negotiations with Mexican officials, and provides important details on the manner and timing of how monies were transferred to government personnel. As noted earlier, Sacharov ascribes a key role in the operation to Sourasky.

149. "Nathaniel (Nat) Ratner — American Veteran of Israel, 1946–1949," p. 2. According to Ives, however, some of the "75 mm caisson type guns, manufactured in Paris in 1887 . . . were stored in an arsenal in the center of town in Mexico City," Los Angeles Report, 19 April 1950, File No. 2-105, Bureau File 2-1004-198, p. 71. See also New York Report, 26 April 1949, New York File No. 2-434, Bureau File 2-1004-79, pp. 1–6 (an earlier FBI interview with Ives that contains much of the same essential details about the arms operation in Mexico).

150. Letter of Ratner to Greenspun, 11 April 1967; document provided to me by the Ratner Family. Added Ratner, "Knowing what those arms would mean to Israel, it took extreme will power to leave anything behind at the arsenal."

151. Letter of Ratner to Leonard Slater, undated and apparently never sent. (Clearly, the letter was written after *The Pledge* was published.) This document was also provided to me by the Ratner family.

152. *Where I Stand*, p. 122.

153. All three documents cited in notes 139–141 reference this fact.

154. Oko, "1960 Account," p. 11. See note 73.

155. Oko, "THE KEFALOS,"p. 4: "I can also state that I have never seen such a low grade of arms."

156. Ben-Gurion, *The War of Independence: Ben-Gurion's Diary. 2*, p. 684. While these figures are probably correct in the main, there are additional reports and estimates of the armament transported by the vessel. See Bureau file 64-32444-7, Mexico City, 5 August 1948, pp. 1–2 (partial list of arms loaded); and enclosure A ("Mexican dock checker's list of cargo loaded in KEFALOS"). The latter is a far more detailed list of armament and other items loaded. On the aviation gasoline, see Slater, *The Pledge*, p. 308. See also New York Report, 26 April 1949, New York File No. 2-434, Bureau File 2-1004-

79. According to Ives, "the Palestinians were anxious to buy gasoline, and that Greenspun and [name redacted] came to see him about this matter" (p. 4). In the same interview, Ives mentioned Abraham Phillips, who was "in the oil and gasoline business" (p. 5). It is likely that Phillips, given his commercial dealings in Tampico, might well have been the individual who purchased the gasoline for shipment in the *Kefalos*. On this point, see Mordechai Nisiaou, "on the other hand, it is imperative to recall the airplane fuel — high octane — that was purchased by the Jewish community in Mexico" (Archive: Yad Tabenkin 15-46/168/6); reference provided to author by Yehuda Ben-Tzur. See also Kollek, Teddy, Kollek, Amos, *For Jerusalem: A Life* (New York: Random House, 1978), p. 87. Ratner wrote that there were "drums of aviation gasoline" loaded on the ship; "Nathaniel (Nat) Ratner — American Veteran of Israel, 1946–1949," p. 2. See also the notes that Moshe Oren wrote over fifteen years ago in preparation for a book about the secret project "Rechesh" that was never written. The following is asserted: "13 June — airplane fuel critical situation in Israel" […] "Beginning Aug' 1948 — Eli Shalit finished through his men in Mexico to load airplane fuel drums on board the Kefalos in Tampico"; e-mail to author from Yehuda Ben-Tzur, 23 November 2010. Important information on Rechesh in Amitzur, *The Origin*, p. 64ff. The detailed itemized list labeled "Mexican Dock Checker's List of Cargo Loaded in Kefalos," in F.B.I. file 64-32444-7, enclosure (A), 5 August 1948 as already cited above in this note. This document was received by the author after the book was finished from the Department of Defense, Defense Intelligence Agency, United States Government, 6 November 2013.

157. *Where I Stand*, p. 122.

158. Ever the self-aggrandizing, would-be swashbuckler, Greenspun claimed that he had pilfered the documents from the Chinese Embassy (*Where I Stand*, pp. 143–147). Sacharov, on the other hand, and far more realistically, wrote that he and Greenspun had bought the papers in question (pp. 185–186).

159. See AJA, 883, for a copy of the document.

Chapter 4. *The Crew and the Long Voyage*

1. Documents provided to the author by the Ratner family.

2. Stricken from this list were chief engineer, Peeter Ilves, a recently naturalized U.S. citizen; third assistant engineer, August Karjus, Estonian; and electrician, Peter Stojnic, Yugoslavian. For various reasons, these three individuals failed to make the trip. Also crossed out is no. 37, Philip Kellison, officer, who was not on the ship.

3. Oko's mistake; he was Peruvian, not Portuguese.

4. For reasons that are not clear, on this list Oko crossed out the names of Kesselman and Elazaroff. Although the latter continued to use his original name for some time, he eventually changed it to Alvin (Al) Ellis, the name he would use the rest of his life. Below these four entries, for reasons that remain unknown, there appears the name of Ruth Tartakoff, and below it,

simply "Tartakov."

5. Ilves and Manresa, also from that vessel, as noted earlier, failed to go on the trip for different reasons. Although José Blanco's second last name is not found in any of Oko's documents, he is listed in another crew manifest as hailing from the town of Peralta in Navarra. See Ancestry.com, New Orleans Passenger Lists, 1820–1945, NARA, Series No. T905_186; and FamilySearch.org, https://familysearch.org/pal:/MM9.1.1/KZQ2-G8F. My father clearly remembers Blanco as a "*vasco-navarro*." According to his birth certificate, his full name was José Blanco Arbeloa, born on 30 January 1913. He was the brother of Félix Blanco Arbeloa (b. 1911), also from Peralta and executed by the fascists in October 1936 (see www.intxorta. org/izendegia/?page_id'5). Their younger sister, Juana Blanco Arbeloa (b. 1920), eventually obtained political asylum in Mexico (see http://pares. mcu.es/MovimientosMigratorios/viewer2Controller.form?nid'8532&accion'4&pila'true).

6. It is not always possible to know some of the crew members' exact age because of discrepancies in the ship manifests listed in Ancestry.com; some documents, in fact, provide estimates rather than precise ages.

7. As in the case of ages, here, too, there are discrepancies and uncertainties. If anything, in general less is known about length of service at sea than about ages. A few crew members had little or no seagoing experience (e.g., Blanco Aguinaga, Kesselman, Gladys, of course, and a couple of others).

8. Such were the cases of Suarez and Oliva Mateos, Valebona Estada and Cacheiro, Piñeiro and Torrealday, and Ellis and Ratner.

9. *Por el mundo*, chapter "*Navegando*." Apart from a few scrapes and disagreements, my father recalls that harmony generally reigned among the crew.

10. "And It Was So," chapter 2, p. 10. At another point, Oko recalled Forbes was "a thorough seaman, a forthright Scotch-American redhead who can be trusted to see a job through" (Ibid, p. 71). (Fragmentary pages of this work exist that do not appear to belong to any chapter. In all, there are six different pages: three with the number 70, two with the number 71, and one with the number 72.)

11. Ibid. According to notes prepared for the manuscript, "Apaolaza doted" on the poetry of Lorca and gave one of the poet's books to Oko. The captain reciprocated with a copy of *Don Quijote* in Spanish ("And It Was So," Notes, 3). Important information on Apaolaza's hard-scrabble life after the Spanish Civil War can be found in *El Correo Español-El Pueblo Vasco*, 5–6 October 1985.

12. "And It Was So," pp. 70–71 of fragmentary pages of this work.

13. "And It Was So," Notes, 3.

14. "And It Was So," chapter 2, p. 10.

15. Oko, "1960 Account," p. 12.

16. Ibid., p. 7.

17. Ibid., p. 12.

18. "And It Was So," Notes, 2. Under circumstances that remain unclear, crew members picked up a pregnant cat in Tampico (and aptly named her Tam-

pico), and she made the trip to Tel Aviv. Ratner wrote a wonderfully funny short account of the adventures and misadventures of "Tampico." (This document was made available to the author by the Ratner family.) During part of the voyage, the cat slept on Borrego's bunk, which, according to Oko, the steward "regarded as a badge of honor" ("And It Was So," Notes, 2).

19. Blanco Aguinaga, *Por el mundo*, p. 234ff.
20. Irargi — Centro de Patrimonio Documental de Euskadi. Archivo histórico del Gobierno Vasco. Beyris. ARCH. 20. LEG. 289, DOC. 41-5.
21. Blanco Aguinaga, *Por el mundo*, pp. 234–238.
22. Listed erroneously in Ancestry.com as Jaquin Terrealday, he appears on several manifests of the website's New York Passenger Lists, 1820–1957.
23. Blanco Aguinaga, *Por el mundo*, pp. 250–253. Oko's reaction was a way of signaling that he did not entirely disapprove of Torrealday's and my father's actions.
24. Ibid., pp. 246–247. Oko recalled the events somewhat differently if, on the main, he confirmed Blanco Aguinaga's account ("And It Was So," Notes, 2). The captain related that he needed another mess boy, and that he preferred "a Spanish Loyalist." When asked about Totoricagüena's passport, Oko told Apaolaza and Sánchez, "[W]e will take care of it."
25. Some of what follows, unless otherwise specified, is from a memorial tribute posted at http://palyam.org/Izkor/The86/the86. According to the 1930 United States Census, Rothman was then employed as a draftsman in an electric company. More on Rothman at http://www.machal.org.il, see "Volunteer Database."
26. Although the college was closed in 1985, information on the school can be found at www.upsala.org and http://en.wikipedia.org/wiki/Upsala_College.
27. *Upsalite* (1934). It also lists him as president of the Alpha Sigma Upsilon fraternity.
28. 29 March 1950 letter of Al Ellis to Mrs. Daniels, most likely Rothman's sister. A copy of this letter reached Shoshana Yadin-Kesselman, sister of Arieh Kesselman. This document was provided to me by Yehuda Ben-Tzur. See the latter's references to Rothman in Ben-Tzur, http://palyam.org/English/ArmsShips/kefalostranslationlatest1by, pp. 8 and 13.
29. "Plane Crashes in Italy" (1 January 1949). *New York Times* (1923–current file), p. 5. Retrieved 15 September 2011, from ProQuest Historical Newspapers, *New York Times* (1851–2007) (Document ID: 96609117). See also American Foreign Service, Report of the Death of an American Citizen, American Embassy, Consular Section, Rome, Italy, 12 January 1950; Ancestry.com, Reports of Deaths of American Citizens Abroad, 1835–1974. The *Palestine Post* carried news of the crash with the names of the victims in a front-page article on 2 January 1949.
30. AJA, 883: (a) Rothman's ship identification card appears to be the only in existence along with Forbes's; (b) 1950 undated speech; and (c) an excellent photograph taken by Oko or Gladys on board.

31. Retrieved from http://en.wikipedia.org/wiki/Illinois_Institute_of_Technology.

32. "With AMERICA'S FIGHTERS" (17 May 1942). *Chicago Daily Tribune* (1923–1963), p. SW1. Retrieved 15 September 2011, from ProQuest Historical Newspapers, *Chicago Tribune* (1849–1987) (Document ID: 473178712).

33. "Nat Ratner: 'I wasn't about to leave 2,000 people in — boxcars,'" *Daily Herald*, p. 30, April 1998. According to this article, he was involved in both invasions of Borneo and Okinawa. The Ratner family provided me in September 2011 with Ratner's war record. I cite it exactly as I received it from his daughter, Nancy: "According to the Notice of Separation from Active Duty papers, Dad enlisted on 9/15/42 and was commissioned on 8/23/44. His date of 'entry into active service' was 1 July 1943. He was released to inactive Duty in July 1946. His rank was Lieutenant (jg) (E) USNR. He served on the USS Muir DE770, USS Ray DE338 and the USS Dufilho DE423. The medals and awards listed on his notice of separation included: 'American Area, Asiatic-–Pacific Area (1 star), Philippine Liberation, World War II Victory, European Theatre.' My father stayed in the Naval Reserves until retirement as a LCDR, lieutenant commander." See also Ratner, Nathaniel, 1967–1995, MACHAL and Aliyah Bet Records, I-501, Box 24, Folder 9. American Jewish Historical Society, Boston, MA, and New York, NY.

34. *Daily Herald*, 30 April 1998.

35. "Nathaniel (Nat) Ratner — American Veteran of Israel, 1946–1949," p. 1. For the *Altalena* affair, see Judith Rice, "The S.S. Ben Hecht: 'The Mandate of Conscience,' *The Jewish Magazine*, June 2010. The articles concerning this vessel can be found at Palyam.org and www.navsource.org/archives/10/16/160138.htm, with information on the ship and photographic evidence of its demise.

36. "Nathaniel (Nat) Ratner — American Veteran of Israel, 1946–1949," p. 1.

37. Ibid. According to Ancestry.com, New York Passenger Lists, 1820–1957, Ratner returned from Naples aboard the *Nea Hellas* on 9 February 1948. He had left the United States on 28 November 1947.

38. "Nathaniel (Nat) Ratner — American Veteran of Israel, 1946–1949," p. 1. I assume he meant that he was impartial between the factions, but *not* "non-political."

39. Ibid. His daughter Nancy informed me that Ratner left so hurriedly that he was unable to pack properly, and that this greatly concerned his family, who did not know for a good long time where he was or what had happened to him.

40. ROBERT LINDSEY. (9 October 1983). "Al Ellis: Have Drone. Will Travel." *New York Times* (1923–current file), p. E20. Retrieved 16 September 2011, from ProQuest Historical Newspapers, *New York Times* (1851–2007) (Document ID: 283559342). See "And It Was So," Notes, 1. According to these jottings, Ellis was an orphan, and his "motive for going" to Israel in 1948 was "to have 'people' at last." Similar observations on page 3 of the

same notes: "Hoped to belong somewhere. At last have 'people of his own.'" However, I have doubts about Ellis's actual birthplace. The ship manifest of the *Sinaia* lists the Elazaroff family as having arrived at Providence, Rhode Island, from Jaffa on 31 December 1926. The mother, Savia, is listed as twenty-two years old and married to Isidore Elazaroff, an American citizen. She was accompanied by her son, David, age two, and Abraham, listed as a one-month-old child (see Ancestry.com, Atlantic Ports Passengers Lists, 1820–1873 and 1893–1959). This last fact alone would seem to raise serious questions about his birthplace, unless, of course, the manifest listed his age incorrectly. However, phone conversations with Al Ellis's brother, David, and with his second wife, Ilene, appear to confirm that he was born in Los Angeles. Until a reliable birth certificate can be found — something that has eluded me — I will continue to harbor some doubts as to Ellis's place of birth.

41. The Elazaroffs took several voyages between Jaffa and the United States in the 1920s. See Ancestry.com, Atlantic Ports Passengers Lists, 1820–1873 and 1893–1959. In a telephone conversation, David Ellis informed me that Savia had been born in Iraq, a fact I have been unable to verify.

42. *New York Times* article cited in note 40. Ellis had enlisted in the U.S. Army on 27 July 1944; see Ancestry.com, U.S. World War II Enlistment Records, 1938–1946.

43. The *H.H. Raymond* arrived in San Francisco on 1 November 1947 from Fusan, Korea, and the *Iran Victory* arrived in San Francisco on 15 May 1948; see Ancestry.com, California Passenger and Crew Lists, 1893–1957. On both vessels, Ellis is listed as "O.S." (ordinary seaman). On the *H.H. Raymond* manifest, Ellis's ethnicity is listed as Russian and Turkish, and on the *Iran Victory* simply as American.

44. Sacharov, *Out of the Limelight*, p. 186. However, Ellis, like the other volunteers, collected a salary. Ratner significantly characterizes Ellis as an "armed guard" on board the ship (see "Nathaniel (Nat) Ratner — American Veteran of Israel, 1946–1949," p. 2). Ratner also asserts that "Al during the trip to Israel cleaned all the Idalia machine guns and test fired them," a claim that does not accord with the recollections of Blanco Aguinaga, and that is lacking any evidence that might corroborate it (see undated letter of Nathaniel Ratner to Leonard Slater, p. 2).

45. See note 28.

46. Ibid.

47. See note 28 and http://palyam.org/Izkor/The86/the86. A photograph of Ellis with his new Israeli Navy underwater demolition unit, and other American volunteers, can be found at www.mahal-idf-volunteers.org/about/Machal.pdf, p. 29.

48. Slater, *The Pledge*, p. 118. This author also describes him as a "tall, lanky attractive fellow," information that does not completely square with the fact that Keller, according to his son, Eytan, was around 5'5" and weighed 115–120 lbs.

49. Ancestry.com, New York Passenger Lists, 1820–1957.

50. Slater, *The Pledge*, ch. 21–22. There are a number of articles in *The New York Times* on this incident dated January–June 1948.

51. Slater, *The Pledge*, p. 192.

52. The United Press (21 May 1948). "Lebanon Imprisons 41 Americans, 28 Others From Haifa-Bound Ship: LEBANON HOLDS 69; 41 ARE AMERICANS." *New York Times* (1923–current file), p. 1. Retrieved 16 September 2011, from ProQuest Historical Newspapers, *New York Times* (1851–2007) (Document ID: 109559537); see also related articles from the same newspaper dated 22, 24, 29, and 31 May, and 5, 12, and 29 June.

53. Ancestry.com, New York Passenger Lists, 1820–1957.

54. Retrieved from http://palyam.org/Izkor/The86/the86. Much of what follows is taken from the short memorial.

55. Goldman to Kesselman, 17 July 1947. Letter made available to me by Yehuda Ben-Tzur, who obtained it from the Kesselman family.

56. Regrettably, there is no record of Kesselman's arrival in Mexico or when he enlisted on the *Kefalos*.

57. The main sources for these endeavors are the following: (a) Ellis letter, "The first days we spent in painting the entire ship a different [word crossed out] color, giving it a new name "S.S. Pinzon"; and in general changing the appearance of the ship to escape recognization [sic?] from the British and U.N."; (b) Oko, "1960 Account," p. 12; (c) "And It Was So," Notes, 5; (d) Blanco Aguinaga, *Por el mundo*, pp. 249–250: (e) Blanco Aguinaga, "A crew member's story" (typescript), pp. 12–14; (f) "Nathaniel (Nat) Ratner – American Veteran of Israel, 1946–1949," p. 2; and (g) photographic evidence: pictures showing *Pinzon* stenciled on lifeboats, lifesavers, and so forth.

58. "And It Was So," Notes, 5.

59. Ibid., and Blanco Aguinaga, *Por el mundo*, pp. 249–250.

60. "And It Was So," Notes, 5. Clearly, Oko's self-satisfaction was misplaced. For one thing, the official name of the real *Pinzon* was *M.V. Pinzon*. More significantly, the real *Pinzon* and its imposter (ex-*Kefalos*) did not resemble each other in the slightest, no matter how clever the Haganah brain trust might have felt their stratagem was to confuse the British. More on the *M.V. Pinzon* at http://www.clydesite.co.uk/clydebuilt/viewship.asp?id=4638.

61. "And It Was So," Notes, 5.

62. Oko, "1960 Account," p. 12. Oko thought that after the changes to the ship's appearance a "quick glimpse [would] be confusing to anyone with photo of ship in New York or Tampico." Relates Ratner, "The trip across the Atlantic was spent building false bridge extensions to disguise the ship from the British who monitored all ships clearing Gibraltar"; full reference in note 57.

63. "And It Was So," summary for chapter 10, titled "Abeam Gibraltar: August 27th."

64. Ibid.

65. Ibid. Notes, Gibraltar, 5. Continued Oko, "[I]t was like the crisis in a surgical operation with a toss-up whether the patient would hemorrhage and

cash in his chips or survive."

66. Oko, "1960 Account," p. 13. I do not have a photograph of Sánchez, but I do have one of Apaolaza, and he does not appear to have been particularly swarthy. Perhaps they had acquired a tan after twenty-six days at sea?

67. "And It Was So," Notes, Gibraltar, 5. Explained Oko, "I banked on our failure to respond to the blinker question 'What ship?' being interpreted as a sloppy skipper's assumption that the question was being directed at some other ship making the passage through the channel."

68. Oko, "1960 Account," p. 13. Somewhat fancifully, Oko also imagined that perhaps what had saved the ship from being picked up by a British patrol was "the laziness of the man on watch [...] not being particularly concerned or interferring [sic] about his dreams about his girl back home, or whatever situation did arise that kept the alertness from being really alert; I guess we will have to have to thank some little English girl, British girl or some situation or tea time [...] but in any event we were not challenged."

69. "And It Was So," Notes, Gibraltar, 5.

70. Ibid., summary for chapter 10, titled "Abeam Gibraltar: August 27th."

71. Blanco Aguinaga, *Por el mundo*, p. 254. Much of what follows is from pp. 254–255.

72. Ibid.: "*vestidos de gala [...] galones y todo. Uniformes blancos.*"

73. "And It Was So," "In the Mediterranean to Tel Aviv," Notes, 6. "About an hour later saw hogsback of rugged pinacles."

74. Ibid.

75. Blanco Aguinaga, *Por el mundo*: "*Y para que contar los gritos de aquellos dos al puente de mando y los violentos golpes de timón hacia el sur que siguieron a los gritos! Salvamos el escollo y todo volvió a la calma durante un par de días más*" (p. 256).

76. Ibid., pp. 256–258.

77. Ibid., p. 258. The mystery of the warship and its identity has never been solved.

78. Oko, "1960 Account," p. 14.

79. See (a) Ben-Tzur, "An Arms Ship to Israel in the War of Independence. S/S Kefalos > 'Dromit'" (http://palyam.org/English/ArmsShips/kefalostrans-lationlatest1by, pp. 10–12); (b) Oko, "1960 Account," p. 13; (c) Oko, "THE KEFALOS," pp. 3–4; (d) Oko, "And It Was So," Notes, 6; and (e) Blanco Aguinaga, *Por el mundo*, pp. 258–259. Oko kept copies of the communications sent out by the *Kefalos/Pinzon* for 2–7 September 1948. There were eleven messages (QTCs and calls) sent out during those six days. The texts of the communications are in AJA, 883.

80. Ben-Tzur piece cited in note 80, p. 10.

81. Ibid., p. 12. Oko's bitter words are from "THE KEFALOS," p. 5.

82. Oko, "1960 Account": "[W]e were supposed to have contact two days out of Israel in the Mediterranean with a shoo-shoo station, as they call it, in Prague, an illicit radio station, and would be given further instructions. We received no instructions. We could not make contact with out illicit radio station in spite of the fact that my radio operator had wave band and every

other thing" (p. 13). This relation, which, as noted earlier, was taped, may have some transcription problems or errors that render it somewhat ungrammatical.

83. Ben-Tzur piece cited in note 80, p. 12.

84. Oko, "1960 account," p. 12. It is not clear whether the exact amount of fuel was 190 or 290 barrels, as the numbers >1' and >2' are superimposed upon one another in the typescript. However, in "And It Was So," heading "In the Med[iterranean] to Tel Aviv," Notes, 6, Oko says the ship had only 330 gallons of fuel left, or about a day's supply. Whatever the precise amount, the ship was running extremely low on fuel.

85. Ratner to Greenspun, 11 April 1967.

86. "Nathaniel (Nat) Ratner – American Veteran of Israel, 1946–1949," p. 3. These were eerily prophetic words of what would occur less than a week later. Ellis wrote, "we were completely out of fuel, had run out of water three days earlier" (see note 28 for full reference).

87. "And It Was So," summary for chapter 12, titled "Tel Aviv: Sept 8th to 12th." Even so, the captain confessed that "Tel Aviv looked like a chance to relax and recover from the shakes brought on by knowing that our supplies of fuel and water were running low." Oko was pleased: "This was the end of our voyage *to* Israel. From here on, we would be sailing *for* Israel."

88. Oko, "1960 Account," p. 14. The transcription is somewhat garbled. I believe it should read "call for patrol planes from Israel to protect us." In Oko's notes for "And It Was So," there is a telling annotation prior to entering Tel Aviv: "What ship? PINZON carrying sugar from Tampico."

89. *Marin Independent Journal*, 22 April 1961, p. 13. A small snapshot of almost certainly the same flag in Bancroft, Mss 68/39c, carton 2. See earlier reference to the captain's pajamas and this flag in chapter 1, note 78. Arieh Kesselman is reported to have shown Gladys the layout and colors of the Israeli flag (Oko's "1960 Account," p. 9).

90. Blanco Aguinaga, *Por el mundo*, p. 259. See A'aron Yironi (ship chandler), "List of Arm Ships arrived to Tel Aviv Anchorage," Haganah Archives, Tel Aviv. According to this document, the "m.a. 'PINZON' (at present 'DROMIT')" arrived on 8 September 1948. The list was provided to me by Yehuda Ben-Tzur. See the wonderful photograph of the ship's crew in Tel Aviv shortly after its arrival in Ben-Tzur, "An Arms Ship to Israel in the War of Independence. S/S Kefalos > 'Dromit,'" captioned "Tel Aviv – the 'Pinzon' crew weren't allowed to leave the ship," p. 14. The lifesaver still sports the name "S/S. M.A. PINZON. PANAMA." Ben-Tzur obtained the photograph from one of Arieh Kesselman's relatives.

91. Blanco Aguinaga, *Por el mundo*, pp. 259–260; Oko, "1960 Account," p. 14; Oko, "And It Was So," chapter 12, titled "Tel Aviv: Sept 8th to 12th," Notes, 7; and "Nathaniel (Nat) Ratner – American Veteran of Israel, 1946–1949," p. 3.

92. Blanco Aguinaga, *Por el mundo*, p. 261.

93. Cited in Ben-Tzur, "An Arms Ship to Israel in the War of Independence: S/S Kefalos > 'Dromit,'" p. 13.

94. Ibid. Ben-Gurion kept close tabs on the arms that had been delivered. See

p. 14 of this piece for a list he wrote in his diary on 13 September. It is important to underscore again that the arms were unloaded at night.

95. 10 September 1948. The original is at the Bancroft Library in Oko's papers. A copy can also be found at the AJA, 883; see also chapter 6, note 42, this volume. The note appears to have been delivered to Oko in Naples. On Skolnik's visit to the ship and subsequent developments with this aide and his wife, see Oko, "1960 Account," pp. 14–16. Skolnik changed his name to Levi Eshkol, and served as the third Prime Minister of Israel from 1963 until his death in 1969. According to Oko, at the time of his visit to the vessel, Skolnik was Under-Secretary of Defense and Minister of Immigration. Ratner relates that "Top Israeli government officials came aboard the Kefalos to express their appreciation for our success," in "Nathaniel (Nat) Ratner — American Veteran of Israel, 1946-1949," p. 3. According to Oko, Skolnik brought with him the port director of Tel Aviv, a former barrister in France named Alexander Zevstein (more correctly Zipstein, the spelling used henceforth). As port director, he was in an ideal position to facilitate the smuggling of arms; see www.machal.org.il/index.php?option'com_content&view'article&id'267&Itemid'241&lang'en.

96. See http://unispal.un.org/unispal.nsf/udc.htm, S/RES/54 and S/RES/56. A good account of the truce violations by all sides can be found in the YEARBOOK OF THE UNITED NATIONS, 1947–48, DEPARTMENT OF PUBLIC INFORMATION, UNITED NATIONS, NEW YORK, p, 9. The Question of Palestine. Document dated 13 January 1949. Available online at http://unispal.un.org/UNISPAL.NSF/0/5CE900D2DE34AAD-F852562BD007002D2.

97. United Nations — Archives and Records Management Section, S-0636-0015-04, U/N. Mediator for Palestine. Senior United Nations Military Observers' Records (SUNMO Records by Area) — Tel Aviv — Daily Reports. 05/09/1948–31/10/1948.

98. Ibid. Oko's ruse of putting the "M.A." as closely as possible to "Pinzon" (if still misspelled as "Pinson") had apparently fooled Fleury or one of his inferiors. It is impossible to know how the ammonium, sulphate, farm machinery, and general cargo made it into the report. Had the Israelis perhaps prepared false papers for this subterfuge? (See note 105.) It is also possible that the papers may have been delivered to the ship by one of the two small boats that immediately approached the *Kefalos* upon its arrival in Tel Aviv? Disguising arms as farm machinery or equipment was a common practice well known to the British; see *Schenectady Gazette*, 24 June 1948, "Cyprus Docks Loaded With Arms Shipments Bound For Israel." Some heavy crates intercepted by the British were marked as "farm equipment."

99. Ibid. I use the term "apparently" because the date is crossed out before the brief report in question.

100. AJA, 883, "S/S KEFALOS. TAMPICO TO TEL AVIV," p. 2.

101. Oko, "1960 Account," p. 15. See also note 89, this chapter.

102. Ibid., p. 16. The apparent normalcy was highly deceptive. Arriving at the docks, Zipstein made it known that they were not alone, but were in fact

surrounded by arms and armed personnel cleverly hidden everywhere.

103. Blanco Aguinaga, *Por el mundo*, pp. 260–261. During the unloading operation, captain Oko had apparently given orders not to lock anything up on ship; he so absolutely trusted those involved in the unloading that he was convinced that nothing would be stolen from the vessel, as occurred in other ports. And even though the ship's steward, Borrego, was not so sure about this, when the ship was totally empty, the crew discovered that "not even a single spoon had disappeared," p. 261.

104. Oko, "1960 Account," p. 17 (emphasis added). There is no actual record of the forged arrival papers; see note 99, this chapter.

105. Ibid. Whether these names were adopted in the arrival papers, or used informally, is unknown. More on these assumed names in Oko to Agron, 15 March 1950 (AJA, 883), and in "And It Was So," Notes, 7, chapter 12, titled "Tel Aviv: Sept 8th to 12th."

106. Ibid., pp. 17–18. Oko's account is incomplete and unclear on this point. He relates that the "French chap was poured off the gangway — drunk? — on his way back to shore full of pernod," and the only thing port director Zipstein could get out of him was an allusion to Gladys's alluring figure. Suggestive comments on the U.N. observers in the notes prepared for "And It Was So," section Naples, 9. After drinking much absinthe, the Belgian U.N. officer is said to have remarked, "It sort of makes you dreamy and sends your conscience on vacation."

107. For where the arms were sent, see Slater, *The Pledge*, pp. 307–308; Oko, "1960 Account," p. 16; Ben-Tzur, "An Arms Ship to Israel in the War of Independence. S/S Kefalos > 'Dromit,'" p. 16; and Ratner, "Nathaniel (Nat) Ratner — American Veteran of Israel, 1946–1949." Though he does not specify their destination, Ratner makes at least two other important points. First, he reports being told that the arms were "rushed to the fronts and were in use within 12 to 24 hours." Second, he notes that "the aviation gas had arrived in time to replenish empty tanks and allow the few planes to fly again" (p. 3).

108. Oko, "1960 Account," pp. 17–18.

109. Ben-Tzur, "An Arms Ship to Israel in the War of Independence. S/S Kefalos > 'Dromit,'" pp. 15–16.

110. Ibid., p. 14.

111. Blanco Aguinaga, *Por el mundo*, p. 261. The crew member deduced that the person in question was a Sephardic Jew.

112. "Nathaniel (Nat) Ratner — American Veteran of Israel, 1946–1949," p. 3.

113. Blanco Aguinaga's chronology of events does not square with the date of the vessel's departure; see *Por el mundo*, p. 262.

114. AJA, 883, "S/S KEFALOS. TAMPICO TO TEL AVIV," p. 2. By the time the ship reached Tel Aviv, it had traveled 9,127 miles — 2,031 from New York to Tampico, and 7,096 from Tampico to Tel Aviv.

Chapter 5. *Neapolitan Interlude*

1. According to Oko's ship log, as noted previously, the ship left Tel Aviv at

6:15 a.m. A notation reads, "standing off, various courses and speeds"; AJA, 883. Blanco Aguinaga vividly describes the fury of the engineers and firemen (*maquinistas y fogoneros*) when told to put salt water in the boilers (*Por el mundo*, p. 262). Some wondered how well the machinery was going to work, given that it was already old and run down; crew members also pondered how long it would take to clean out the boilers in Naples.

2. Blanco Aguinaga, *Por el mundo*, pp. 262–63.

3. Ibid., pp. 263–264.

4. Oko, "1960 Account," p. 19. The spelling error is certainly not Oko's; it occurred during the interview's transcription.

5. Personal recollection of Blanco Aguinaga.

6. Yehuda Ben-Tzur, "An Arms Ship to Israel in the War of Independence: S/S Kefalos > 'Dromit,'" p. 13 (http://palyam.org/English/ArmsShips/kefalostranslationlatest1by). He changed his name to Ambash. Additional details on Aryeh Mambush-Ambash in an interview conducted by Ben-Tzur on 23 March 2009. He was a full-time member of Haganah's procurement unit, specializing in forging documents. He had been sent to Naples on the *Kefalos* to prepare documentation for the ship so that it might operate as a "kosher" freighter (i.e., "legal"). Personal e-mail from Ben-Tzur, 27 March 2009.

7. *Marin Independent Journal*, p. 13. Unfortunately, the original photograph has been lost. It is unknown if the vessel still bore the name *Pinzon* on its bow and aft upon leaving Tel Aviv on 12 September. However, a caption of the original photograph reads verbatim, "CAPT. A.S. OKO with PURSER GLADYS ** bound for Naples to convert the "Kefalos" (PINZON) into a refugee carrier." (Source: Untitled list of notes for the photographs that accompany "And It Was So," Bancroft Library, Mss 69/39c, carton 3.)

8. Ben-Tzur, "An Arms Ship to Israel in the War of Independence. S/S Kefalos > 'Dromit,'" p. 16ff (http://palyam.org/English/ArmsShips/kefalostranslationlatest1by). Perhaps the indecision helps to explain why during the ship's prolonged layover in Naples Oko received continual offers of ships that could be converted to passenger carriers by Ignazio Lizzio's company. The letters of Lizzio, and of his representative P. J. Randall, continued through much of his stay at port; in fact, the last offer of ships was dated 2 November. Significantly, the very first letter to Oko from Lizzio was dated 14 September 1948, that is, the day after the *Kefalos* left from the coast of Haifa for Naples (all communications can be consulted in AJA, 883).

9. Oko, "And It Was So," "Naples — Sept 19 to Nov. 8," Notes, 8–9 (five unnumbered pages); "1960 Account," pp. 18–19; Blanco Aguinaga, *Por el mundo*, p. 265; and Ratner, "Nathaniel (Nat) Ratner — American Veteran of Israel, 1946–1949," p. 3. Until now it has not been possible for this author to identify precisely in which shipyard, or by which entity (or entities), the work was conducted. Oko in various places refers to an organization spelled "Emees," "Enees," and even "Imy's," which may stand for *Industrie Marittime Italiane*. However, an invoice of work on the Pfo. [*piroscafo*] "Kefalos" also lists an organization labeled "O.N.I.," which may be *Officine Na-*

vali Italiane; see Haganah Archives, 14/1496, invoice titled "Documento Di Spesa No. 80," Naples, 31 October 1948. I obtained this document from Yehuda Ben-Tzur. As of this writing, I have been unable to determine the relationship between the I.M.I. and the O.N.I., or whether they were separate entities.

10. Oko, "1960 Account," p. 18.
11. Ibid., p. 19.
12. Ibid., p. 18.
13. Ibid.
14. Ibid.
15. Ibid., pp. 18–19; Ratner, "Nathaniel (Nat) Ratner — American Veteran of Israel, 1946–1949," p. 3, "over the side, out-house toilets were also constructed." Some of these facilities are plainly visible in photographs of the vessel in its voyages from the Balkans to Israel. For example, see the outhouses in the *Marin Independent Journal* article, 22 April 1961, pp. 5 and 13. The wooden structures are located immediately below the lifeboats.
16. Many of his orders, requests, and suggestions can be consulted in AJA, 883. For instance, see Oko to Rosenberg, 24 October 1948, on outhouses and disposal lines running down the side of the vessel.
17. Oko, "And It Was So," "Naples — Sept 19 to Nov. 8," Notes, 8. Oko repeats this in his "1960 Account," p. 18. The individual who had a fondness for opera may have been Zeev Rotem; see www.palyam.org/English/IS/Rotem_Zeev. He very much enjoyed church music, concerts, and opera.
18. Oko, "1960 Account," p. 18. Oko fails to identify the veterinarian. He also does not provide Rosenberg's first name, which unfortunately does not turn up in the documents. At another point, Oko refers to a certain Kram — again, without details. This may have been Mundek Kramer (suggestion courtesy of Yehuda Ben-Tzur). Additional important remarks on the "unfortunate selection of certain Israeli shipping personnel" in Italy, letter of Oko to Lizzio, 9 September 1949, AJA, 883.
19. "And It Was So," "Naples — Sept 19 to Nov. 8," Notes, 8–9. The captain relates in his notes that there were "some pretty hungry people in Naples, and they used ingenuity, sharpened by hunger, to get themselves on the dock." Another annotation reads, "DOCKSIDE — as in Tampico, such poverty! Fed as many as could." There are additional remarks in these pages about extensive local poverty. See also Blanco Aguinaga for important observations of devastation and poverty in post-war Naples, *Por el mundo,* p. 265.
20. "And It Was So," "Naples — Sept 19 to Nov. 8," Notes, 8–9.
21. AJA, 883. Much of what follows in this paragraph is from this communication. Oko's notes assert that he tried to fly to Israel to complain about overpayments and about the danger of putting refugees aboard the ship ("And It Was So," Notes, 9, Naples — Scio story). See also Oko's important observation that the "conversion of the EX-KEFALOS seemed blocked at every turn" in "And It Was So," "Naples — Sept 19 to Nov. 8," Notes, 8. (No explanation for the term "Ex-Kefalos." Perhaps he or the ghostwriter may have meant "ex-Pinzon.") Perhaps it was far from coincidental that one

of the bills for work on the vessel (perhaps for repairs and reconversion?) was dated the same day as Oko's letter to Skolnik. The sum was not small: 438,540 lire. Had Oko been presented the bill prior to writing Skolnik? It seems highly probable.

22. AJA, 883, Oko to Minieri, 7 November 1948. Minieri's first name does not appear on the letter.

23. See AJA, 883, for claims in later years for unpaid bills.

24. AJA, 883, letter of separation, 29 September 1948. He had signed on in New York on 11 June 1948. Oko merely states that Apaolaza was paid off by mutual consent (a common formula), but adds blandly that he "is a competent engineer," a far cry from the glowing praise heaped earlier by the captain upon this "guerrilla," whose harsh post–Spanish Civil War years were certainly known by Oko; see *El Correo Español: El Pueblo Vasco*, 5–6 October 1985.

25. AJA, 883; (a) Almeidas letter of separation, 29 September 1948. He had signed on in New York City on 11 June. (b) Núñez letter of separation, 29 September 1948. He had signed on in New York City on 11 June 1948. (Almeidas and Núñez both apparently headed for Portugal). (c) letter from G. C. Stern to Oko, from New York, 15 October 1948. In this communication, Stern notified Oko that "the Chief Engineer, the Cook and one of the seaman" had arrived there. The seaman is not identified. (d) Blanco Aguinaga letter of separation, 26 October 1948. Generously, Oko wrote that he had served on the *Kefalos* since 1 June 1948, when, in fact, he had only arrived in Tampico in mid-July. Supposed illness in the family caused his departure. More about the circumstances of his exit from the ship in *Por el mundo*, pp. 266–267. Not every sailor left the ship willingly and in good standing. Hector Pineda and Honorio Román Cortinas Fernández, had both been arrested and had been in trouble with the law. Pineda was paid off "by mutual consent," according to his letter of separation, 3 November 1948 (see also Oko's letter to the Panamanian consul in Naples, 26 October 1948); and Cortinas Fernández was — or had been — in jail on a drug charge, and was fired from the ship on 26 October, although to mitigate matters somewhat, Oko arranged a "mutual consent agreement" with the sailor, paid him off, and repatriated him to New York, document signed by both on 26 October 1948.

26. See Marie-Thérèse Chabord, "Les Archives de l'Organisation Internationale des Réfugiés (O.I.R.), *Gazette des Archives*, No. 58, 3e trimestre, 1967; and A.N.P., AJ/43, Organisation Internationale Pour Les Réfugiés (OIR).

27. AJA, 883. The positions of four of these individuals on board the ship is known: Álvarez (fireman), Herrero Poza (wiper), Echeverría (cook), and Morales (messman). The positions of Miralles and Ramón Ruiz are not specified. The place of birth of these persons is usually noted. The official discharges from Bagnoli are signed by the camp commander, Sampson, whose signed first name is illegible. In "And It Was So," Oko's notes assert that he "took some men from Bagnolo [sic] through International Red Cross prison camp. Men screened to check out any Blue Legion." These

last garbled remarks appear to be the ghostwriter's. Not much is known about these individuals except for Benito Echeverría; see Irargi-Centro de Patrimonio Documental de Euskadi. Archivo Histórico del Gobierno Vasco. Fondo del Departamento de Presidencia. Secretaría General (París). Correspondencia General. Correspondencia-E. Caja 64, Legajo 02, imagenes 11-16/192, correspondence between Echeverría and Basque officials in France, 1947–1948 (with important biographical information); Centro de Patrimonio Documental de Euskadi. Archivo Histórico del Gobierno Vasco, Fondo del Departamento de Presidencia. Caja 81, legajo 04, imagenes nos. 218-9/318, letter of Gortazar to Durañona, Bayonne, 24 March 1948. Echeverría is described as living in a "Campo de Recogida de Prófugos" in Italy. He had written a letter to a friend complaining of being destitute: "se queja de estar a falta de todo (ropa y dinero)." During the Spanish Civil War, Echeverría had been a lieutenant of the Battalion Loyola, Company Azkatasuna.

28. AJA, 883. Both of their recommendations are dated 24 September 1948 at Naples.

29. AJA, 883. Their names appear on an undated master list of salaries drafted by Oko. Castaldi may well have been the "pantryman at Hotel di Napoli" described in Oko's notes as an Italian national.

30. Lloyd's Voyage record card for *M.V. Pinzon*. The *M.V. Pinzon* arrived in Naples on 3 October from Leghorn, and departed on 5 October for Gibraltar. The copy of the *Informatore Maritimo Di Napoli* that Oko saved is barely legible. Attempts to secure a better reproduction have been unsuccessful.

31. Oko, "1960 Account," p. 19. The incident occurred at the still unidentified "Emees" or "Enees" yard.

32. AJA, 883, letter from G. C. Stern to Oko, from New York, 15 October 1948. Blanco Aguinaga notes that once the boilers were cleaned, the vessel was taken out to sea to verify that the machinery was working well (*Por el mundo*, p. 265).

33. "And It Was So," "Naples — Scio Story," Notes, 9. Much of what follows is from this source. At the top of this page of notes, below the heading, is the notation, "Salvage of ship full of aviation equipment for Israel."

34. AJA, 883, (a) note from Captain Amendolia Angelo to Oko (undated); (b) letter from "The Institution in Italy" to Oko, Rome, 12 October 1948; (c) letter from Oko to the captain of the *Scio*, 12 October 1948, with the monetary conditions under which the towing to Naples was to take place; and (d) taped interview of Ratner by his daughter, Nancy, 5 January 2000, provided to the author by Ratner family. According to the captain's notes, "Kefalos sailors signed slips [that they] would accept two days bonus and pay in lieu of salvage to keep down inquiries." Later the *Scio* transported arms to Israel from the Balkans; see Ben-Tzur, "An Arms Ship to Israel in the War of Independence S/S Kefalos > 'Dromit,'" p. 20 (http://palyam.org/English/ArmsShips/kefalostranslationlatest1by); see also http://www.palyam.org/English/IS/Rotem_Zeev, and other allusions to this vessel in accounts at palyam.org.

35. Blanco Aguinaga, *Por el mundo*, p. 265.
36. Ibid.
37. Ibid., p. 266. Young Blanco Aguinaga's heady days in Naples would soon end. In late October 1948, he received a telegram informing him that his mother was ill and that he should return to Mexico, which he did immediately. His perfectly healthy mother awaited him at the airport; it had been a ploy engendered by the fear that something might happen to him in a dangerous region. He sadly resigned himself to the fact that he would never be a sailor, as he had often dreamt of becoming (pp. 266–267).
38. "And It Was So," Notes. Naples, unnumbered page.
39. Ibid., Notes, 8. Naples. What follows is from these observations.
40. Ibid. Notes. Naples, unnumbered page: "Troc [adero] in Naples, Pia following dance with Forbes."
41. AJA, 883. Forbes to Oko, 19 February 1949. Forbes continued to sail for Israel for several months in 1949 before returning to the United States. See his discharge papers from the *S.S. Theodor Herzl*, where he served as chief mate from 16 February until 16 June 1949 (document made available to me by his son, Eric A. Forbes).
42. The four melavim were Meir Falick, Aharon Peled (Rosenfeld), Willie Rostoker, and David Stern/Shtern, and the radio operator was Chaya'le/Haya Kozlovzky. See Palmach Museum, Photographs Catalogue, Collection titled "From Ma'apilim to Olim, at the time of the Declaration of the State of Israel," photograph number 11477 (http://www.palmach.org.il). The functions of the Israeli Defense Forces officers in the photograph are unknown. A later list asserts that there were five melavim on board, not four (see chapter 6, this volume, note 3). There is no explanation for this discrepancy. Did another melave board the ship at the very last minute before leaving Naples? Although the term *melavim* (accompanists or protectors) was first used on board illegal immigration (Aliya Bet) ships, its use was carried over in the case of the two trips from the Balkans to Haifa, and this despite the fact that at that point nothing legally prevented refugees from migrating to Israel.
43. See note 6.
44. Jon Kimche and David Kimche, *The Secret Roads: The "Illegal" Migration of a People, 1938–1948* (Farrar, Straus and Cudahy, 1955), p. 114; see also pp. 144 and 147. Melavim received their orders from Palmach/Palyam.
45. See note 6.
46. "1960 Account," p. 21. The transcript mistakenly calls them "mellowbeam," a clear phonetic transcription error.
47. Palmach Museum, Photographs Catalogue, Collection titled "From Ma'apilim to Olim, at the time of the Declaration of the State of Israel (see www.palmach.org.il). At least one of the melavim, Aharon Peled (Rosenfeld), assisted in Naples with preparing the ship and loading it with food and water (see www.palyam.org/English/IS/Peled_Aharon_Arke). Also working to get the ship ready, although in a different capacity, was Zeev Rotem, who worked on outfitting and procurement (see www.palyam.org/

English/IS/Rotem_Zeev).

48. Palmach Museum, photograph number 11472 (see http://www.palmach. org.il). [Photograph 18 in this book]

49. AJA, 883.

50. See note 21. On the day before departure, the Panamanian Consulate in Naples granted the *Kefalos* official permission to leave Naples for Split/*Splato (Yugoslavia)*; "*despacho no. 36, patente de navegación no. 997*" N.Y.; AJA, 883.

Chatper 6. *Rescues of Refugees*

1. Oko, "1960 Account," p. 22.

2. AJA, 883, Clearance Certificate, Haifa, 26 November 1948, Number of Crew, 42.

3. The melavim were Meir Falick/Falik, Aryeh Mambush, Willi/Willie Rostoker, Aharon Rozenfeld (later changed last name to Peled), and David Stern. The IDF representatives were Joseph Cohen and Ephraim Pilarsdorf. I have decided to consider the new radio operator, Chaya/Haya Kozlovsky, also an Israeli, as a member of the crew and not among these individuals. Their names appear in AJA, 883, communication from *Hadromith* (ship) to Hamosad (Mossad Le'Aliya Bet – Shoham – Zim.), 20 November 1948, signed by Oko. See chapter 5, note 42. (After 15 May 1948, the "Bet" was omitted and the entity was named Ha'Mossad Le'Aliya. Information provided to me by Yehuda Ben-Tzur, who also translated the names written in Hebrew in the document).

4. The ship's itinerary for the next two months can be closely followed through the captain scrupulous log (AJA, 883). Oko, as noted earlier, carefully recorded the vessel's position, speed, course, and distance and added brief relevant comments for the voyages. The captain's log is supplemented by "The daily status of the Dromit as listed by the Mosad Le'Alia in Italy," a document from the Haganah archive (call number 42.1), generously provided to me by Yehuda Ben-Tzur. As employers of the *Kefalos*, Israeli officials kept a close watch on the ship's movements and whereabouts.

5. "1960 Account," p. 20.

6. "As soon as we arrived, word was sent that the refugees from Bulgaria, Romania and Hungary could be sent by train for transport to Israel. Within a week train loads of boxcars filled with refugees began arriving. Close to 4,000 were embarked, along with several Israelis who controlled the refugees," in "Nathaniel (Nat) Ratner – American Veteran of Israel, 1946–1949." 3. The *Palestine Post* front-page article of 24 November 1948 announced the arrival of the *Kefalos* in Haifa and noted that most of the 4,000 passengers were from Bulgaria.

7. From AJA, 883. Caption in back of photograph in Gladys's hand reads "Refugees waiting on [illegible abbreviation]." This photograph was submitted for publication in the *Marin Independent Journal* article of 22 April 1961. Oko wrote below Gladys's caption, "Oko file. Please Return." The picture never made it to print. In a list of photographs that accompanies the

unpublished manuscript "And It Was So" (at the Bancroft Library), a type-written notation by either Oko or Gladys reads, "(10) Refugees waiting on the dock at Bakar. November 14, 1948" (underlined in original).

8. "1960 Account," pp. 20–21.

9. Oko, "And It Was So," summary for chapter 20, "Bakar: November 14th to 15th."

10. "1960 Account," p. 21. Aharon Peled (Rosenfeld), one of the melavim who escorted refugees from the Balkans, wrote in remarkably similar terms: "I am proud of the fact that I took part in the saving of the remnants of the Holocaust" (see www.palyam.org/English/IS/Peled_Aharon_Arke). Recall that he had also helped prepare the ship at Naples "by building the bunks for the Olim and loading it with food and water."

11. AJA, 883. Both photographs are alongside other materials in the correspondence and papers relating to the rescue of European Jews by Captain and Mrs. Oko, 1948–1949. In a list of photographs that accompanies the unpublished manuscript, "And It Was So" (at the Bancroft Library), a type-written notation by either Oko or Gladys reads, "(11) Loaded and bound for Haifa," and "(11) Bound for Haifa with over 4300 refugees on board. November, 1948." Whether the duplication in numbering was intentional or not is unknown. In all there are five photographs of the rescue of refugees in the Balkans at the AJA.

12. "1960 Account," p. 21. According to a list at the Central Zionist Archives (Jerusalem), S104/609, 4,038 passengers arrived on the vessel in this voyage. This 62-page list, however, appears to be incomplete and *may* have included more individuals; in fact, the last page is torn at the bottom. Unless a full list emerges, we may never know the exact number. There are, of course, other estimates; see *Palestine Post*, 24 November 1948 (4,000); "The daily status of the Dromit as listed by the Mosad Le'Alia in Italy," call number 42.1, Haganah archive ("installations in N[aples] for 4,000 passengers, she will be able to carry 4,000 persons"); and Haya (Chaya) Kozlovzky (www.palyam.org/English/IS/Kozlovsky_Haya, p. 4): 4,500 from Bulgaria; "some of them spoke Hebrew"; and 300 from Hungary.

13. "1960 Account," p. 21. Aharon Peled (formerly Rosenfeld), a melavim on both voyages, in an email to me (see note 66), writes: "the language I spoke with the immigrants was mainly Hebrew (with most of the Bulgarian), Yiddish and sign language." See note 12; see also note 66.

14. Ibid.

15. Ratner to Greenspun, 11 April 1967.

16. "1960 Account," p. 21.

17. Ibid., pp. 21–22. There are several striking photographs of musicians performing during this voyage: (a) AJA, 883 (accordionist and singer), no. 12, with caption "there was music aboard en route to Haifa" in notes from "And It Was So" [Photograph 28]; (b) *Marin Independent Journal*, 22 April 1961, p. 12: "Music provided by the Kefalo's [sic] refugee passengers was one of the many cheering incidents of two voyages to Haifa, Israel." In this photograph there are two accordionists and a guitarist; (c) Palmach Muse-

um photographs: one with a tambourine player (no. 11487), another with an accordionist and a man to his right who seems to be leading the crowd in song (no. 11491), and a third one with someone who appears to be singing (no. 11486); (d) another photograph shows a violinist and an accordionist performing on the second tier/balcony of the deck (see United States Holocaust Memorial Museum [USHMM], no. 24748). The last photograph may be from the second voyage, according to the caption, which is dated December 1948. However, this is far from definitive proof because the two voyages are closely related in time and the photograph could well have been post-dated by the photographer or the museum. It remains unclear exactly to which trip the nine photographs at the USHMM belong, although I tend to believe that they are from the first voyage. More on music and musicians in Peled's account cited in note 72, "the Bugarian [sic] had music instruments and they played as well."

18. "And It Was So," Bakar, Notes, November 14th to 15th. An annotation reads, "HORA – Heb[rew] folk dance." Haya/Chaya Kozlovsky notes that the refugees (olim) "organized their own program of singing and dancing, and I was impressed by their cooperation" (www.palyam.org/English/IS/Kozlovsky_Haya, p. 4).

19. AJA, 883, Duplicate (no.) 13. Interestingly, despite Gladys's explanation, Oko noted later that he "was grateful that I did not have to perform marriages," ("1960 Account," p. 23). This might be interpreted as meaning that he had merely presided over the wedding ceremony as ship captains are wont to do, but that the effective aspect of the marriage had been conducted by the rabbi on board and reinforced by a marriage contract (see next note).

20. USHMM, "Marriage ceremony of a Yugoslavian-Jewish couple on board the SS *Kefalos*, sailing from Bakar to Israel" (Photograph no. 24749); and "A witness signs the ketubah [marriage contract] at the marriage ceremony of a Yugoslavian-Jewish couple on board the SS Kefalos, sailing from Bakar to Israel" (Photograph no. 24744). It cannot be determined as of this writing whether these photographs are from the first or second voyage. Additional research is needed to establish which trip they depict. Oko's remarks are not helpful on this matter: "we had five marriages in the course of two voyages" ("1960 Account," pp. 22–23). There are four photographs of marriages on board during the first voyage in the Palmach Museum collection, (nos. 11482-5). It is clear that they occurred during the first trip because the vessel's radio operator, Chaya/Haya Kozlovsky, is clearly visible in all of them.

21. "1960 Account," pp. 23–24. Oko recorded the names of those married aboard the ship, and he stayed in contact with some of them and their families in future years.

22. See www.palyam.org/English/IS/Kozlovsky_Haya, p. 4.

23. Front-page article, 24 November 1948; more on this later in the chapter as well as in note 38. See also Oko, "1960 Account," p. 22–23; and Chaya/Haya Kozlovsky's chronicle at www.palyam.org/English/IS/Kozlovsky_

Haya. She explains that two were twins. Although she was the radio operator, the young twenty-year-old was called upon to assist with one of the women who had given birth — and possibly with others as well. She specifically relates that she was also responsible for the women and their babies.

24. See www.palyam.org/English/IS/Kozlovsky_Haya; "And It Was So," Bakar, Notes, 10, handwritten notation at bottom in Aline Merritt's hand. According to Nancy Ratner, her father did something similar for one of the newlyweds, giving up his room so that they could have privacy on their wedding night. Personal communication to the author.

25. "Nathaniel (Nat) Ratner — American Veteran of Israel, 1946–1949," p. 3. Oko's log for 17 November records the following: "3:30p Pt San Cataldo 8 mi," (AJA, 883). I have been unable to find this location or where the ship might have taken shelter off the Italian coast, if indeed it did, as Ratner suggests. There is no entry for this day in the "The daily status of the Dromit as listed by the Mosad Le'Alia in Italy," (see note 4). And for 18 November, the list simply says "Near Island ... [?] Going to Arnon' [Israel]," without further details.

26. "Nathaniel (Nat) Ratner — American Veteran of Israel, 1946–1949," p. 3. When the Israelis decided to seize control of the ship, since they felt that Ratner was on their side, they gave him a gun. And when Oko was determined to resist the Israelis' demands, he, too, provided Ratner with a gun. With a mixture of humor and irony, Ratner remarks that since he still had the gun from the *Idalia* (given to him by Greenspun), he now had three guns.

27. Ibid.

28. AJA, 883. Though it has no heading, the list was clearly meant for Oko. The document carries Ratner's signature.

29. AJA, 883, Hamosad to *Hadromith*, 20 November 1948.

30. AJA, 883, *Hadromith* to Hamosad, 20 November 1948. The communication also endorsed Ratner's recommendations on other matters (boilers, vapor pressure, valves, and water pumps). In response to a question from Hamosad, Oko replied that he required a licensed radio operator. Whether this was meant to show dissatisfaction with the work of Chaya/Haya Kozlovsky is unknown, but there was clear tension between the two. She did not speak English, and Chaya considered herself a "Gid'onit," or radio operator, although she claims that Oko insisted on referring to the position as "ship's communications officer." This meant that she would eat her meals with the officers and not with her fellow Israelis.

31. I strongly suspect that if any review or "survey" (as Oko called it) was carried out, it was probably at best a very cursory one. The vessel arrived at Haifa on the morning of 23 November and was off again on its next voyage in barely five days.

32. AJA, 883, two reports of Dr. Heinrich Keller to Oko, 19 November 1948, and one dated 21 November. At Bakar, Keller wrote an interesting note to Oko, whose meaning is ambiguous at best:
    "Dear Captain,

On the open sea*, between heaven and earth,
The clock of life strikes forty-four.
It is the time of life when a man's life begins.
May the Almighty give His blessing to all your heart's desires.
May He hold you in the circle of your loved ones,
In health, joy, and happiness enclosed.
From the bottom of my heart, I wish you much health and many blessings
in your family life."
I owe the translation from the German to my colleague Richard S. Levy.
Dr. Keller *may* have been alluding to Oko's upcoming forty-fourth birth-
day (12 December).

33. "1960 Account," p. 22.
34. There was another doctor on the vessel whose last name was Feidman. Unfortunately, his first name is unknown. See AJA, 883, *Hadromith* to Hamosad, 20 November 1948. Chaya Kozlovsky, the radio operator, also cared
for the sick children (see www.palyam.org/English/IS/Kozlovsky_Haya,
p. 4).
35. "1960 Account," p. 22. Its location is unclear from the transcript. Oko
writes that the hospital was "in number 3 up between deck."
36. AJA, 883.
37. AJA, 883, Oko to Quarantine Medical Officer, Port of Haifa, 27 November
1948. Apparently, there was a small incident when the ship's third officer
lowered the flag "after hearing the order given by a Harbor Official per-
mitting the passengers to disembark," to the dissatisfaction of the medical officer. According to Oko's log, the vessel entered Haifa at 7:53 a.m. A
photograph of the ship steaming toward port taken by Baruch Geller, chief
engineer of the Israeli vessel *INS Maoz*, K 24, can be seen at www.palyam.
org/English/ArmsShips/hy_Dromit, p. 2.
38. The article was written by Judith Avrunin. Oko clipped a copy of it and
kept it in his files. All of the quotes in this paragraph are from this piece.
39. "In Haifa we were received by soldiers and by many Israeli officials, and
there was general rejoicing and singing" (www.palyam.org/English/IS/
Kozlovsky_Haya, p. 4).
40. See note 11.
41. AJA, 883. There may well have been other communications given Oko's
insistence for a meeting.
42. AJA, 883. 23 November 1948; the note is written on Manuel Enterprises
stationery.
43. AJA, 883, undated and unsigned communication to Oko on a small scrap
of paper. It read, "Cpt. Oko. 1) Arieh rang up, is not going to T.A. because
he could not get a car. 2) He arranged with Tzvi Yechieli [might be "Jechieli"], Tel No. 4543 to contact Cpt. Oko for arranging the meeting with Mr.
Skolnik. 12:30 – 24.XI.48." It is not clear whether the time and date pertain
to when the note was sent, or whether this was the stipulated time for the
meeting to take place. Yehuda Ben-Tzur, who interviewed Mambush about
this matter, informed me that the latter took it upon himself to arrange the

interview between Oko and Skolnik.

44. For Oko's remarks about the Skolniks, their visit and gifts, see the captain's "1960 Account." The original note from Skolnik to the Okos, dated 10 September 1948, is at the Bancroft Library, Mss 68/39 carton 2. A copy of the note in AJA, 883.

45. AJA, 883, Yechieli to Oko, 28 November 1948.

46. Ibid. This communication also has instructions regarding the use of the ship's wireless and how cables should be sent as well as a list of melavim (six) and nurses (three) for the voyage.

47. Ibid. At note's end, Yechieli politely authorized Oko to make all necessary arrangements with respect to the *owners'* obligations.

48. For the vessel's itinerary during the second voyage, see note 4 for sources.

49. "And It Was So," rubric titled "Anxiety in Bakar (2nd time)," Notes (11).

50. "Nathaniel (Nat) Ratner — American Veteran of Israel, 1946–1949," p. 4.

51. Ibid. According to Oko's notes, the "situation [was] disturbed by Yugoslav munition ship coming in and lying at anchor, demanding us to give up berth." "And It Was So," rubric titled "Anxiety in Bakar (2nd time)," Notes (11).

52. "Nathaniel (Nat) Ratner — American Veteran of Israel, 1946–1949," p. 4.

53. "We were tied off to bollards on the beach with every conceivable thing on ship — wire, rope, etc. Force of winds tremendous. Winds from east — we were on east shore near cement plant. Short section of concrete dock. Had to shift ship fore and aft to take on passengers. Not convenient, but the only facility." "And It Was So," rubric titled "Anxiety in Bakar (2nd time)," Notes (p. 11).

54. They can be consulted in AJA, 883.

55. "Nathaniel (Nat) Ratner — American Veteran of Israel, 1946–1949," p. 4.

56. "And It Was So," rubric titled "Anxiety in Bakar (2nd time)," Notes (11). Oko's notes are haphazard and not entirely clear on these points. There are also spelling errors and typographical mistakes. "Developed" could also be read as "enveloped."

57. Tommy Lapid's story about his Aliya to Israel. A segment translated from Yayir Lapid's book *Memories after My Death: Joseph (Tomy) Lapid*, published by Keter, 2010. Tommy, 17 years old, made Aliya on board the *S.S. Kefalos* on its second voyage with olim from Bakar, Yugoslavia, to Haifa. Also on board during this trip was Arieh Rona, a future admiral in the Israeli navy. He was kind enough to send me an extremely interesting account of this journey: "These are memories of six year old child. The 'Kefalos' made two trips to Israel. I came on the second trip in December 1948. On board there were several hundred people which were accommodated in the ship's holds that was used previously for general cargo voyages. I came with my family we arrived to Haifa on the 28th of December, 1948 after a voyage of 12 days at sea departed from a small port in the Adriatic Sea named Bakar. The voyage was very rough and according to my mother the Jewish community in my home town [of] Subotiza gathered in the synagogue [to] hold a special prayer to pass peacefully the voyage because the news about our difficulties

at sea already reached them. As you know, and Yehuda [Ben-Tzur] knows better, the people of the Palyam escorted the new arrivals (Olim). The captain was an American merchant mariner who had a very difficult task to take care of the several hundred people, feed them and treat them in this rough voyage which took 12 days. We arrived in early morning to Haifa Bay and saw the mount of Carmel in front of us with dawn, (first light), I can remember even today the excitement and the emotion of the people on the ship when we arrived to Haifa. We had been accepted by the Israeli agency officials and sent to Beer Yaakov, which was a camp for the immigrants previously being a British army barrack/post. Even today being an old man I can still feel the excitement of that special morning. [...] Arieh Rona," (email to author, 21 April 2011). In a subsequent email, in reply to a question from me, Rona wrote that "some Jews [on board] spoke Ladino, which is pretty close to Spanish" (email to author, 30 April 2011).

58. *Daily Herald*, 30 April 1998.

59. "Nathaniel (Nat) Ratner — American Veteran of Israel, 1946–1949," p. 4; see also *Daily Herald*, 30 April 1998. Even so, there occurred another incident prior to departure, an incident not recorded anywhere else. According to Ratner, "our radio operator had to be released from jail. He had transmitted while in port to the U.S. Navy for a weather report, and he was released only after they [the authorities] were sure he had not transmitted any intelligence information" (see "Nathaniel (Nat) Ratner — American Veteran of Israel, 1946–1949," p. 4).

60. "And It Was So," rubric titled "Anxiety in Bakar (2nd time)," Notes (p. 11).

61. See http://www.palyam.org/English/IS/Bar-Lev_Yehoshua, p. 3. Bar Lev relates that on their way to Bakar the ship received a telegram from Barpal, an Israeli official, "asking if we have sufficient food and fuel to pick up some passengers. We answered that we had enough food for 1,500 people for ten days or more. Barpal was a secretive person. He did not tell us that we might have to take a few more than 1,500 olim, but he did ask us if we had checked our figures well." More on the ramifications of this episode later in the chapter.

62. Ibid.

63. *Daily Herald*, 30 April 1998.

64. Ratner to Greenspun, 11 April 1967.

65. Tellingly, Oko recorded no speed for 19 December. The slow speeds occurred on 20–21 December. A cryptic remark at the end of the captain's notes for the second trip to Bakar is difficult to interpret, though it *may* refer to conditions shortly after leaving that port: "Almost cost the ship. 2 days later on our own — 2 islands of South Pelopensia [sic]. Lights — headed into a rocky bite (Soljac)?" Interestingly, the document "The daily status of the Dromit as listed by the Mosad Le'Alia in Italy" has no entries for 20–21 December. Full reference in note 4.

66. See www.palyam.org/English/IS/Bar-Lev_Yehoshua, p. 3. The recollections of Aharon Peled (changed last name from Rosenfeld), another of the melavim, are remarkably similar. Peled made the two trips as an es-

cort. Unfortunately, he is not precise about the journey (or journeys) he is recounting. See also www.palyam.org/English/IS/Peled_Aharon_Arke: "The voyage was a difficult one as the sea was very rough and the helm broke [...] [T]here were many more who wanted to get onto the ship when we left Bakar, but there was not enough room." An email account from Mr. Peled to this author of March 2011 gives additional important details of his experiences as a melavim. He notes that "most of the immigrants were laying in bed vomiting," and that they "were sick and didn't want to eat much, which it turned [out] to be good [be]cause the food was enough for the all [sic?] journey." As the individual in charge of distributing the food, Peled provides interesting details of how the food was allotted and what kind of foods and drink were made available to the immigrants. He also provides fleeting insights into their language, culture, and customs. Two additional excellent photographs of happy groups of immigrants during the second voyage in Yad Vashem Photo Archives; see http://collections.yadvashem.org/photosarchive/en-us/7725109.html [Photograph 26]and http://collections.yadvashem.org/photosarchive/en-us/7725230.html [Photograph 27], items 88071 and 88072, respectively, titled "Young people on the deck of the illegal immigrant ship 'Kefalos,' 1948." This is factually incorrect because it was no longer illegal to migrate to Israel.

67. See www.palyam.org/English/IS/Bar-Lev_Yehoshua, p. 3.
68. Ibid.
69. Ibid.
70. Ibid.
71. Ibid. Oko's log for 24 December reads, "Christmas eve and no proper GROG aboard," and for the next day, "Merry Christmas. Arrival Hiafa [sic]. To go: 60 mi." The arrival was not entirely routine. It appears that on the night of the 24th the ship had tried to put into port but could not do so because of an Egyptian air raid. According to Oko, "the port was blacked out. We couldn't use the harbor lights to guide us, and a small boat came out to give us instructions to put over to Akra and anchor for the night and await daybreak to discharge our passengers" ("1960 Account," p. 24).
72. *Daily Herald*, 30 April 1998. Aharon Peled recalls that when "the immigrants saw the Carmel Mountain, they were very happy. Some of them cried, and some start [sic] sing they [sic] national Israel song "Hatikva'" (according to an undated account of Mr. Peled titled "Kefelus's [sic] journey from Napoli to Baker [sic], Yugoslavia and to Haifa, Israel, 1948," sent to this author in March 2011). Unfortunately, it is impossible to discern from this text whether this occurred during the first or second voyage.
73. "1960 Account," p. 22: "subsequent voyage carrying 3800 odd people."
74. *Palestine Post*, 26 December 1948. Of course most, although not all, had arrived on the *Kefalos*.
75. "1960 Account," p. 23.
76. Ibid., p. 22. As early as 15 March 1950, Oko asserted that the *Kefalos* "had carried 7,737 refugees into Haifa" (AJA, 883, letter of Oko to Agron). Although Oko consistently advanced this figure, there may have been dis-

crepancies in his calculations. For instance, in the "1960 Account" Oko asserted that there were "4,300 people aboard" on the first voyage. Therefore, if there were 3,800 on the second one, as he also wrote, the total would be closer to 8,100. The exact number may only be determined through a careful study of the lists of immigrants at the Central Zionist Archives, although these also may not prove totally reliable inasmuch as they appear to be incomplete. See list with call number S104/611 for arrivals on the second voyage. This 40-page list, like the one from the earlier voyage, seems to be missing pages. The total is only 2,410 persons, which is far below other estimates.

77. "1960 Account," p. 23. Written this way in the transcription; he clearly said or meant "Negev."

78. "Within a year they delivered 7,737 Jews from Europe to their promised land. The Okos regard this as their ultimate contact with 'the essential verities,'" *Independent Journal*, 22 April 1961, pp. 6–7.

79. See Ben-Tzur, "An Arms Ship to Israel in the War of Independence S/S Kefalos > 'Dromit,' p. 18. This author asserts that the ship, "while en route [...] was ordered by Barpal to enter the port of Bari, most probably to check if she is suitable to load the tanks, in addition to the Olim."

80. See www.palyam.org/English/IS/Bar-Lev_Yehoshua, p. 2. I assume this means *more* than the number the ship was slated to transport. All subsequent quotes from Bar Lev are found in this account.

81. AJA, 883. This and subsequent exchanges — though not all — between ship and land are found among Oko's papers.

82. Reference in note 79.

83. AJA, 883, Barpal to *Kefalos* (emphasis added).

84. The reference to "again" is difficult to interpret because to the best of my knowledge the ship had not put into Bari before. Perhaps there is a problem with the translation to English?

85. AJA, 883. Thirty minutes after this cable, Oko noted the ship's position and wrote "Sailing Nemedri. Courses Split. 54.5 miles to Split." Nemedri stands for "North European and Mediterranean Routeing Instructions. Contain routeing instructions to enable vessels to avoid passing through mined areas after World War II"; see Layton, C. W. T., Peter Clissold, and A. G. W. Miller, *Dictionary of Nautical Words and Terms: 8000 Definitions in Navigation, Seamanship, Rigging, Meteorology, Astronomy*. Glasgow: Brown, Son & Ferguson, 1994, p. 237.

86. Cited in Ben-Tzur, "An Arms Ship to Israel in the War of Independence S/S Kefalos > 'Dromit,' p. 18 (emphasis added).

87. Ibid. Bar Lev admits that he and the other melavim — and perhaps Oko as well — "knew nothing of what was to transpire, nor in what a 'catch-22' Barpal himself was entangled."

88. See note 45 above.

89. AJA, 883. The communication carries Oko's signature, and the exact time it was sent.

90. AJA, 883 (emphasis added). The last name of the sender's signature is diffi-

cult to make out. It is signed by a certain Simon S. [?] The note appears to have been delivered or sent at 20:00 hours on that day, although the handwriting in not clear on this matter. The sender says that he regrets sending the note in writing, but asserts he could not board the ship – one assumes to deliver its contents personally – because there were no gangway facilities.

91. "And It Was So," rubric titled "Bakar" Notes (10): "[after the] second trip, Gladys and I called on camps to see first trippers."

92. "1960 Account," p. 23. He went on to note that he and his wife still received letters from some of them addressed to "Dear Parents." Some of this correspondence can be consulted in AJA, 883. Although Oko does not mention it, it is *possible* that in early January 1949 the captain and Gladys may have learned of the 31 December crash in Italy that killed Rothman and several Israelis.

93. AJA, 883, Jechieli to Oko.

94. AJA, 883. The information that follows is from these two sets of severance papers. I assume that they are the only ones in Oko's papers because the others were given to the crew members concerned. There is no master list of all those who were paid off. It is worth noting that the papers carry the ship's official seal; the typewritten heading of the Consulate of Panama atop the front page; and the official registry number – N.Y. 997 – of the vessel.

95. Two interesting observations: the subsistence allowance was twenty-five dollars per day. In other words, he was charged for 120 days of subsistence by the ship owners. Also, he was not paid for 1–6 January 1949, most probably the days he and Gladys had been away from the ship visiting the camps of refugees. Unfortunately, there remains little documentation of the payout, although it is clear that Oko was not pleased with the process. Without providing details, a remark in the unfinished "And It Was So" (structural outline, p. 5), tellingly reads, "Haifa: December 25th to 26th [...] Battle for crew's pay [...] Israel tried a Bonicos trick, but failed"; an unflattering reference to Bonicos's failure and/or resistance to pay the crew the previous year.

96. On the previous day, 8 January, Oko had used the ship's official seal to write a glowing letter of recommendation for Dr. Heinrich Keller; see Oko to Horowitz, of the American Joint Distribution Committee in Rome. The captain noted that the doctor's services "to the immigrants aboard my vessel were exceptional" (AJA, 883). Keller had served on board during both voyages from the Balkans to Israel.

97. AJA, 883. Although essentially similar, the letters nevertheless contain subtle nuances in content. Interestingly, the recommendations have the Manuel Enterprises name and address typed at the top. Since he no longer had access to the ship's stationery and seal, Oko added in each letter that it was advisable to have the recommendations notarized. For Oko's return to San Francisco, see SAC, San Francisco, report of Douglas G. Allen, 7 April 1949, subject: Adolph Sigmund Oko, Jr. – was, File No. 100-28664.

"On February 3, 1949, [source] T-1 further advised that subject [Oko] had returned to the United States and had telephoned an attorney, Mr. Elkus, in San Francisco, from New York City" (p. 3 of report); and source "San Francisco T-3" advised on January 17, 1949 that "the subject had returned to New York and would arrive in San Francisco in a week or two. T-3 again advised on March 2, 1949, that the subject had returned to San Francisco" (p. 4).

98. AJA, 883, Oko to Marvin Lowenthal, 24 February 1949. In an effort to show that he was above board and had nothing to hide, on the same day Oko telephoned the FBI to inform them that if the bureau "desired to talk to him for any reason he was available" (in FBI report of Douglas G. Allen cited in note 97).

99. Very little is known about what became of most of the ship's crew members after the last voyage and payout, although the record is not entirely blank. In addition to those former crew members who ended up in the San Francisco area, there are interesting details about Ratner and Forbes. The former, in his words, "toured around Israel and ended in a Negev desert outpost," and experienced several adventurous and dangerous moments. When the cease-fire took effect, he decided to return home (see "Nathaniel (Nat) Ratner — American Veteran of Israel, 1946–1949," p. 4). He was then indicted, along with Ellis and Greenspun, for arms smuggling. As for Forbes, he married an Italian (Neapolitan?) woman in late January or early February 1949, and then, as noted earlier, served as chief mate on the *S.S. Theodor Herzl*, an Israeli vessel. Some time soon thereafter, Forbes, too, returned to the San Francisco region. At least two other sailors of the *Kefalos*, Lorenzo Aldalur and Casiano Totoricagüena, also ended up in the United States, both residing in the New York region. See Totoricagüena, Gloria P., Emilia Sarriugarte Doyaga, and Anna M. Renteria Aguirre, *The Basques of New York: A Cosmopolitan Experience*. Vitoria-Gasteiz: Eusko Jaurlaritzaren Argitalpen Zerbitzu Nagusia 'Servicio Central de Publicaciones del Gobierno Vasco, 2003, pp. 153 and 140, respectively. (A few additional details on some of the crew after the *Kefalos* in the Epilogue to this volume.)

100. Ben-Tzur, "An Arms Ship to Israel in the War of Independence S/S Kefalos > 'Dromit,' pp. 21–22.

101. Bancroft Library, Mss 68/39, carton 3.

Conclusion

1. Oko, "And It Was So," Bakar, Notes (10) (emphasis added). I have adjusted the punctuation for greater legibility.

2. Oko, "1960 Account," p. 1 (emphasis added).

3. See José Antonio Lisbona, *España-Israel: Historia de unas relaciones secretas,* pp. 373–375, (these pages contain several errors); Iñaki Beobide, Rocio Satrústegui, Koldo San Sebastián, and Steven Spielberg, *Entre Dos Patrias* (documentary film, ETB, 1991); "Los vascos de sión," *El Correo Digital*, 31 May 2007 (www.elcorreo.com/vizcaya/prensa/20070531/sociedad/vascos-sion_20070531.html); Jessica Kreimerman, "Basque rescue: The

Basques played a secret role in illegal Jewish immigration to Palestine," *The Jerusalem Report* (Jerusalem, 20 February 1992); Fernández Díaz, Victoria, *El exilio de los marinos republicanos* (Valencia: Universitat de València, 2009, 292); and J. M. Romaña Arteaga, *La Segunda Guerra Mundial y Los Vascos* (Bilbao: Mensajero, 1988, 104–108). The latter book contains the testimony of Victor Gangoitia Bañales, which appeared in *El Correo Español–El Pueblo Vasco*, 1 July 1985. Gangoitia, along with Hilario Zarragoitia Guezuraga, are the two main individuals featured in the documentary *Entre Dos Patrias*. Zarragoitia Guezuraga was one of the sailors on the *Pan York* and was interned for some time in Cyprus (see note 5). His name appears often in correspondence between himself and Basque authorities in exile; see IRARGI – Centro de Patrimonio Documental de Euskadi, Archivo Histórico del Gobierno Vasco, Fondo del Departamento de Presidencia. On Jewish immigration and refugees during the British mandate, see Arieh J. Kochavi, "The Struggle against Jewish Immigration to Palestine," *Middle Eastern Studies*, Vol. 34, No. 3 (July 1998), pp. 146–167; and by the same author, *Post-Holocaust Politics: Britain, the United States, and Jewish Refugees, 1945–1948*. Chapel Hill: University of North Carolina Press, 2001.

4. Biographical information on Hernandorena's birth, including some remarks by his daughter, Maria Pilar, are available at http://mareometro.blogspot.com/2008/09/esteban-hernandorena-zubiaga.html. More substantial facts about his life in *BIL*, Mensuel Hendayais, nos. 137, 138, and 140, October and November 1991 and January 1992, respectively. See "Captain Steve Tells Us About Himself," interview by Ayala Dan, in *Public committee to commemorate Captain Steve's Memory,* edited by Moshe Gutter under the auspices of Zim Co., El-Yam Co., and the National Seamen Union, n.d.; translated from Hebrew and edited by the Palyam.org staff. Information regarding his merchant service at sea available through Ancestry.com; see Massachusetts Crew Lists, 1917–1943; Seattle Passenger and Crew Lists, 1882–1957; and New York Passenger Lists, 1820–1957. Captain Steve is remembered fondly as well in several accounts that can be consulted at www.palyam.org, notably those of Gad Hilb (with whom he served), "The Voyage of the 'Pans,'" and others. In addition, I have received testimonials about Hernandorena from Professor Nissan Liviatan, Captain Hillel Yarkoni, and Willi Rostoker. He is buried in Israel, and his tombstone bears this moving Spanish-language inscription: "*Sr. Don Esteban Hernandorena. 'Captain Steve'. Heroe de la Immigración Clandestina (Aliya Bet). Uno de los fundadores de la Marina Mercante Israeli . * 1905 Bilbao + 1965 Haifa.*"

5. IRARGI – Centro de Patrimonio Documental de Euskadi, Archivo Histórico del Gobierno Vasco, Fondo del Departamento de Presidencia, Caja 65, Legajo 3, imágenes nos. 20-1/117, J.A. de Durañona to Andima Eguiluz Ibiñagabeitia and fourteen others at Famagusta, Cyprus, 24 February 1948; imágenes nos. 21–24, Andima Eguiluz Ibiñagabeitia to J.A de Durañona, from Famagusta, Cyprus, 13 March 1948; and Caja 81, Legajo 4, imagen 199/318, J.A. de Durañona to Javier de Gortázar, 24 Febru-

ary 1948, with a list of the internees; imagenes nos. 203–204, Gortázar to Durañona, 25 February 1948. Additional information in imágenes nos. 204–205/318, Durañona to Gortázar, 25 February 1948, with a list of the internees and annotations on the margins of their political affiliations. It appears that nearly all the Basques interned in Cyprus had arrived there on 1 January 1948; see www.mahal-idf-volunteers.org/about/Machal.pdf, p. 14.

6. I have been unable to ascertain when and how Oko and Manresa met, but there is *some* reason to believe that they *might* have been introduced by Manuel Galdós, captain of the fishing vessel *Mistral*, which formed part of the PYSBE fleet (see note 8). The *Mistral* and the *Tramontana* (the ship captained by Manresa), were sister vessels, and it is beyond doubt that Galdos and Manresa knew one another at PYSBE. Oko returned to San Pedro, California, from Shanghai on 2 August 1946, aboard the *Mindoro*. Also on board was Manuel Galdós; see Ancestry.com, California Passenger and Crew Lists, 1893–1957. On the ship manifest, Galdós is listed as having been born around 1909 at San Sebastián, a fact that coincides with known biographical facts. It is difficult to imagine that the two did not interact during the two-week voyage (the ship left Shanghai on 17 July). Even though Galdós's precise role in China remains unknown to me, he had seen action in the Pacific during World War II (see http://www.marinavasca.eu/en/biografia-manuel-galdos-uzcanga.php). And at some point after the conflict he resided or spent time in China (see chapter 2, note 53). Despite the possible Oko–Manresa connection through Galdós, another point to consider is that Manresa probably sailed in the mid-1940s from Cuba to San Francisco on the Lloyd's Shipping Company with cargos of sugar. I have not been able to confirm this fact, but two of Manresa's family members have so indicated to me in personal correspondence.

7. Oko profoundly trusted and admired Manresa, welcoming his counsel on a range of delicate matters. Recall Manresa's assistance in New York with the recruitment of crew members. The episode of the *Vita* has been the object of numerous controversies and polemics. The story has been recounted by one of its crew members; see Antonio de Ertze Garamendi, *Mis memorias* (To-Sand Sur 81 No. 380, Coi. Lorenzi Buturini 5768-6787. 1999, p. 72ff). Additional details on the episode, related to Ertze Garamendi's account, available at http://nauticajonkepa.wordpress.com/2009/11/16/fotos-del-vita/, and in the site's links. More on the *Vita*, Manresa, and its Basque crew in Juan Pardo San Gil, *Euzkadiko Gudontzidia 'La Marina de Guerra Auxiliar de Euzkadi: (1936–39)* (2nd edition. Donostia-San Sebastián: Untzi Museoa-Museo Naval, 2008, pp. 151–152); the book is also available online at http://um.gipuzkoakultura.net/pdf/libro_marina_de_guerra.pdf. More on the *Vita* at http://ianasagasti.blogs.com/mi_blog/2011/02/los-vascos-y-el-vita.html; and in Victoria Fernández Díaz, *El exilio de los marinos republicanos* (Valencia: Universitat de València, 2009, p. 280, n. 34).

8. PYSBE was an acronym for *Pesquerías y Secaderos de Bacalao de España.* Con-

siderable information on PYSBE in Juan Pardo San Gil, *Euzkadiko Gudontzidia 'La Marina de Guerra Auxiliar de Euzkadi: (1936–39)* (2nd edition.
Donostia-San Sebastián: Untzi Museoa-Museo Naval, 2008), pp. 19–23
and elsewhere in work. On Manresa, the *Tramontana*, and the *Vita*, see
pp. 151–153. More on PYSBE in Artemio Mortera Pérez, *Los bacaladeros
de PYSBE* [Valladolid]: Quirón, 2002; and available at www.menkalinan.
com/html_metopas/metopa_gipuzkoa.htm.

9. The others were Ellis, Kesselman, Ratner, and Rothman; see chapter 3.
10. I am mindful that the *Kefalos* was not unique in this respect. Other Israeli
vessels with sizable Spanish crews likewise brought together populations
and diasporas with similar shared histories. Considerably more work remains to be done on this and related questions.
11. An explanation of *Palyam* and *Palyamniks* available at www.palyam.org/
English/Palyam_overview_en. The Palyam was the naval operations unit
of the Haganah; its members were known as *Palyamniks*. The main page
of Palyam's website (Palyam.org) contains important recollections of its
members regarding Basque *and* Spanish participation in its actions, especially during the era of Aliyah Bet ("illegal immigration") prior to the
end of the British mandate. The accounts are too numerous — nearly two
dozen — to detail separately. See also Joseph M. Hochstein and Murray S.
Greenfield, *The Jews' Secret Fleet: The Untold Story of North American Volunteers Who Smashed the British Blockade of Palestine* (Jerusalem: Gefen Pub.
House, 2010, revised edition, pp. 84 and 154).
12. Ben-Gurion references here from *The War of Independence: Ben-Gurion's Diary*, 2, p. 684. See also chapter 4, note 94.
13. I owe this suggestion and phrasing to Yehuda Ben-Tzur.
14. "And It Was So," structural outline, p. 6.

Epilogue

1. Bonnie Shrewsbury Arthur, *The Inverness Tales: And Views of the Point Reyes
Peninsula*. Penngrove, CA: HawksEye Press, 2002, pp. 50–52. The loan
from Rabbi Fine (AJA, 883).
2. Oko was the key promoter of the Drake Navigators Guild from its incep-
tion. He was an original member and founder in 1949 (e-mail from Mr.
Robert Allen, 27 March 2012). See Raymond Aker and Edward P. Von der
Porten, *Discovering Francis Drake's California Harbor* (Palo Alto, California:
Drake Navigators Guild, 2000, pp. 13–14). Oko explored the ocean; see
the expedition of the *Salvager*, employed by the Drake Navigators Guild
under Captain Adolph S. Oko, Jr., exploring Drake's Bay near San Francisco. Photo Credit: UC San Diego Library, identifier bb7338996x, cakhsuia_
mc76-14-0065, 92-34. (The photograph was published in the *San Francisco
Chronicle*, September 23, 1951.) The captain also engaged in scholarship;
see Oko, Adolph S. Jr., *Francis Drake and Nova Albion*. San Francisco, 1964.
(Cover title: "Reprinted from the California Historical Society Quarterly,
vol XLIII, no. 2, June 1964"). In conjunction with these subject matters,

Oko cultivated friendships with prominent individuals, such as Fleet Admiral Chester W. Nimitz, United States Navy, who also wrote on Drake.

3. Oko was a fierce critic of those he derided as "bird-watching-do-gooders" and "tyrannical government land grabbers," see Bonnie Shrewsbury Arthur, *The Inverness Tales*, p. 57. More on Oko's participation in these affairs in Ann Lage and George L. Collins, *George L. Collins: The Art and Politics of Park Planning and Preservation 1920–1979: An Interview* (Berkeley: University of California Press, 1980); and Paul Sadin, *Managing a Land in Motion: An Administrative History of Point Reyes National Seashore* (Washington, D.C.: National Park Service, US Dept. of the Interior, 2007).

4. See Chapter 6, note 96; see also *Baywood Press* (later renamed *Point Reyes Light*), 3 October 1963.

5. Journal of the Assembly, Legislature of the State of California, 1964, First Extraordinary Session, House Resolution No. 7, Relating to the Death of Captain Adolph Sigmund Oko. Note: The full text of House Resolution No. 7 appears at page 8 of the Assembly Daily Journal for 3 February 1964.

6. See Chapter 6, note 96.

7. Forbes obituary, *Contra Costa Times*, 14 May 1981; Larrauri obituary, *Monterey Peninsula Herald*, 10 July 1985; Sánchez and Corino are mentioned in AJA, 883, letters of Oko, and in FBI documents.

8. For Aldalur and Totoricagüena, see Chapter 6, note 99; more on Aldalur available at www.ancientfaces.com/research/person/14820855/lorenzo-aldalur-profile-and-genealogy.

9. "Robert Keller Appointed Jewish Agency Director for West Coast." *Jewish Telegraphic Agency*, 23 July 1962; and "Israel Fashion Industry Schedules Largest U.S. Promotion Next Month." *Jewish Telegraphic Agency*, 18 August 1971.

10. See Chapter 4, note 40.

11. Wolfgang Saxon. "Raphael Recanati, Philanthropist, Dies 75: Shipping and banking leader aided many institutions." *New York Times* (1923–current file), 2 June 2 1999. Available at http://www.proquest.com.proxy.cc.uic.edu/ (accessed 17 February 2012).

12. Steven Erlanger and Marilyn Berger. "OBITUARIES: Teddy Kollek Dies at 95; Led Jerusalem." *New York Times* (1923–current file), 3 January 2007. Available at http://www.proquest.com.proxy.cc.uic.edu/ (accessed 17 February 2012).

13. Ta'as is an abbreviation of the Hebrew for "Military Industry" (Hebrew: *Ta'asiya Tzvait*). Additional information received from Yehuda Ben-Tzur from his personal information and sources.

14. See www.palyam.org/English/ArmsShips/hf_Dromit; and www.hma.org.il/Museum/Templates/showpage.asp?DBID'1&LNGID'1&TMID'84&FID'1753&PID'5055.

Bibliography

Archival Sources

American Jewish Archives (AJA) (http://americanjewisharchives.org)

American Jewish Historical Society (http://www.ajhs.org/)

Bancroft Library, University of California, Berkeley (http://bancroft.berkeley.edu/)

Central Zionist Archives (CZA) (www.zionistarchives.org.il/ZA/pMainE.aspx)

Federal Bureau of Investigation/Department of Justice (FBI)/(DOJ)

The Haganah Archives (www.irgon-haagana.co.il/). Hebrew.

Irargi — Centro de Patrimonio Documental de Euskadi. Archivo Histórico del Gobierno Vasco. Beyris. (http://eah-ahe.org/)

The Israel Defense Forces (IDF) and Defense Establishment Archives (http://www.archives.mod.gov.il/pages/ENG/default_eng.asp)

Maine Maritime Museum (http://www.mainemaritimemuseum.org/)

National Archives and Record Administration (NARA) (www.archives.gov)

Palmach Museum (www.palmach.org.il/show_item.asp?itemId'8096&levelId'42798&itemType'0)

Property Management & Archive Record System (PMARS) (https://pmars.marad.dot.gov)

U.S. Coast Guard, National Maritime Center, Martinsburg, West Virginia (http://www.uscg.mil/nmc/)

United States Holocaust Memorial Museum (http://www.ush-mm.org/)

United Nations, Archives and Records Management Section (https://archives.un.org/content/united-nations-archives-and-records-management-section)

Yad Vashem (http://www.yadvashem.org/)

Primary Sources

Full and Down — U.S. Maritime Service Officers' Training Station, Government Island, Alameda, California. Class of Summer 1942.

National Organization of Masters, Mates & Pilots of America Membership Book.

Norske Veritas (Organization). *Register of Norwegian, Swedish, Danish, Finnish and Icelandic ships and of other ships classed with Det Norske Veritas*. Oslo: Det Norske Veritas, 1900s.

San Francisco City directories.

U.S. Federal Census (1910, 1920, 1930, 1940).

United States. *Merchant Vessels of the United States*. Washington, D.C: U.S. Government Printing Office, 1866–1960s.

Official Government Journals

Gaceta Oficial. Órgano de Estado (Panamá)

Newspapers, Magazines, and Journals

Baltimore Sun
Chicago Daily Tribune
El Correo Espanol–El Pueblo Vasco (Bilbao)
Daily Herald (Arlington Heights, Illinois)
Excelsior (Mexico City)
Los Angeles Examiner
Los Angeles Times
Marin Independent Journal
El Mundo (Tampico)
Pacific Sun (Stinson Beach, California)

Palestine Post (Israel)
Portland Press Herald
The New York Times
San Francisco Call-Bulletin
San Francisco Chronicle
Sea Magazine
Stars and Stripes
La Tribuna (Tampico)
El Universal (Mexico City)

Unpublished Sources

Avigor, Shaul. "Copybook." Originals are kept at Archives of the Israeli Defense Forces. Manuscript. (I obtained copies and translations of these documents from Yehuda Ben-Tzur.)

Blanco Aguinaga, Carlos. "A crew member's story of the SS Kefalos in the summer and early fall of 1948." Undated. (Typescript.)

A. S. Oko Jr., "And It Was So." In late 1957, Captain Oko began to write a book-length account of the *Kefalos* saga "as told to Aline Merritt." The manuscript was never completed, most probably because of Oko's failing health. Sometime that year he traveled to England for an operation to repair heart problems that had lingered since being wounded in China in 1945, problems aggravated in part during the eight months at the helm of the *Kefalos*. The unfinished manuscript is at the Bancroft Library (Mss. 68/39 c., carton 3), in several large folders containing handwritten notes by Merritt, as well as several typewritten chapters. I have made use of those chapters that appear to be the most complete or nearly finished (numbers 1–9 that cover the period from the start of the story through Tampico). I also made extensive use of detailed typewritten notes and other materials compiled by Merritt in preparation for the eventual work. Some of these materials carry Oko's handwritten revisions. It is worth noting that the book was to be illustrated by Merritt's husband, Warren Chase Merritt, a well-known artist. Although the work was to carry the title ". . .And It Was So," I have decided to omit the opening ellipsis for clarity and simplicity. (According to the institution that holds these documents, the preferred citation for the collection is Adolph Sigmund Oko papers: additions, BANC MSS 68/39 c, The Bancroft Library, University of California, Berkeley. The collection also goes by the title Adolph Sigmund Oko papers: additions, 1929–1965.)

A. S. Oko Jr.,"THE KEFALOS." Undated, but in all likelihood written in early 1949. (In AJA, 883. Typescript with author's handwritten revisions.)

A. S. Oko Jr., "1960 Account." (Taped interview of Oko, conducted by Mr. Edward P. Von Der Porteren at Point Reyes Station, California, on 28 December 1960.)

[The tape has been lost, but Mr. Von Der Porteren, Oko's friend and collaborator on marine matters, fortunately transcribed this important and lengthy interview, and kindly made a copy available to me.]

Nathaniel Ratner. "Nathaniel (Nat) Ratner — American Veteran Of Israel, 1946–1949." Typescript.

————. Letter from Ratner to Hank Greenspun, 11 April 1967.

————. Letter to Leonard Slater, undated and apparently never sent.

"The daily status of the *Dromit'* as listed by the Mosad Le'Alia in Italy," Haganah Archives, call number 42.1. List obtained from Yehuda Ben-Tzur.

"List of Arm Ships arrived to Tel Aviv Anchorage," Haganah Archives, Tel Aviv. By A'aron Yironi, ship chandler.

Web Sources

www.history.com/history/shipyards/1major/inactive/bethsan-francisco.htm
www.sjohistorie.no/skip/d/Dicto%201917
www.hma.org.il/Museum/Templates/showpage.asp?D-BID'1&LNGID'1&TMID'84&FID'1753&PID'5055
www.warsailors.com/freefleet/norfleetd.html
www.shipscribe.com/usnaux/AK/AK59.html
www.palyam.org/English/ArmsShips/hy_Dromit
www.de.wikipedia.org/wiki/Dvora
www.convoyweb.org.uk/hague/index.html

www.ibiblio.org/hyperwar/USN/Admin-Hist/173-Armed-
Guards/173-AG-2.html

www.americanjewisharchives.org/aja/FindingAids/oko.htm

http://freepages.genealogy.rootsweb.ancestry.com/~nzbound/
nautical_terms.htm

http://ia600308.us.archive.org/14/items/lifeinprintinglawt-
00kennrich/lifeinprintinglawt00kennrich.pdf

www.history.navy.mil/photos/sh-usn/usnsh-a/ak51.htm

www.shipscribe.com/usnaux/AK/AK51.html

https://pmars.marad.dot.gov/detail.asp?Ship'510

www.navsource.org/archives/09/49/49037.htm

http://en.wikipedia.org/wiki/USS_Aries_%28AK-51%29

http://www.convoyweb.org.uk/ports/index.html?search.
php?vessel'ARIES~armain

http://www.palyam.org/English/IS/Rotem_Zeev

http://resources.ushmm.org/inquery/uia_query.php/pho-
tos?hr'null&query'kw133272 (All nine *Kefalos* photographs
from United States Holocaust Memorial Museum.)

http://resources.ushmm.org/inquery/uia_doc.php/pho-
tos/21085?hr'null

http://resources.ushmm.org/inquery/uia_doc.php/pho-
tos/18121?hr'null

www.elcorreo.com/vizcaya/prensa/20070531/sociedad/buque-
canones-obuses-para_20070531.html

www.palyam.org/English/ArmsShips/The_Idalia_caper

http://palyam.org/English/ArmsShips/kefalostranslationlatest-
1by (Titled "An Arms Ship to Israel in the War of Independence S/S *Kefalos* > *Dromit*")

www.palyam.org/English/IS/Peled_Aharon_Arke

http://palyam.org/Izkor/The86/the86. (Memorials to Arieh
Kesselman and Jack Rothman. Hebrew.)

www.upsala.org

http://en.wikipedia.org/wiki/Upsala_College

www.navsource.org/archives/10/16/160138.htm

www.mahal-idf-volunteers.org/about/Machal.pdf

www.palyam.org/English/IS/Kozlovsky_Haya

www.palyam.org/English/IS/Bar-Lev_Yehoshua

www.elcorreo.com/vizcaya/prensa/20070531/sociedad/vascos-sion_20070531.html ("Los vascos de sión," *El Correo Digital*, 31 May 2007).

http://ianasagasti.blogs.com/mi_blog/2011/02/los-vascos-y-el-vita.html

www.jewishvirtuallibrary.org/jsource/judaica/ ejud_0002_0015_0_15056.html (Source: Encyclopaedia Judaica)

http://collections.yadvashem.org/photosarchive/en-us/7725109.html (Yad Vashem Kefalos photograph)

http://collections.yadvashem.org/photosarchive/en-us/7725230.html (Yad Vashem Kefalos photograph)

Secondary Sources

Aker, Raymond, and Edward P. Von Der Porteren. *Discovering Francis Drake's California Harbor*. Palo Alto, CA (2605 Waverley St., Palo Alto 94306): Drake Navigators Guild, 2000.

Álvarez Chillida, Gonzalo. *El antisemitismo en España: La imagen del judío, 1812–2002*. Madrid: Marcial Pons, 2002.

Álvarez Chillida, Gonzalo. "La eclosión del antisemitismo español: De la República al holocaust." In Álvarez Chillida, Gonzalo, and Ricardo Izquierdo Benito, *El antisemitismo en España*. Cuenca: Ediciones de la Universidad de Castilla-La Mancha, 2007.

Arthur, Bonnie Shrewsbury. *The Inverness Tales: And Views of the Point Reyes Peninsula*. Penngrove, CA: HawksEye Press, 2002.

Baughman, James P. *The Mallorys of Mystic: Six Generations in American Maritime Enterprise*. Middletown, CT: Published for the Marine Historical Association by Wesleyan University Press, 1972.

Ben-Guryon, David, David Ben-Guryon, and G. Rivlin. *The War of Independence: Ben-Gurion's Diary*. 1–2. Tel-Aviv: Verl. des Israel. Verteidigungsministeriums, 1982. (Hebrew)

Beobide, Iñaki, Rocio Satrústegui, Koldo San Sebastián, and Steven Spielberg. *Entre dos patrias*. Spain: E.T.B., 1991. (Documentary film).

Bercuson, David Jay. *The Secret Army*. New York: Stein & Day, 1984, c1983.

Blanco Aguinaga, Carlos. *Por el mundo: Infancia, guerra y principio de un exilio afortunado.* Irun: Alberdania, 2007.

Bjørkelund, Leif M., and E. H. Kongshavn. *Våre gamle skip: Skipshistorisk billedbok for Haugesund, Kopervik og Skudeneshavn.* [Aksdal]: Lokalhistorisk stiftelse, 1996.

Bowman, Carroll R. "The Spinozism of Adolph S. Oko," *Southern Journal of Philosophy*, Vol. 6, Issue 3: 172–180. Fall, 1968.

Calhoun, Ricky-Dale. "Arming David: The Haganah's Illegal Arms Procurement Network in the United States, 1945–49," *Journal of Palestine Studies*, Vol. 36, No. 4 (Summer 2007).

Carreño A., Gloria, and Ethel Gerbilsky de Glusman. *El Estado de Israel en la opinión de la prensa mexicana: Abril, mayo, junio de 1948.* México: Centro de Documentación e Investigación de la Comunidad Ashkenazí de México, 1995.

Chabord, Marie-Thérèse. Les Archives de l'Organisation Internationale des Réfugiés (O.I.R.), *Gazette des Archives*, No. 58, 3e trimestre, 1967.

Christen, Arden G., and Peter M. Pronych. *Painless Parker: A Dental Renegade's Fight to Make Advertising "Ethical."* Baltimore, MD: Distributed for the American Academy of History of Dentistry by Samuel D. Harris, National Museum of Dentistry, 1995.

Larry Collins, Dominique Lapierre. *O Jerusalem.* New York: Simon & Schuster 1972; paperback edition, 2007.

Øyvind Eitrheim, Jan Tore Klovland, and Jan F. Qvigstad. "Historical Monetary Statistics for Norway 1819–2003," Norges Bank Occasional Papers No. 35, Oslo 2004.

Fernández Díaz, Victoria. *El exilio de los marinos republicanos.* Valencia: Universitat de València, 2009.

Greenspun, Hank, and Alex Pelle. *Where I Stand: The Record of a Reckless Man.* New York: D. McKay Co., 1966.

Hadari, Ze'ev Venia. *Second Exodus: The Full Story of Jewish Illegal Immigration to Palestine, 1945-1948.* London, England: Vallentine Mitchell, 1991.

Hochstein, Joseph M., and Murray S. Greenfield. *The Jews' Secret Fleet: The Untold Story of North American Volunteers Who Smashed the British Blockade of Palestine.* Jerusalem: Gefen Pub. House, 2010.

Ilan, Amitzur. *The Origin of the Arab–Israeli Arms Race: Arms, Embargo, Military Power and Decision in the 1948 Palestine War*. New York: New York University Press, 1996.

Kimche, Jon, and David Kimche. *The Secret Roads: The "Illegal" Migration of a People, 1938–1948*. New York: Farrar, Straus & Cudahy, 1955.

Ignacio Klich. "Latin America, the United States and the Birth of Israel: The Case of Somoza's Nicaragua," *Journal of Latin American Studies*, Vol. 20, No. 2 (Nov., 1988).

Kochavi, Arieh J. *Post-Holocaust Politics: Britain, the United States, and Jewish Refugees, 1945–1948*. Chapel Hill: University of North Carolina Press, 2001.

———. "The Struggle against Jewish Immigration to Palestine," *Middle Eastern Studies*, Vol. 34, No. 3 (July 1998).

Kollek, Teddy, and Amos Kollek. *For Jerusalem: A Life*. New York: Random House, 1978.

Lappîd, Yā'îr. *Zikhronot ahare moti: Sipuro shel Yosef (Tomi) Lapid*. Yerushalayim: Keter, 2010. (Hebrew)

Lisbona, José Antonio. *España–Israel: Historia de unas relaciones secretas*. Madrid: Temas de Hoy, 2002.

Mason, Jack. *Point Reyes West: Fourteen Stories*. Inverness, CA: North Shore Books, 1984.

Pardo San Gil, Juan. *Euzkadiko Gudontzidia: La Marina de Guerra Auxiliar de Euzkadi (1936–39)*. Donostia–San Sebastián: Untzi Museoa, 1998. (Available at http://um.gipuzkoakultura. net/pdf/libro_marina_de_guerra.pdf).

Rother, Bernd. *Franco y el Holocausto*. Madrid: Marcial Pons, Historia, 2005.

Romaña Arteaga, J. M. *La Segunda Guerra Mundial y Los Vascos*. Bilbao: Mensajero, 1988.

Sacharov, Eliahu. *Out of the Limelight: Events, Operations, Missions, and Personalities in Israeli History*. Jerusalem: Gefen, 2004.

"Adolph S. Oko." In Skolnik, Fred, and Michael Berenbaum, *Encyclopaedia Judaica*. Detroit: Macmillan Reference USA in association with the Keter Publishing House, 2007.

Slater, Leonard. *The Pledge*. New York: Simon & Schuster, 1970.

Starke, Tony, and William A. Schell. *Register of Merchant Ships*

Completed in 1917. Peer-reviewed Kent, World Ship Society, 1999.

Strohmier, Daniel. "A history of the Bethlehem Steel Company Shipbuilding and Ship Repairing Activities," *Naval Engineers Journal*, 77: 2, 1963.

Totoricagüena, Gloria P., Emilia Sarriugarte Doyaga, and Anna M. Rentería Aguirre. *The Basques of New York: A Cosmopolitan Experience*. Vitoria-Gasteiz: Eusko Jaurlaritzaren Argitalpen Zerbitzu Nagusia 'Servicio Central de Publicaciones del Gobierno Vasco, 2003.

Wertheimer, Andrew B. "Oko, Adolph S," in Garraty, John A., and Mark C. Carnes. *American National Biography*. New York: Oxford University Press, 1999, Vol. 16, pp. 661–662.

Index

Page numbers in *italics* indicate photographs. Numbers followed by n indicate endnotes.